T0380690

Of Ecclesiastes and More

Science and Faith Unraveled in One Life

Salvestian Teller

WESTBOW
PRESS®
A DIVISION OF THOMAS NELSON
& ZONDERVAN

WestBow Press books may be ordered through booksellers or by contacting:

WestBow Press
A Division of Thomas Nelson & Zondervan
1663 Liberty Drive
Bloomington, IN 47403
www.westbowpress.com
844-714-3454

ISBN: 978-1-9736-6762-9 (sc)
ISBN: 978-1-9736-6763-6 (e)

Library of Congress Control Number: 2019908816

Print information available on the last page.

WestBow Press rev. date: 03/22/2021

Contents

Dedication vii
Preface.. ix
Acknowledgments..xiii

Part I   A Time for Everything

Prologue.. xvii
Chapter 1   A Time To Be Born 1
  1.1 Across the Balkan 1
  1.2 The Word Imprinted.. 8
  1.3 A Born-Again Nation 11
  1.4 Summer in the Old Mountain...................................... 17
  1.5 A Little Town in the Skirts.. 24
  1.6 The Atom Was Split, and the World Followed....... 35
  1.7 A Curtain of Iron.. 41
Chapter 2   The Race for Technology.................................... 48
  2.1 A Time for War and a Time for Peace..................... 48
  2.2 In the Beginning Was the Calculus 53
  2.3 Computers Go General 61
  2.4 Man in Space.. 67
  2.5 Mere Bulgarian 73
  2.6 The Making of an Engineer 78
  2.7 Men on the Moon.. 89
Chapter 3   The Golden Age.. 98
  3.1 A Time to Love 98
  3.2 Fatherhood 107
  3.3 From Plums to Computers.. 111
  3.4 Apogee.. 117
  3.5 Leisure when You Can.. 125
  3.6 Missiles and Bread 129
  3.7 Super Supercomputers.. 132

Chapter 4   The Imprisonment of the Mind 142
  4.1 A Hole in the Soul 142
  4.2 Managers and Leaders 147
  4.3 A Time to Be Silent 157
  4.4 Computers Go Personal 163
  4.5 Cracks in the Concrete 168
  4.6 Postdoctoral 171
Chapter 5   A Time to Tear 179
  5.1 Seismic Waves 179
  5.2 The Fall of a System 184
  5.3 And Marriage Follows 187
  5.4 A Time to Give Up 190
  5.5 Exodus 193
  5.6 Believing without Seeing 197
  5.7 Amazing Grace 203
Chapter 6   A Time to Mend 207
  6.1 Baptism in Medicine 207
  6.2 A Time to Dance 211
  6.3 A Time to Build 219
  6.4 A Time to Scatter Stones 224
  6.5 A Time to Gather Them 233
  6.6 The Science of Life 241
  6.7 A Time to Mourn 247
Chapter 7   Epilogue 255

Part II The Wonder of Life

Chapter 1   The Wondrous You 265
Chapter 2   Matter and Spirit 272
Chapter 3   Smartest Animal or Temple of God 275
Chapter 4   Ambassadors in the World 286
  4.1 The World of Nations 290
  4.2 The World of Science 299
Chapter 5   The End of Time 315
Bibliography 319

Dedication

На сестра ми, На мама, На бате, На татко,

с обич и вяра, че ще извикат

името на Господа когато се върне!

To my sister, to my mum, to my brother, to my
dad, with love and trust that they will call on
the name of the Lord when he returns.

Preface

One of the readers' questions to the first edition was "In what way the book of Ecclesiastes speaks about our generation of baby boomers?" Ecclesiastes is a popular book and even non believers often endeavour on reading it disregarding the rest of the Bible. As a result they miss the point. Many do not realise that the Teacher actually is just a character in the setting, probably King Solomon, who speaks out his life experience and observations, but the Author of the book is someone else, perhaps a priest from the Temple who wrote it down and presented it. He introduces the Teacher in the beginning and makes the conclusion in the end (Eccl 1:1 and 12:9). The depressing words of the Teacher are not intended to drive out hope. Rather they are meant to give a hard lesson to the reader; to humble and direct her/him to the only person who can fulfil all life aspirations and make them meaningful, who ultimately brings justice in the world even on a cosmic scale- God alone.

In a similar way this book is twofold. Part I is a life story of a person, who was blind to the presence of God and his goodness. Those who expect a short straightforward Christian testimony here will be disappointed. It comes at the very end of that part. Part II is written by the same author, a different person, who is now a believer and who tries to open the eyes of the reader to the wisdom and power of God. It is more scholarly, philosophical in style but I hope not too dry and devout of emotion. In fact it extends an open invitation for joining the cheerful company of those strangers, who chose to step with one leg in the kingdom of heaven and who one day will be together again in the new heaven.

It is assumed that the reader of this book is interested in both: technology as well as moral loyalty between humans, engaged in creating it; I presume you, like me, aspire to the heroic human endeavour to understand and subdue nature in order to alleviate suffering and make life on this planet sustainable, safer and more enjoyable. To understand the technical side of this writing you do not need special technical knowledge or qualifications. Some readers found the numerous technical details boring but to understand them you do not need more knowledge than secondary education provides. I decided to leave most of them untouched, trusting they are a good account of the birth of the modern computer and the information age that followed. Those events pushed the world into an unprecedented, exponentially increasing, speed of change in all aspects of life, never seen before. For that reason the technical details cannot be simply dismissed. System-centred, engineering minds would always love reading how that technological explosion started, while other, people-centred minds, could skip over the technical bits.

Having received responses from readers of the first edition I became more aware of the fact that there were disagreements between atheists at least about the language they use and how they tolerate other views. There is a new consensus forming on the terminology. Atheists believe that there is no God but some of them are secular members of our society which are generally tolerant to other views if they see consistency and clarity in them. Other atheists, however, are intolerant. They not only reject God but are actively involved in eradicating theistic views in society by law and force. They insult indiscriminately all Christians and other religious groups, dismissing them as dishonest, hypocritical, small minded bigots. For that reason these people are now more precisely identified as *anti-theists*. A distinction is made in the new edition in that respect. I acknowledge the fact that many Christians are intolerant too and I address that point in Part II. No one can deny there are many strands of Christianity, identified or self identified with various terminology and the issues are vast. However it is not the goal of this book to debate all of them systematically, but to seek unity. Everyone who speaks out the Apostles Creed from their heart sincerely is our brother or sister regardless of the differences in opinion on other matters. At this point I am usually asked "How do you know they are sincere in their heart?" Jesus said "By their fruit you will recognise them" (Matthew 7:16). To me this is a mystery. You somehow know it for sure when they are sincere! More on the Apostles Creed can be found in A. McGrath's booklet *I believe*.

There were some typos and stylistic errors that needed to be fixed by revisiting some places and making the text more readable. This edition also contains some small additions and changes in hope to make the exposition more accurate and entertaining.

Salvestian Teller

Acknowledgments

Originally I deemed unnecessary to write formal acknowledgments because an autobiography should, though implicitly, say everything of that sort in the text anyway. It proved to be wrong. I realise I seldom said the words of thanks in the book literally and I should have done so, even though most of the people are not among the living now.

I give thanks to members of my kin: grandmother, father and my mother for giving me life and supporting me through it with great care and love; my sister and my brother for encouraging, mentoring, helping and supporting their youngest sibling when I was little and throughout my education.

I give thanks to all my teachers in secondary education which were very responsible and loving people. Lots of thanks go to all my lecturers and tutors in the Technical University in Sofia. I later realised most of them taught a very dynamic modern field during the communist era, an area difficult to master in a society, isolated from the rest of the world during the cold war. But they did. They taught their subjects of maths, electrodynamics, computers and electronics to a very high standard even on a global scale.

I also thank all those of my superiors and colleagues on my first job in Bulgaria for doing a lot to shield their teams from political harassment and provide interesting and challenging projects to work on in relative peace even though the environment and the system we all lived in was horrendous.

I thank to all my colleagues and team workers who were very generous people. Now I have the opportunity to extend my thanks even to my enemies, though by the end of this project I realised I did not really have any true enemies, apart from the enemy all of us have in our very self. It is true also that God sometimes allows our enemies to take advantage of us for a very good purpose. I hope I explained that concept in the book well and it does not need repetition.

I thank my late wife and her parents for accepting me in their family and for the love and care they showed to me.

A very special gratitude goes to my wife and best friend Tricia for taking interest in my past and for wanting to marry me, though she knew what a bad husband I was in my first marriage. I acknowledge her criticism and comments to the first edition. She also truly showed me how to love and enjoy life in a way I never realised was possible, although the book of Ecclesiastes is not short of that wisdom when it says:

"Enjoy life with your wife, whom you love, all
the days of this fleeting life that God has given
you under the sun (Ecclesiastes 9:9).
Salvestian Teller

PART I

A Time for Everything

Prologue

We were born only yesterday and know nothing, and
our days on earth are but a shadow. (Job 8:9)

For God will bring every deed into judgement,
including every hidden thing, whether it
is good or evil (Ecclesiastes 12:14)

When we are young, life stretches so far ahead into the unknown that time does not seem to bother us at all. Time passes so slowly that we seldom think of it as a resource we may run out of one day. These days, I am beginning to realise, like the biblical character Job, with a sense of urgency, that all my life, and perhaps life generally, is just a tick in the passage of time in the universe. Maybe everyone at a certain point in life receives that kind of urgency, and a strong desire comes with it, to leave some mark behind, something to make one remembered after one is gone. Perhaps when the material world we live in is the only thing we know from experience, the temptation to leave a tangible mark in it before we leave becomes unbearable. We are tempted to redress our personalities and put a final make-up on them or even to rewrite the history by explaining the facts in a way favourable to us.

This of course is vanity, yet it is good to share thoughts that might be of use to other people and especially future generations. But I realise I am not a celebrity, nor am I famous for my professional achievements. I am asking myself, "Is my life experience and my understanding of it valuable to anyone, indeed? Is the reading going to be at least enjoyable to the reader? I'm not an experienced writer, either." After pondering a lot over these questions, without finding answer to them, I decided to just let go of what was inside me and make peace with my past. A sense of peace came upon me that moment, which made the existence of a recipient irrelevant to what I was compelled to produce, as if I was giving an account to a superior who was paying not with money but with granting peace, stretching to eternity.

Life is interesting and valuable, at least just because it is unique. Billions of us are living on the planet, and thousands are born and die every minute. Yet no two of them are the same. Each life contains a valuable message in some form, but not every message gets passed further.

There was a moment when I realised that my life carried a unique experience from a journey across technological advances and science, nations, cultures, world views, politics, and social systems, which changed dramatically at the end of the millennium and are still changing. Our baby boom generation in Europe did not experience major wars with live weapons on a global scale. However, the cold war and the collapse of the Communist system afterwards were not less dramatic and painful for many human beings on both sides of the Iron Curtain. There are many lessons to be learned from that experience.

Mixing work experience and technological history with intimate family life and thoughts on faith and science may look like intellectual snobbery and not very professional for the sake of the art of writing. However, this mixture, I believe, is the only way to perfectly understand the context in which particular relationships and human behaviour develop as well as to link them to a common denominator of all times: the truth from the scripture, which transcends time.

It could also, I hope, help untie the jargon of science for non-academics, who might be interested in the relations between faith and science and are looking for thoughts on how to address the issues. But equally, I hope it would be interesting and encouraging for non believing academics to look in the mind of a colleague who chose to believe and who, although not famous for his achievements, could engage with both faith and science without endangering the integrity of his professional career.

The story here may also help explain humanity through the life of our generation: its upbringing and realisation, the aspirations, the challenges, the successes, the failures, and the disillusionment as we were searching for something firmer to hold on to, for the truth and the meaning of life. As it happened, we experienced turbulence and trauma just in the apogee of our age, when people are usually most productive and expected to bear fruit and enjoy it. Instead, we had to make life changing decisions and dramatic moves that were very similar to the flying of an adult bird kept in a cage since birth. That often included a complete change of our world views and value systems, and called us to step out of the narrow profession, engaging more actively with social and ethical issues.

Perhaps the most important conclusion in the Bible's book of Ecclesiastes is the awareness that without God, life is ultimately meaningless. Consequently, we are compelled as humankind to either accept the truth that what motivates us here in this world is of primary importance, something we will be called to account later, or alternatively fall into a meaningless world of traumatic oblivion, destined for nonexistence.

As we grow older, we tend to get tired from life experience and relationships, and think that young people are bored from them too. But far from it. Some of them have high interest in real-life experiences, although I do not attend to detail on facts, dates, or names. If they are brought, it is to highlight the experience, which gave rise to a thought or a concept in my mind, and also to preserve authenticity.

This is a Christian testimony. It is a product of nostalgia for the age of innocence and romanticism, but also a witness to the triumph of goodness over wrongdoing, even when we were the wrongdoers in certain situations. Remembering should not so much vindicate the past as to be a faith-filled analysis that prepares for the future. Bringing life back with a new understanding helps cast out gloom and despair, and allows light and optimism to reign in the life of future generations, our children.

I believe a story of a sinner, just as I am, is an unequivocal witness to God's magnificent grace which can turn forgiven sinners into his children, princes able to partner and even reign with Him. The reader might have come through many books, telling about how good it is for humanity to think that god exists. I hope I have done a little bit better by helping you realise that actually God IS.

All Bible quotations are from the NIV translation.

1

A Time To Be Born

There is a time for everything.... A time to be
born and a time to die. (Ecclesiastes 3:1–2)

1.1 Across the Balkan

The mountain chain, rich of beech forest, dividing Bulgaria
into northern and southern parts, is called Old Mountain
(Стара Планина). The locals who lived there for centuries
called it simply "the Balkan." It is the mountain that gave the
name to the whole peninsula stretching from the Carpathian
Mountains and Danube river down to the Mediterranean on
the south.

Our village was on the northern slopes of the Balkan near
Tryavna. A story goes that when the nearby Turnovo, then the
capital of the Bulgarian Kingdom, fell under the Turks in the
fourteenth century, and the leader of the church, Patriarch
Evtimiy, was exiled to Anatolia, people followed the cortege on
foot, weeping all the time. Some of them stopped and settled
in the entrance to the pass across the mountain. The settlers
were called Plachkovtsi (weepers).

The village became important in 1913 when a railway
crossed the Balkan, and a key station was built right here. The

1

trains coming from Ruse, through the Danube Plain, were pulled by steam locomotives and had to change engines before entering the pass with a type suitable for steep slopes. It was the ideal place for a base station and soon became a well-known holiday destination, when artists, poets, and writers like Ivan Vazov, for example, came here to draw inspiration from the beauty of the mountain slopes and the scenic railway, with many tunnels and stunning views.

It must have been a big challenge for the civil engineers who built this railway, with some twenty-five tunnels and numerous bridges to cross the mountain here, where an Alpine cog wheel would perhaps be more suitable for transporting passengers. But it was not built for holiday makers. There was an important coal mine with coke ovens nearby. Further up the mountain the rail track weaves, making a "6" on the highest point and then an "8" just after that on the way down to the Thracian Valley to the south.

One day, we were picking wild raspberries there and shortly after that boarded the train on the station up the hill. A man said, "I saw you near the track ages ago. Have you run after the train?" Travellers on the coaches could have a funny experience of seeing mountain hikers through the window walking up the hill near the rail track and then fifteen minutes later, the same hikers again, as if they were running with the train, not realising the train had actually turned back but was higher on the slope.

My mother was born in a house on the crest of the mountain ridge, where a little railway stop called Buzovets and a station further on called Crestets were built. From here on, the train started its descent into southern Bulgaria. My other grandfather was a tradesman for the army, and he built his house here to use the stop for his trade. A little hamlet grew around it as a result of it, with beautiful views to the south and to the north. His father in law was mayor of the nearest town, called Stanchev Han (Stanchev's Inn). When my father married the old man's granddaughter, he gave him a few beehives as a present. However, my father did not have the patience of a beekeeper, and after a few years, the bees died. His hungry family liked the honey, but no one fed them sugar during the winter. After hearing the bad news, the old man came to Dad's house, just a few miles down the slopes, flourishing his club high in the air. "Do not complain to me of the exploiters, your employers," he said, "because you are one of them." Dad had just had an accident in the factory with his arm nearly severed at the shoulder by a belt. That saved him from being whipped for the loss of his bees.

The railway at the time also served an important commercial route between the town of Ruse, on the Danube river, and Stara Zagora and Plovdiv, on the southern side of the Balkan and further across the Rodopy Mountains to the Ionian Sea in the Mediterranean. Transport of cargo by ships from central and eastern Europe via the Danube across the Black Sea and destined for the Mediterranean through the Bosphorus could be cut down by days. It also passed through important agricultural areas.

More importantly this railway represents a symbol of the unification of the nation and its independence. Against all odds, in 1885, people denounced the Russian administration on the north and the Turkish rule on the south; united, they later declared independence. No wonder Tsar Boris III, a great fan of modern technology, liked coming here, driving the royal train himself. My father remembered him on the annual village fair, coming off his train and mingling with the crowds wearing a machinist's costume and worker's cap, all dirty from the coal.

In the summer, I stayed in my granny's house a mile up the mountain on a southern slope facing the hill with the ninth tunnel. The railway was on the opposite slope a hundred yards away from the house. Trains passed by almost every hour or so after leaving the station from the north or coming to it from the heights on the south. My friends and cousins were ten years old and never tired watching the trains. Most interesting were the cargo trains, which had two locomotives: one in front and another one on the tail. Sometimes, the train was so long and heavy that the engines were puffing and panting like slow-moving animals so that one could jump on and off the train easily. We sometimes did.

To be kept away from trouble, we always had something to do: chop wood, tend the animals on the common grazing fields, and so on. When there was nothing to do, we read books suggested from school for the summer, including world classics like *Uncle Tom's Cabin*, *Treasure Island*, *Robinson Crusoe*, *King Arthur and the Knights of the Round Table*, and many others.

The land, being on the crossroads from Europe to to Asia and Africa, was the home of the most ancient civilisations in the world, predating the Sumer, Egyptian, and Mycenaean cultures. Later, in antiquity, the Thracians established some forms of statehood. They were influenced by the Hellenistic culture on the south of the peninsula, where people later were blessed to have enough time and resources not only to indulge in pleasures but to exercise their minds with natural philosophy.

Homer's *Odyssey* and *Iliad* were on the curriculum, and we took interest in them, given that many of the events, though mythological, took place near here. The Thracians were skilful craftsmen and goldsmiths. Numerous treasures, unearthed from the barrows of our land, showed they liked not only the gold itself but also beauty in all its forms. The Argonauts sailed through the waters of the Black Sea to retrieve the Golden Fleece. Colchis is believed to be in the Caucasus Mountains across the sea from Burgas on the eastern shores of the waters. Also favoured in our culture were the mythical heroes of Orpheus and Eurydice. Their love story took place in the Rodopy Mountains on the south. The Greek myths inspired love, strong characters, physical strength, and endurance, but they also glorified crafty minds and cunning behaviour, which children often found disturbing. The stories about chivalry and trust in *The Knights of the Round Table* sounded much more cheerful and reassuring.

Granny had a clock, but she seldom looked at it. I rarely saw her setting up the alarm. Instead, she had two other very reliable clocks: The rooster crowed at about four o'clock in the morning, when she had to feed the animals. Her roosters were always very beautifully coloured with red, green, and gold. Only one was selected to "rule" over his harem for an year or so. This was a big fierce creature, which the little kids were afraid of, but the older ones liked irritating with a stick, especially when they went on top of a hen to mate, misunderstanding the lovemaking for violence. Over the years, Granny carefully selected her roosters and their replacements from the young generation of chicks so she could proudly put her name on the breed if she was to sell one. And the roosters crowed beautifully.

The other clock Granny had were the passenger trains passing on the rail track on the opposite slope: one in the morning at roughly nine, and one in the afternoon around five. This clock she could see or hear wherever she went in the village during the day. The noise of the passenger train was not like the heavy cargo train. It had fast rail-track wallops, and the engine was breathing quick, hooting along.

When I became a student in Sofia, I loved coming home on this rail route whenever possible, though the connections were not that convenient. The other one possible was to leave Sofia and cross the Old Mountain on the pass along River Iskar. That was the route from Sofia to Varna on the east coast, which required changing at Gorna Oriahovitca.

The mountain people on both sides of the Old Mountain have lived for centuries; it was a hard but surprisingly self-sufficient, sustainable, and yet prosperous life by today's standards, surviving through helping each other like a big family. They produced almost everything they needed locally. In the old times, the only things they bought from far away were salt, sugar, spices, oil, and kerosene. For this, they would go with convoys on donkeys or horses across the mountain to the southern towns of Stara Zagora and Plovdiv, where the climate was warmer. Sometimes, they'd go farther across the Rodopy Mountains down to the White Sea (the Bulgarian name of the Ionian Sea in the Mediterranean). They mainly barter-traded, offering their produce of wool and fabrics, meat, cheese, dried fruits, and grain. Because of no significant surplus, not much was traded then for money. The other trade route was northwards to Bucharest across the Danube river, where my grand-grandfather sold his meat produce.

The Greeks, who occupied the very southern part of the peninsula and had a big influence on the pre-Christian period of the Roman empire, had a language and culture quite different from theirs. Even in their golden age of Pericles, did they not seek the inlands of the surrounding three continents, but colonised the islands and the coastal areas around. They were people of the sea in their heart. When the Roman empire split in AD 395, the western part, with Rome as a centre, continued to use Latin, whereas the eastern part, with a centre in Byzantium (Constantinople), was dominated by the Greek culture and gradually established the Greek language. Sadly, the political division was followed by a schism in the church in 1014, when the Eastern Orthodoxy, based in Constantinople, ceased to be aligned with the pope in Rome.

In the ninth century, people on the Balkan peninsula received the Christian message through the missionary work of Cyril and Methodius. They worked initially among the western Slavic population of Moravia and Pannonia (today territories of Czech, Slovakia, Austria, and Hungary). They used the so-called Glagolic script and translated and circulated the Gospel in that script, promoting the liturgy in the language of the people there. The pope originally supported the mission, but after he met with resistance from the German bishops, he withdrew his permission to use the local language in liturgy, and people got stuck with Latin.

Later in the tenth century, the disciples of Cyril (Clement of Ochrid, Naum of Preslav, and others) began to teach the people of the Balkans. They adapted the alphabet to better serve the Bulgarian language. One letter for each sound: simple to learn and apply. A few letters were used to pronounce differently which largely accommodated the dialects at the time east to west. Their work here was in a sense a continuation of the broader mission of the Gospels among the barbaric tribes of Europe, which were gradually converted into a community in the Roman Empire, based on Christian ethics. Christianity in the Balkans would help amalgamate the dialects of a multitude of ethnic groups of local Thracians and numerous nomadic tribes.

The politics in the Eastern Roman Empire, later named Byzantium, dictated that the "eastern barbarians" would be integrated into their culture much quicker if the Greek alphabet was modified to suit their language. That is what Cyril's disciples did. They were engaged by prince Boris I, an established ruler on the Balkans, who was converted to Christianity by the Byzantium emperor himself, to translate the Gospel from Greek to Bulgarian using the new script. They also translated other useful literature from Latin and Greek. The old script was used in Bulgaria till it fell under the Turks in 1396 (the battle at Nikopol). The Gospels of Tsar Ivan Alexander of 1355, which can now be seen in the British Library, are an example of the high artistic values of the manuscripts created at that time, written in Middle Bulgarian.

Christianity on the Balkans, after the fall of the Roman Empire, was a religion of kings and their nobles, established under Byzantine model, in multiple rival kingdoms of which Bulgaria was a dominating power for some time. Ordinary people of the feudal economy throughout the land never truly lived in strong communities united by faith, but were divided by their rulers in pursuit of power. Naturally they could not compete with the much stronger militant theocratic society of the Turks, based on Islam, which were expanding from the south-east across the straits of Bosphorus and the Dardanelles.

After the fall of Bulgaria and the rest of the peninsula, under the Turks, the majority of churches were destroyed in multiple waves of Islamisation. Yet Christian life continued in the monastic communities in the mountains, behind fortified walls of the monasteries, which were painstakingly rebuilt each time after religious onslaughts and looting raids. The monasteries helped preserve Bulgaria's language and national identity. After centuries of persecution, churches were allowed to be built again. However, the authorities insisted that they should be not taller than one floor, so in order to gain space, they often were burrowed below the ground level.

1.2 The Word Imprinted

> One generation will commend your works to another;
> they will tell of your mighty acts. (Psalm 145:4)

A revival period came about at the beginning of nineteenth century; people started to perform liturgies in open-air altars, often in connection with village fairs. The industrious people of the Balkans became valued ethnic members of the Ottoman Empire because they were the main producers for the army. Skilful craftsmen, they provided hand-woven clothes from wool and leather as well as important agricultural produce: grain, meat, dairy, and various utensils. The expansion of this trade eventually made a class of well-off middle-class Bulgarians and encouraged architecture and art. Young people were hungry for education and a new way of life, away from the feudal Ottoman culture in decline. Many of them were sent by their wealthy parents to study abroad, where they got familiar with other cultures and political systems.

In 1840, a new translation of the New Testament (NT) was performed by Neofit Rilski from the old manuscripts as well as from new Greek translations to modern Bulgarian in the western dialect, as the language changed over the centuries. This work was sponsored by the British and Foreign Bible Society. Since the printing press was banned from the Balkan lands by the Turks, it was pressed in Smyrna (Izmir) in several revisions, helped by Konstantin Fotinov.

At the same time, British and American missionaries coordinated their work and promoted new educational programmes in Bulgaria. They sponsored building new schools and publishing newspapers, magazines, literature, and history, geography, arithmetic, and medicine books. New churches were established with the help of the American Congregational Church and the Methodist Church centred in Britain. After many years of hard work, in 1871, a whole translation of the New and Old Testament in modern Bulgarian was printed in Tsarigrad (Constantinople).

The success of the British-American mission was secured by employing the most educated and knowledgeable scholars of the land, who knew the language and the dialects very well. The team worked from old Bulgarian and Greek manuscripts and even English texts, but the most important was that they knew the language of the people they were translating for, so readers could get the right meaning of the verses. They adopted a modern approach by translating not word by word but by meaning. This translation, which also included the eastern dialects, was performed by a team including the poet Petko

Slaveykov from Tryavna, Konstantin Fotinov from Samokov, Christodul Kostovich, Nicola Michaylovski, and Elias Riggs. Riggs, from the Congregational Church, learned Bulgarian to a high degree of proficiency from Fotinov and was able to take a hands-on approach in the project.

All this work was open and legal. The Turkish administration was not against it because they realised that there was a spiritual vacuum among the people, which could be quickly filled with influence from Christian Russia, their major foe. Their only concern was converting people from Islam, which was punishable by death. For that reason, Christian missions in the Turkish Empire were still a very risky business.

The Tsarigrad edition of the Bulgarian Bible was an outstanding achievement. The text was in great demand and was used in the years to come. Its distribution, however, was strongly opposed by the Greek Orthodox clerics, who tried to push the Greek language northward among the Bulgarian-speaking population. In 1830, Greece gained independence with the help of her Western allies, Britain and France, and had geopolitical aspirations, just like Russia. In many traditionally Bulgarian-speaking churches north of Greece, the liturgies were performed in Greek, without understanding. So people were very excited about the new translation in their own language. The governing clerics from the Greek Orthodoxy, however, collected copies of the new translation, which was in the Protestant tradition, and burned them. These actions alienated people from the clergy and provoked a campaign for autonomy among the Bulgarian churches, based on two principles: free election of their leaders from their own people and freedom to perform the services in the Bulgarian language. In 1870, this request was granted by the sultan in a *ferman* (charter). It established the Bulgarian Exarchy (independent church), a very important step towards a full national independence for Bulgaria.

1.3 A Born-Again Nation

Independence does not always need to be won with violence. When the time is right, it can also be granted to an assertive, determined request. But naturally, most examples of gaining independence in history are with a physical onslaught on the oppressor, with the intention to harm and kill. Yet it is justified only when rebellion is the last resort in achieving a good cause. This was not the case for Bulgaria in the years after 1870, when so much had just been achieved through prayer, campaigning and diplomacy. Would the Turks agree to a demand for national independence in the next step? Well, why not? Would they prefer to have a breakaway hostile neighbour with Russia on their doorstep, or would they not show wisdom by granting independence and having a friendly neighbour afterwards, who they could still have as an ally?

There had to be a fight. Otherwise, how could we convince others we were absolutely determined and able to run our own affairs yet without causing harm to our neighbours when shaking the grounds? But fighting does not always mean revolution with rifles. An example of this way was the independence of India, which came as a result of nonviolent protests led by Gandhi.

I realise I am not very convincing. You may say there is no such example in the early history, and you might point to the Bible passage, "Beat your ploughs into swords" (Joel 3:10). And you'd be right. Travelling through Bulgaria recently, I passed by a monument to a local revolutionary hero of the revival. There was an inscription there echoing the same call: "Sell your field and buy a gun!" The ultimate answer to this, I think, comes from Matthew 27:21–23. But our rebellion was not an act of terrorism that thrived in the absence of faith, that good is stronger than evil. That is the very essence of Christianity. Yet if the faith is weak, it undermines the commitment with doubt. Will God really hear our petition?

Will he give us good things or just fool us with an ersatz? Is there God at all?

After five hundred years under foreign rule, Bulgarians ran out of patience and took to the gun. The revolt in 1876, encouraged with Russian support, was of course quashed by the Ottomans. Russians had good reasons to invade. A year later, they crossed over the Danube river and marched across the Balkan, all the way down to Constantinople on the Bosphorus. But what was the cost? Our national heroes, Vasil Levski, Christo Botev, and many others, gave their lives in a violent revolt. The lives of thousands of Ukrainian soldiers, fighting for the Russian Emperor, were sacrificed too. Alongside them were many volunteers from Bulgaria, Romania, and others. And our history never counts the Turkish soldiers here because they were the enemy. But what then are the moral grounds of the new order we aspired to? Was it a crusade? Was it a war for hegemony? Or was it a war in a wilderness: the stronger kills the weaker, and the weaker is no more?

Whatever we may think it was, God agreed to it. It was God's gracious act of redemption for a people, which long ago were one of the first in the world to translate and proclaim the Gospel, his Word, in the language of their land and beyond. After generations in servitude, they were changed and now called to serve the Lord of love in freedom again. A time of hunger and thirst for righteousness was going to be filled with a time of restoration and rebuilding. But as one might expect the war brought about enormous difficulties on the road to independence.

In the Treaty of Berlin in 1878, the West agreed that northern Bulgaria (Moesia) should be annexed by Christian Russia but insisted southern Bulgaria (northern Thrace) to be given back as autonomy under Turkey. Macedonia, on the west, remained under the Turkish yoke. A tremendous wave of resentment among the people in the land against the treaty was gathering momentum.

Eight years after the Russian-Turkish war ended, people on both sides of the Balkan stood up and declared the unification of the north to the south. The revolt went well, almost without casualties. However, none of the great powers or neighbouring country dared to acknowledge the unification of Bulgaria. Serbia even attacked from the west but they were defeated by the outstanding heroism and enthusiasm of the new Bulgarian army, which marched from the eastern border with Turkey to the west for just a few days and engaged in battle almost straight away. It required nearly superhuman effort from the infantry. This operation is recorded in the world military history as a heroic achievement without a precedent.

In the mean time Russia suspected the West was playing games. They caused Prince Battenberg, in charge of their principality, to abdicate. The West presumed Russian manipulation. In reality, no foreign powers were involved. The action was spontaneous and truly inspired by the people's determination to be free from foreign rule. However Battenberg's abdication caused a deep political crisis in Bulgaria, which rippled across Europe. It was a time of testing for the newborn nation.

Stefan Stambolov, from Veliko Turnovo, used a modern tool of communication- the telegraph, during the revolt to take control; the only politician who responded promptly to the local actions in Thrace and managed to get on top of them with a vision. In the following years, a delegation of renown Bulgarian scholars, intellectuals, and politicians, led by this outstanding politician, toured Europe in search for a king. Representatives on his mission team now were unwilling to establish yet another republic in troublesome Europe and decided that the royalist network was a safer option to win support for the cause. Eventually, they made a proposal to a German prince, Ferdinand Sax Coburgota. He accepted. In 1908, Ferdinand declared the third sovereign Bulgarian Kingdom; the ceremony was held in the ancient capital, Veliko Turnovo. It was a remarkable day of the birth of a new nation through the power of unity.

Russian influence still remained strong in the following years. During the Russian administration in northern Bulgaria, before the unification, many positive achievements were made: foundations of a strong disciplined army, reliable healthcare and medical tuition, educational progress, achievements not fully accomplished even in the vast empire far away, which was soon to be crippled by civil war and revolution.

Macedonia remained under the Ottomans and continued their struggle for independence. The Ilinden uprising in 1903, instigated by now independent Bulgaria, was crushed with cruelty by the Ottomans. Ironically, united Bulgaria, now established as a major economic and military power in the Balkans, with its geopolitical ambitions, was taking over the role Russia used to have. However, people in Macedonia had to wait till the First Balkan War in 1913, when all the newly hatched Balkan states—Serbia, Romania, Greece, and Bulgaria—united against Turkey and won. But the result was not what Macedonian people expected- partitioning. Consequently, Tsar Ferdinand I, who felt Bulgaria sacrificed too many of its own people for the liberation of the rest of the Balkan population from the coalition, ordered the fighting to continue, now against his former allies. It was a bad decision, but it would be unfair to put all the blame on the tsar. He actually responded to the sentiments and the aspirations of the newly hatched oligarchs and industrialists who dreamed of a new imperial Bulgaria and badly exploited the desires of all Bulgarian-speaking people in Moesia, Thrace, and Macedonia to live united. As a result of this second war, he had to give back some territory. The disputed land was divided between Greece and Serbia.

A wave of cultural onslaught began against Bulgarian literature, churches, and organisations in all lands outside mainland Bulgaria. Vardar Macedonia, annexed by Serbia under the name Banovia, was subjected to a ruthless domination of Serbian language and culture. In Greek Macedonia, Greek was declared the only official language. In the following years, Bulgaria received up to a million immigrants from Macedonian and Thracian lands outside the borders, which created huge problems, exacerbated by the following WWI, ending with military defeat, political and economic crisis. Its influence on the Balkans was greatly diminished. Despite this, the country was prepared to support Macedonian independence, and in 1918, the Bulgarian government of Malinov offered to surrender land for a new independent Macedonia. However, Serbia and Greece opposed the plan. In 1929, Vardar Macedonia and Ohrid, the spiritual heartland of many Bulgarians, was included in the artificially created state of Yugoslavia. Its language further diverged from Bulgarian.

The constitution of 1879, under Russian influence, established the Bulgarian Orthodox Church as the national religion of Bulgaria, which helped infuse Christian ethics in society, with freedom for other faiths and a pluralistic political system, allowing a transition from feudal order to capitalism. The newly formed Protestant evangelical churches during the revival period, although few in number, remained the powerhouse of Christian life in the country for years to come. Their work was in peace with the Orthodox Church and the other denominations.

However, the conversion of the majority of people after the liberation, in one way or another, took place under the coercive power of the state, which produced a religious nation that recognised Christianity just as a good moral code, enforced by the government. Bulgarians remained nominally Christian. It did not result in spiritually stronger mature Christian communities by studying the Bible and infirming their faith, which had the power to transform societies beyond the narrow aspirations of nationalism and politics. Politics uses institutional religion to ameliorate and control the society by imposing ethical standards. But only faith in the spirit can transform and change, as God intended. As a result, the Bulgarians were given political power before they grew up spiritually in their faith and established a stable long-lasting foundation of their identity and authority. Naturally, that power was weak and transient.

Nevertheless, the invaluably positive effect was that after hundreds of years of cultural oppression under the Ottomans, the country was able to rejoin Corpus Christianum, the community of Christians, in Europe. Although the Eastern Orthodox churches were not in communion with the churches of the Western world since the schism, the society was still able to join the club of cultures in Europe, where all private and public life was controlled, or at least under the strong influence, by the Christian church. Those cultures had been shaped for hundreds of years by the Christian values of the Bible, while Ottoman Bulgaria was out of it.

Alongside the cultural changes, the country underwent serious economic ones. Elin Pelin's short stories, despite their too harsh cynicism, truthfully depict the country life and the relation of ordinary people to authorities and religion at the time. His novel *Гераците* (*The Gerak Family*) is a very moving story about the changes in the new liberated Bulgaria, where the traditional generational family enterprises were gradually being replaced with mechanised manufacturing. The idyllic work of the craftsmen in old Bulgaria turned into labour. Young people had to leave their families and migrate to places with jobs. The traditional families, where knowledge and love passed from older generations to the younger, no longer existed, and old people became redundant, useless. The division of work in mechanised manufacturing caused workers to no longer see the result of their work; they were treated as units without identity, as if the meaning of their life evaporated.

Yet the amalgamation between state and church in these early stages of establishing the capitalist order in Bulgaria worked well to secure Christian ethics in society, to restrain the unbound aim to self-interest, against unrestrained profits, interest on loans, and so on. Entrepreneurs were called to behave responsibly and even practice self-denial. Monarchy was also about to come out of its inept, private image and become public and popular. The rituals were part of a concerted attempt to make the monarch a symbol and focus of nationhood.

1.4 Summer in the Old Mountain

The first settlers in the villages near Tryavna apparently came from Stara Zagora in the region of Thrace. They were all Christians, finding it difficult to adapt to the hectic commercialised lifestyle in the valleys, looking for more peaceful and uncorrupted life. The population in all the mountain regions of Bulgaria, with the exception of the Pomaks in the Rodopy Mountains on the south, had remained Christian during the Ottoman rule because the lands with warmer climate and more fertile valleys would always be left to the ruling Turkish administration. The Pomaks were coercively converted to Islam in the 17th century, but they were allowed to preserve their own language.

In the nineteenth century, most houses in Tryavna were built with timber; walls were a double layer of woven tree branches, plastered with clay. They were nicely washed with white lime. The roofs were made with beautiful slabs of stone, looking quite heavy for the light structure beneath, which nevertheless was tough and durable. Lifestyle in these houses was very primitive. The loo usually was a latrine outside. The drinking and washing up was provided with water drawn from the nearby well. Grandfather was a stone mason. He was building the church in Ressen, near Turnovo, when he was called into the army for World War I. He fell in the Battle of the River Cherna (Crna) in 1916, leaving behind a widow with five infants.

When Grandfather was called into the army, he had only managed build the ground floor of his house. My Dad, still an adolescent, had to finish it little by little, with the help of relatives. He was very proud of his achievement and remembered an earthquake in the 1930s; they were sitting outside and saw how the house canted quite a lot in one direction like a toy, as if trying to bow to someone, and then returned back to its straight position. The only repair they had to do was to plaster the cracked walls and replace some of the slabs fallen from the roof. At the same time, many buildings in the town collapsed, and many casualties were reported.

My granny, the mother of my father, was a tough Christian. Faced with the task of raising five orphans on her own, she turned quite strong in character and managed to provide for all the children. The villagers had a nice little stone church they built a century ago. The church was still full of worshipers on Sundays in the early fifties, when I used to go there for summer school vacations.

Granny had an oil lamp ("кандило") in a little niche, which was continuously burning and where she would make the sign of the cross and pray. For most villagers, Christianity was not just going to church and observing rituals. They did practice what they believed by sharing and helping each other in every aspect of life. One could feel the genuine spirit of togetherness at that time by the way they greeted each other. If a worker in the field was passed by someone in the road, they would say, "God helps" ("Помага Бог"). The other would respond, "God is good" ("Дал Бог добро") The service on

Sunday, unlike most Orthodox churches, sometimes had a short lesson and comments on the scripture from the priest. He would instruct and attend to the needs of every individual personally.

In 1947, Granny had me baptised here as a baby, keeping it secret from my father. Naturally, I have no remembrance of that event, but I do believe it made a positive difference in my life, at least with the firm determination with which Granny dedicated me to a life of trusting in good. One day, when I was older, she revealed to me that my Dad did not want a third child (me). She opposed his thoughts fervently, and I came into the world. In my childish optimism and forgiving nature, I did not make a drama out of it; neither she did, but it was good to know. I knew I was not planned by my father because of the hard life my ancestors lived. In the past, adding more children to a family was like adding more workers, but after the war, they would like to see them educated as well. My Dad himself wanted to be educated, but life was just too hard. He was a bright and intelligent chap, but an orphan in a poor mountain area. He wanted his children to be educated, but he couldn't see that happening with more children in the family. Yet life was going to change soon in his favour.

The generation of my parents were raised in the tough years after the Balkan Wars and the following World War I, which fuelled extreme socialist movements. Ferdinand I was forced to abdicate. Despite his failures, he managed to unite the people in the land, ultimately leading to territorial expansion and to establishing the Bulgarian state as the most powerful country in the Balkans. After his abdication, the fragile constitutional monarchy of his son Boris III struggled.

After the 1917 revolution in Russia, the fear from Communism spreading westward brought to life totalitarian-style governments, which quickly precipitated the shift from social democratic trade unionism towards Marxism. The political landscape in Central Europe was heading in a similar direction, with the Nazis on the rise. There was an apparent polarisation in geopolitics, east to west. Bulgaria was always tossed between the two cultures.

On the east, life in Russia now was based on Communism. God was expelled from public life altogether and was restricted in the minds of those being governed. Private liberty was therefore sacrificed for the sake of equality. The eastern model was on the rise and admired by working classes across the world. However, since God was not in it, He had to be replaced by perishable personality idols. In theory, any government is supposed to rule for the sake of those governed, but sin corrupts and undermines order with hypocrisy and lies. There was little love and no purpose or meaning in life, other than material gain. Yet the material prosperity was a merit on a national not personal level. People were taught they were mere mortals, and there was no afterlife. Consequently, they did not genuinely believe they would see the end goals fulfilled: the utopia of material abundance and equality.

On the other hand, the theocratic image of Western capitalism, which gave rise to the Industrial Revolution and promoted peace and stability, was in decline. The old school of economics employed science and postulated that self-interest, as an objective fact, is the motor of society. The long-term view of it, however, was that the economic system would work like a clock, according to the laws of physics. In fact, no system involving humans can work automatically without the conviction and sincere support of those who exercise it or otherwise become corrupt. Capitalism, driven by unrestrained self-interest and without ethics attached to it, is a delusion, a delusion that greed is a natural law which could power the economy to produce wealth for everybody, even when it is not distributed equally. Equality is sacrificed and left in the hands of social programmes which do not always believe what they preach. At the same time liberty, including that of production as well as of personal life, is praised.

This meant that the old capitalism had also an atheistic or secular model for the society. In such a system, there is no much love but a merciless law of the wild nature, where the fittest survives, and the rest die. Such philosophy wrongly postulated this law as an objective truth, on an equal basis with the laws of physics, and considered personal beliefs a private matter with their own understanding of the truth. But private beliefs actually vary significantly and are generally incompatible and conflicting. Peace, therefore, rests not so much on unity of values as on proper order, enforced by those who govern not for the sake of all their subjects. If there is no love in governing, power becomes for the few and transient.

In little Bulgaria, always in the middle between overwhelming Eastern and Western powers with their -isms, life was swinging one way or another, and willingly or unwillingly, people had to live on grace. Dad, an orphan from the war, had a tsar's bursary and studied carpentry and furniture craft in the town of Tryavna, known for the best carpenters and woodcarvers in the country. He opened his own workshop later on. He was enthusiastic and talented in art and furniture making, but he apparently did not do well on the business side. It was not the time for business, anyway. World War II was coming, and after that, sweeping changes were under way in the country, which was not to see a free-market economy for more than half a century. But for now, with customers failing to pay for commissioned orders, he had to close his shop and work for others. Disappointed by the idea of a free enterprise and the dishonesty of customers and employers, he soon joined ranks with the trade unions, the Workers Party, and the anti-Nazi movement later on. In my parents' view, like many others, religion was an instrument to manipulate and control people for the sake of the ruling class.

In 1936, my father got married, and he and my mother had three children: my brother, my sister, and me. The family moved to the nearby town of Dryanovo when I was three years old (an event I do not remember). There was a factory for repairing railway coaches, providing more secure work for my Dad. This was where I grew up, but I visited Granny during vacations and over the summer.

Summer in the rural mountains was a blessed time for little children of busy parents. While they were becoming increasingly preoccupied with building advanced industrialised socialism in the town, up in the mountains, life was still like it was at the time of Jesus. Agriculture was already quite mechanised in the valleys and the plains of the country, but in the mountain areas, covering two-thirds of the country, it was not.

I remember when we harvested wheat, barley, and oats. This was done manually with sickles. The working parties involved the extended families. We, the kids, were involved in gleaning and bringing cool water from the faraway spring. Almost every other person in the village was a relative: an uncle, an aunt, or a cousin. The most exciting time for us kids was threshing. It was done with cows or oxen pulling a flint-studded threshing board in the threshing yard. One or two of us would sit on the threshing board and drive the cows, happily riding round and round, despite the burning sun. Little by little, the wooden board we were sitting on would cut the golden sheaves beneath and turn them into straw. The ears would fall apart in chaff and grain. The most responsible moment for the drivers was to extend a shovel towards the bottom of the cow when she was to release droppings on the sheaves.

To separate the chaff from the grain, we used a bit more modern technology, taken from before Industrial Revolution. The mix of straw, chaff, and grain was gathered in a heap and taken to the winnower. There, one of us kids would turn the fan with a handle, and another one would start putting the mixture in a wooden funnel, which guided it through a set of moving sieves while the fan blew away all the chaff and straw. The stupid seeds of weeds would go through even the densest sieve, down to an outlet, while the largest seeds of the grain would stay on a highest ranked sieve, going through another outlet destined to become seeds in the autumn. The middle ranks sorted grain for food of various quality. The winnower was such an amazing, magical machine for us the kids; we would fight for a turn to work on it. In the meantime, the sifted straw was piled in the barn, and later, when the work was finished, we would climb up the beams under the roof and jump down into the straw. We were sometimes allowed to sleep in the barn. The memories of the sweet fragrance of hay and straw in the barn in the summer still stay in my mind, as if it were yesterday.

Life in the mountain villages was harder than in the valleys and the plains. Summer came a month later and autumn a month earlier. Some plants did not do well. Potatoes did very well and were valued, as were oats. Plums had a specific Balkan flavour, and plum jam from the region was sold elsewhere. Apples and pears were satisfactory, but vines could not survive the winter at this altitude. People always looked for an additional source of income, like different crafts. Granny had a hand-driven wooden loom, and she weaved nice rugs on it. I was amazed at her ingenuity to make rugs from old cotton fabrics cut in fine strips, dyed, and weaved. The best rugs, however, were made with wool in traditional colourful patterns of the central Balkan region, dyed white, green, and red.

One year, the cooperative wanted to use one spare room at Granny's place to produce silk. We whitewashed the walls, installed wooden shelves, and had a go. It was immensely fun to climb the mulberry trees for leaves to feed the silkworms. And what a good study for children to watch the butterflies laying their eggs and then to see the eggs hatching little worms. Those creatures swallowed enormous quantities of mulberry leaves before they became fat caterpillars and started weaving themselves in beautiful golden cocoons. I could watch a caterpillar weaving its cocoon for hours. And then to see those caterpillars later suddenly emerging from the cocoons morphed in butterflies again. What a wonder.

The kids stripped nearly all the leaves from the mulberry trees in the vicinity. Eventually, the trees nearly died. After all their leaves were gone, swallowed by the hungry silkworms, Granny decided that she had enough of silk producing and returned to her potatoes.

1.5 A Little Town in the Skirts

In September, we went back to school in the town down the river valley, with cheeks and shoulders burned by the sun. I missed the summer in the mountains. But I liked the school in the town too. I was always happy to see my new study books for the year fresh, smelling of printing ink from the press. I would browse for hours on end in the days before the school started.

During the revival period, Dryanovo had three churches and a monastery, hugged in the northern skirts of the Old Mountain. A clock tower, one of the earliest built in the country, showed time-keeping began to play an important role in the emerging industrial transformation of the region.

Apart from agriculture, crafts, and trade, many people were highly skilled in building. In fact, it was the hometown of Kolyu Ficheto, an architect of the national revival who commissioned many projects throughout the country for the Turkish-run municipalities. He became famous for being willing to prove the strength of his design by sitting under a bridge while a heavy gun passed over. This was during the war in 1877, when the Russians were advancing against the Turks and had to move heavy artillery across bridges. Masons and builders from the region seldom got formally trained during

Turkish rule. Instead, they passed the skill from generation to generation, learning on the job as very young apprentices and then certifying with the guilds.

Ficheto had a distinctive architectural style, with yoke-shaped waved roofs and facades, an example of which is the beautiful Holy Trinity Church in Svishtov. The bridge on the River Yantra in Byala, an astonishingly beautiful structure, noted by many Western travellers, was performed in a similar style. St. Nicola Church in his own town, next to the first civil school, Maxim Raykovich, represents the spirit of the national revival in the area, where beauty and art seemed to have taken a good part in the life of the citizens. One quite extraordinary example of revival architecture is the three-floor House of Lafchiev (Лафчиевата Къща), built around 1840 by Kolyu Gaydargiata using only wood, without the use of any metal nails or brackets.

The town took part in the 1876 uprising by providing sanctuary to a small detachment of rebels from Turnovo. The monastery then received heavy shelling from the Ottoman guns on the cliffs surrounding this beautiful spot. Just above the monastery enclave is the entrance of a cave, where remains of a Palaeolithic settlement were found. We used to go there with teachers for lessons on archaeology, stalactites and stalagmites, and the zoology of bats.

We lived on the second floor of a small apartment block on the eastern fringe of the town. It was very near the factory where my father and mother worked. The bedrooms were facing south, looking down the river and the railway bridge over it. In the spring, the dawn chorus would wake us up from dreams in paradise as the darkness was slowly turning into light. When storms came in the summer, the river sometimes burst wildly out of its bed, carrying away fallen logs and broken trees. The view allowed for excellent train spotting, especially in the winter, behind half-frozen windows, wondrously etched by the frost. Trains passed on the bridge every now and then, and the nights were very filled with their whistling and jotting on the track in the distance. They brought dreams of journeying to worlds which little children like us could not go to yet, but we knew they were out there, far away.

The rail track followed an ancient Roman road, up and across the mountain seen in the distance. The remains of Roman cobblestones could be still seen when we played hide-and-seek. One day, my sister found a silver Roman coin, not very rare or valuable, so she kept it. No one went to dig for treasure. Apparently, there was none, since more houses were built there later, and the ground was thoroughly excavated.

In those days, especially in the countryside, we sensed so much more the rhythms of the seasons: the blossom on the trees and the cuckoo in the spring; the burst of green and the fragrance of the linden blossom; the colour of wildflowers in the meadows in the summer; the grass slowly turning gold-yellow as the autumn approached, followed by the gold-ruddy leaves on the trees; the smell of roasted peppers and plum jam from the lawn, where Mum prepared preserves with neighbours; the sparrows and the blue tits on the telegraph line, with snow caps on the poles; and the play of the flames on the ceiling from the iron stove in the winter twilight.

The culture I was brought up in was a mixture of Christian ethics, uncorrupted Communist discipline, and morality. Looking back to paint a truthful portrait of my father, I note that in those years, a boy was expected to be 'fearful' of his father. And not only in our country. I did not see him as someone I could share my intimate feelings and problems with. In fact, I did fear my father, and that fear prevented me from sharing anything with him as a friend or in confidence. Also, a boy was not supposed to be physically pampered, cuddled, hugged, or kissed; he should not even cry or show weakness in any way. Children and women were also not supposed to talk too much. The actual doing of things was much more valued than talking about them. Talking was considered idleness, unless it was while sitting in a circle and knitting. Granny, a Christian, used to say, "Do not talk too much but let your words have their weight." This of course was distorted in the totalitarian vice to the extreme "Keep your mouth shut and work."

The regime in the 1950s gradually began to impose its own culture on society, which inevitably brought up a conflict between her and my father. It was not just the usual conflict between generations. Granny was in union with Dad's moral platform, as far as social justice was concerned. She once told me, "Your father was a zealot, standing up for the oppressed. He was heavily beaten by the police when he spread leaflets appealing for better treatment of the working class. However, he does not know that the painted ones have now taken the power in the government." By "painted ones," she meant those in the Communist government at different levels who were hypocrites and did not practice what they preached. However, as a believer, she knew the truth that set her free in Christ and was able to perceive that it was all going to end up in a brutal Communist dictatorship. She opposed him on many issues, one of which was when she had me baptised as a baby, in secret, against his will.

was staunch and flinty, but he was not a hypocrite or corrupt and would never succumb to mafia-like plotting. He always expected us to trust him and turned irritated if we doubted something he said. He also demanded absolute honesty from us, up to the point of fanaticism. He had little time for his children, but it would be unfair to say that he was not interested in us at all. He checked my school report book regularly, and I remember how happy I was to win his approval with good marks in maths and literature. But I did not do well on others, and then I felt the terrible fear of rejection; I sometimes got a bad mark on discipline at school and often got physical punishment, with a smack or two on the face. I tried to dodge it and sometimes to hit back, but his hand was very heavy. There was little laughter in our family. Everything had to be serious, and Dad did not relax by being silly, as kids usually do. But there were times of ease as well. He sometimes would tell me stories of his childhood and rural life in the mountains. He also often took me on test journeys.

Each month, the rail coach factory in the town produced four or five new carriages, in addition to those they repaired. The new production was supposed to undergo acceptance testing with representatives from the parent company in Sofia. This was done on a hundred-kilometre stretch on the main live rail network in the Danube Plain, near Veliko Turnovo. I got to know the country and also learned some lessons in mechanics and engineering. The most exciting for me, of course, was the emergency stop test, when they accelerated the train to maximum and then pulled the handle for an emergency stop, measuring the time and the distance of stopping and monitoring how the different systems behaved.

I learned a lot from my father: discipline, perseverance, and systematic work. These were also first lessons of technology and manufacturing discipline. If there was something he taught me with zeal, it was to be strong: Spartan. The ancient materialistic culture of Greece, our neighbour to the south, was a strong influence on all the Balkan lands through the ancient philosophers like the Stoics who taught life without emotional involvement but enduring difficulties with passive actions. As an unbeliever, my Dad lived with worries for survival all the time, obviously struggling with the upbringing of three children, but he seldom shared his worries in the family.

I remember once, in order to keep me motivated, he said, "If you end the year with excellent marks, I will buy you a bicycle." For a kid to have a bicycle in those days was a dream. Not even adults could afford a bicycle. I did get the marks, but we couldn't afford to buy a bicycle. There was no money. My brother just went to study engineering abroad, in Poland, and he had to be financially supported. Dad was very depressed by not keeping his word, and I felt truly sorry for him, but I was fine without a bike.

In contrast to my stern father, Mum was meek and loving. I'm saying this not because she was my mother or because it's simply women's nature to nurture. That was her real personality. She was the one who cuddled and hugged, but within a norm. She always tried to compensate and balance my Dad's strict discipline. This meant a lot. Her family lived more side by side. There were seven children, and the brothers and sisters socialised and got together more often.

It was still hard during post war time, buying things with coupons. For a short time, there was even a shortage of bread. All we had on the table was "качамак" (a porridge made of wholegrain corn flour). For a time, even that disappeared, and our family was faced with real starvation. My father jumped on the train and went to Dobrich to the northeast, in Dobrudzha, which was the bread basket region of the country.

My Dad said, "They have a shortage there too, but whoever walks in water never remains thirsty." He brought a sack full of wheat flour, and the following days counted as a feast when mum cooked pita, and we had beans on the table.

My longing for a loving father was to some extent satisfied by my brother. We had ten years difference in age; my sister and I called him *Bátte*, an old Bulgarian way little kids showed respect for their older brother, a term of endearment, familiarity, dependency, and love. There was another loving term for a sister, *kakko*. My sister and I loved each other a lot, but I stopped calling her that when I was still young. However, we kept calling our brother Bátte till late, even after all of us married and had families. There was only two years difference with my sister. Bátte was a handsome young man, very hearty and caring.

Everybody loved him. He was an outstanding sportsman and earned a GTO grade II (Готов за Труд и Отбрана) badge, which literally said "Ready for Labour and Defence." It was a bit like the Duke of Edinburg award for scouts in Britain. However, it included many disciplines: athletics, gymnastics, sports shooting, radiotelegraphy, medical first aid, nuclear attack protection, and so on. The patron, of course, was not the duke but the party.

Bátte encouraged me to join the local amateur radio club, which had a relatively powerful radio transmitter. We had lots of fun, making amateur connections as far away as Australia with both: Morse code telegraphy and audio. There was no consumer television yet, and radio was still considered high-tech. My brother was struggling to build his own receiver with parts supplied by school, mainly from military scrap after the war. At the same time, I was building a galena crystal detector. Galena ore is common in the mountains of Bulgaria. One only needed to fix a sharp needle on the crystal, and the contact acted as a rectifier. It took off the mean from the high frequency, which was in effect the demodulated signal. The design did not need any power and acted directly on the current from the antenna. One could listen to nearby transmitters by using ordinary earphones. That worked on middle waves, which transmitted Radio Sofia. The volume was very weak and could be adjusted by better positioning of the needle. I remember spending hours with the earphones, when the reception was good, listening to music, news, and sometimes even children's programmes. This was my connection to the civilised world.

Later on, when my brother went to study abroad I got a book called *The Radio? It Is Very Simple*. I was planning to finish his dream project and build a real radio out of vacuum tubes. That project never materialised, as I soon got driven away by an even more exciting idea: computers.

During his last years at school, my brother filled the study room with different kinds of tools and junk; I felt like it was the laboratory of a magician. Assembling electronics required a soldering iron and sometimes small quantities of acid for cleaning. I often snuck in there when he was not around. I don't know how it came, but I saw a little yellow bottle hidden behind the chest of drawers. Lemonades in the shops were always yellow, with a locker cap. I took it for lemonade and lifted it to drink. However, it turned to be a new supply of acid from the school lab. I gasped and ran to my mother for help; she worked not too far from where we lived. I must have been weak on arrival because I remember Mum carrying me to the nearby health centre. They gave me a white liquid neutraliser to drink. Recovery was very quick, without any burns. I have no explanation for that; it was a miracle.

On another occasion, I accidentally found a small-calibre rifle hidden in the cupboard. It was a sport gun Bátte had brought from the club. Later, I learned that he took it home to clean out the barrel, which had a bullet stuck in it. It stayed there for ages. Each time I passed by, I looked, and it was still there, beckoning, with a shiny polished barrel and stock. The temptation for me, an eight-year-old boy, was so high. One day, I was bored with my homework, and my parents and brother were not around. I took it out and started playing with it, fantasising and showing it to my sister. I aimed it at a little dot of paint on the wall and pulled the trigger. To our astonishment, the gun fired, and the bullet made a large hole in the wall, just millimetres away from my sister's finger pointing it to me. Apparently, Bátte was preoccupied with too many activities in the last year at school and forgot the gun was loaded. This could have ended up in tragedy.

I followed after my brother all the time, but he was not annoyed. I loved him a lot, and he loved me too. When he went to study engineering to Krakow in Poland, we missed him a lot. He came back during vacations, and that was a time of celebration for me and my sister. We actually got a lot of Western goods and culture through him. Culturally, the West for us was as far as Poland, East Germany, Czechoslovakia, and Hungary, which were together with our country in the iron cage of the Eastern Block. On his coming home, my brother would bring gifts like tea, instant coffee, jeans, Nivea cream, aftershave, and other cosmetics. To this, one could add dozens of vinyl records, including Chopin, newspapers, magazines, and books, which I could only browse through the pictures, because they were in Polish. The local grocer did sell milled coffee, but it was of very bad quality, often musty and expensive. In Bulgaria, people traditionally made Turkish-style coffee, boiled in a copper pot. And suddenly, here was instant coffee. Black tea was exotic, too, and was usually given to people when sick. We drank lots of herbal tea of different varieties, especially linden, which we gathered at summer time. The black tea from Poland was a very high quality: Ceylon grown, aromatic, really exotic for us.

Bátte also gave us both with my sister first lessons on table manners and etiquette. He brought home the first radio in our family from Poland too. Till then, we only listened to the local national radio programme through a wired service delivered locally by the town council. That radio was the first window to the world; from it, we listened to music from the West. For the first time, Bátte and I listened to *Radio Free Europe* and *The Voice of America* programmes, on short wave, in Bulgarian. The transmitters were in Greece and very powerful, so we were content with the reception, despite the fact it was meant to be muffled by the noise killers on our territory. I was astonished that my Dad was not against listening to it but took interest too. He listened to these programmes very often, and we noticed his mind gradually became more balanced, moderate, and tolerant on politics and life generally after he started hearing propaganda from the other side.

I was in the high school at the time, with a mind like a tabula rasa, widely opened to everything that was coming. We had a three-stage system: four years of infant school, three years of junior high school, and four years of high school: eleven years all together. The school had large rooms and high ceilings, but no central heating. It was built in 1898, the time of the revival period, with a donation from the affluent Archimandrite Maxim Raykovich, who was born in the town. It was an impressive three-storey building, where I initially studied till year four. Before I got to high school, they built a brand-new one nearby, well equipped with fantastic instruments and facilities for teaching modern physics and chemistry.

The high school was very well managed, and the teachers were quite sensible and loving. The director was an enthusiastic young man who, despite the tight funding circumstances, managed to build sports grounds and a park by involving the pupils in weekend working parties. Another project was undertaken by our geography teacher. My sister took part in that exciting work, making a large relief map of Bulgaria on the grounds of the park. The team worked all contour lines with equal elevation from an accurate topographic map and scaled them up on panes of polystyrene. They were then stacked and gently covered with cement. My expectation was that the map was for training only and then was to be destroyed. What was my surprise to see it still there, many years later, preserved as one of the landmarks of the town: the most accurate relief map of Bulgaria. And it had all the rivers running there, with real water.

My brother was a basketball star, and I followed in his footsteps by joining the gymnastics club. I loved it, but my body was not very strong, so my participation in local tournaments was very modest. However, my persistence there helped me stay fit and healthy, and I built a character of self-determination and perseverance.

For a certain period, the factory organised a fire-fighting course for the kids. They taught us how to make a water pipeline and connect it to the mains. We had great fun in climbing the tower and extinguishing mock fires with fire extinguishers. If it wasn't for the school activities, we would have been very vulnerable, as most families had both parents working. I was always engaged. If nothing else, I was called to work on our allotment, where Mum grew vegetables and herbs.

At the time, as the area grew more industrialised, the town was chosen as a district centre. The district included the town of Tryavna and numerous villages, large and small alike. One day, out of the blue, Dad was offered a job as mayor of the district. We had a telephone installed at home, at a time when phones were rare beasts to see in private homes. Only the two doctors, the party secretary, and a few other VIPs in town had one. Dad often came and went by chauffeur-driven car, but we could not ride along. We started seeing even less of him than before; he was always stiff and stern and irritable. Some of his friends hinted he might be promoted to a job in the capital, Sofia, in a few years. Instead, one day, he resigned and returned to his factory. He never shared much, even with Mum, but after some time, he explained. "The top governors in the region and Sofia were asking me to lie all the time," he said. "The crops in the mountain, for example, were always harvested a month after they had done them elsewhere because of the climate, but they had a plan and had to report up the ladder that it was already done. We do not mind, they said, if you harvest it later, just report it done."

Dad was not flexible enough to go up the ladder.

1.6 The Atom Was Split, and the World Followed

In the 1960s, engineering, physics, and generally science, were very attractive areas for making a career. In the East, they were also the safest way to make a career without needing to twist your mind away from the truth, like in humanitarian fields such as sociology, political science, economics, and philosophy. Science was popular, and people were more inquisitive then about the physical structure of the world around us. My parents, non-academics, had a good basic understanding of physics and chemistry. Our world seemed to have fallen in love with technology and science.

Curiosity about the structure of the material world surrounding us is deeply instilled in our minds. The ancients believed matter was made of discrete indivisible components: atoms. The view of the Thracian philosopher Democritus was that ordinary matter is discrete and this view still holds in modern science. However, it now looks like the structure is somewhat hierarchically organised, without very distinctive boundaries between the constituents. Atoms have nuclei, containing a cocktail of particles, so elusive that it is difficult to find if they are hard or just oscillations or waves of field energy. Scientists call them hadrons and smash them in large accelerators to find out if there is still something in there hiding to appear in the last final revelation for the foundations of our world.

The scientist's credo is to investigate by breaking down complex entities into smaller parts, with the conviction that when we understood the smallest bits an entity is composed of, we will also understand the forces that made them interact, and then we would have understood the entity in its entirety. Today, experimental physics and engineering, with the help of sophisticated and expensive machinery, are on the hunt for the ultimate structure of the universe. Theoretical physicists are proposing a unified model comprising a set of equations called

Standard Model, which is expected to become the theory of everything (or almost). Looks like science is in a turning point again.

But it wasn't like that in the nineteenth century, when modern science emerged from the obscure world of natural philosophy. Physics and chemistry then played with a very simple model, based on electromagnetism: a positively charged nucleus, surrounded by a number of negative electrons, kept together by the electromagnetic forces of their interaction, making the whole thing electrically neutral. Elements were then nicely ordered in a periodic table and their properties explained in terms of their charge number: the number of electric charges in the nucleus. Neutrons were not yet known, and the concept of a proton was vague. Yet it was this, the number of positive charges in the nucleus, which uniquely identified an element with all its physical and chemical properties; later, it was called the element's atomic number. This was the number of the charges that caused atoms to bind in different ways to each other.

In this simple model, it was not difficult to explain everything observed by the tendency of atoms to bind to each other and form molecules or other similar structures. Nothing in the nucleus could change. There were only electrons, moving about it and binding with others in different combinations. Two oxygen atoms would always bind to each other to form the more stable oxygen molecule, O_2. If hydrogen atoms come near the old bonds of the oxygen molecule, it may break and make a new one with the hydrogen. There you get a water molecule, H_2O. At the time, humanity only knew the world of these chemical reactions. The nucleus was considered firm and unshaken. Chemical reactions were explained by the tendency of molecules to rearrange their bindings from unstable to more stable formations by sharing or exchanging some of the electrons, according to the same principles of electromagnetism.

Electromagnetism was well researched, and Maxwell's theory described it quantitatively in its entirety, including radio waves. It could be measured very accurately. This simple model allowed scientists to calculate with adequate precision the masses and the energies exchanged in these reactions. It was this mathematical model that helped engineering chemistry, during the Industrial Revolution and beyond, make its remarkable progress, providing chemicals for industry, fertilisers for agriculture, and so on. New materials were synthesised and used: Bakelite, nylon, polyester, polyethylene, those marvellous tough plastics. New machines were built, able to generate and utilise new forms of energy in powerful ways: steam engines, internal combustion engines using petrol and other forms of fuel, electric turbines and motors, batteries for storing electricity, gas turbines, and many others. Biochemistry took its first steps as well.

Then, in the end of the nineteenth century, the discovery of radioactivity came as a big wonder. Scientists realised that in addition to the bonds based on electromagnetic forces, there were some others acting at much closer range. By this time, the neutron was discovered, sitting in the nucleus with mass, just like the proton, but without any electric charge. And those particles in the nucleus were held together by this strange new force that did not need electricity to explain it. The presence of neutrons in the nucleus did not substantially change the way the atom behaved in chemical reactions. The mass of the neutron, same as the proton, just made the whole mass of the atom increase with discrete amounts, multiples of the mass of a neutron. So the element became heavier or lighter. These atoms were called *isotopes* of the same element.

In heavy elements, containing many protons and neutrons, it was discovered that a particle may find it too crowded in there and spontaneously escape the nuclear force in the form of radiation. More interestingly, heavy elements could also split in two (or rarely in three) parts with various remaining numbers of protons and neutrons, thus giving birth or transmuting to completely new elements. For example, uranium could split in two new atoms: barium and krypton. This process was called fission.

In the following years, researchers in Germany found that the masses of the elements before and after the split, including the particles that were set free, did not quite add up. They concluded some of the matter disappeared in the form of waves, heat, or something else. It took some time until scientists realised that Einstein's formula, $E = m\ c^2$ (energy equals mass multiplied by a constant: the speed of light squared), devised earlier and for another reason, was not just another abstract relation, but a very real fundamental law of nature. There was a tremendous amount of latent energy hidden in matter, which could be turned into 'real' energy of heat and waves as matter disappears. This unstable process could lead to a chain reaction when the accelerated particles from one atom hit other atoms and cause them to split as well. A new way of making a powerful explosion was discovered by finding the necessary critical mass that would trigger a chain reaction, but this needed to be proved.

On the eve of World War II, when Nazi weaponeers heard about "explosions" from German physicists, they whispered, "Mmm … explosion! Could we not make nice bombs from that?" However, it took more than a whisper and even a shout from the American scientists to their president to take action. Ignorance changed into panic in 1939, when Einstein, already a refugee in the United States from Germany, wrote to the president about it. The Manhattan Project was initiated. In 1942, engineers in America joined physicists to build the first nuclear reactor in order to master the knowledge of a sustained chain reaction and study the particles involved.

The design of the first bombs was a hard and frantic work of thousands of scientists and engineers, many of whom were refugees in America from Nazi-ruled Europe. The Americans raced to make the bomb based on fission, called an atomic bomb (A-bomb), out of fear that the Germans could blow them up first. As a result, they blew up the Japanese first because they fanatically refused to surrender even after millions of people had died in their colonial adventures in Asia for many years. After tests in New Mexico, the first two A-bombs, manufactured not for test but as weapons of war, were dropped on Japan in 1945.

It startled and shocked all the rulers of countries and commanders of armies, especially in Asia, where military activities had been going on since the beginning of World War I. All appetites for more now suddenly drained out. But the Soviets, an established world power now, had to catch up. Eventually, they managed to test their first A-bomb in 1949, soon after the war.

The countries around the globe were in shock. Where do we go from here? Those who were able to conduct expensive research could make powerful bombs. The rest could not. This situation quickly polarised the world in two mighty nations with a tendency for the rest to line behind them. Then the race for even bigger, more powerful bombs started.

The peace treaty of 1945 in Potsdam established a new world order, agreed to by Churchill, Truman, and Stalin. The old empires were punished: stripped, disintegrated, and diminished, to the advantage of just one. The Russian Empire now extended in Eastern Europe, disguised as a 'union of socialist republics'.

Yet another race, that began secretly, was in rocket science and information processing. Those technologies would allow carrying remotely controlled bombs, hitting targets over large distances through ballistic trajectories in the stratosphere or from stations orbiting the globe in space.

Werner von Braun was an engineer in Germany; he was inspired by the works of the Russian scientist Tsyolkovski. Von Braun became the chief designer of the V-2 rocket in Nazi Germany. It was operational before the end of the war, but thanks God, Germany could not master the nuclear bomb till the war was over. However, the V-2 did cause some damage to Britain. Over two thousand people were killed by direct hits from rockets, mainly launched from Nazi-occupied Holland. These casualties were minimal compared to those caused by bombing from the airplanes of Luftwaffe, but the British kept the matter secret because of the demoralising effect they could have. Ordinary people did not have a clue about rocket weapons and were terrified.

During the advancement of the Allied forces in Germany at the end of the war, von Braun made a tremendous effort to surrender to the Americans before the SS could kill him or the Russians capture him. Eventually, the US Army managed to capture him, and after interrogations, he was quickly moved to America, with over a hundred other principal engineers from his team. At the same time, the Russians managed to capture the documentation of the V-2 projects and over two hundred other engineers. Any little know-how mattered in this race, where little delay in the beginning could lead to years of delay later.

The United States and the Soviet Union were allies in World War II. What was it that made them become enemies of the cold war? How can a country, allowing its citizens become rich, trust another one, preaching assault on the rich and war between classes?

The lack of trust between people and nations has been around since the Fall of humanity in the Garden of Eden. The forbidden tree of knowledge of good and evil was not the tree of life. Actually, it was leading to death. Humans did not trust God; they disobeyed Him and ate from it. "Why not try?" they thought. Taking human life followed soon when their son, Cain, killed their other son, Abel, out of envy.

You make take that story from the Bible just as a metaphor, but the character of humanity it depicts is true. So great is our desire to be on top of everything and everyone, to know, to try, and to experiment. Science is a passion that could take people beyond the natural desire for peace, built in everyone of us, and even beyond trusting others. But knowing comes with responsibility. Science is also a tool, like a knife; you can kill someone with it, but you can also crack a nut and have a meal. It all depends on the intentions of the one who is holding the handle.

The invention of nuclear bombs and rocket technology are great examples of how scientific achievements could be used first for evil by people, endowed with free will, and how God can turn this evil into good later out of His love for us.

1.7 A Curtain of Iron

In 1939, after Germany attacked Poland and started the war, Bulgaria officially declared neutrality, which the tsar managed to keep up until 1941; in that turbulent year, German troops invaded neighbouring Yugoslavia. Before that, diplomacy with the British failed to secure peace for the country. Being under pressure by both Nazi Germany and Soviet Russia, Boris III felt he would rather succumb to the country of his ancestors than to Communist Russia. The German troops, desperate to take strategic positions on the Mediterranean, crossed the Bulgarian northern border several hours before the pact was officially signed in Berlin. For Germany, the country was vital to securing southern Europe during their onslaught on Russia to the east, according to a plan secret at the time: the plan Barbarossa. After they barbarically invaded Russia on the 22 of

June same year they used the Balkan territory for safe crossing and built a naval base in Varna on the Black Sea. As a result, strong underground resistance blew up in the following years against the attempts by the political elite to collaborate with them. It was mainly inspired by the underground network inside the country, controlled by the Soviets.

Bulgaria's neutrality, despite formally being in the Axis, was candid. The government, mainly on Tsar Boris's insistence, never committed arm forces to the German military onslaught to the east. The church exerted a remarkable stoicism and resistance to the pressure from the Nazi officials to deport and imprison Bulgarian Jews. They sent letters to the government. Priests were physically present during protests against attempted deportations. The tsar pleaded before Hitler's ministers and opposed the deportation. As a result, nearly fifty thousand Bulgarian Jews were saved by relocating them to other places in the country instead of letting them be deported to the Treblinka camp in Poland.

It is believed that the tsar, who was not of Bulgarian descent, used to say, "My generals are with the Germans, my diplomats are with the British, my wife is with the Italians, and my people are for the Russians. Only I am for Bulgaria." Inevitably, the Nazi spirit gained some ground in the Bulgarian army later. But in many places, it was also infiltrated by spies connected to the underground resistance, controlled by the Allies. General Zaimov, a close friend to Boris, was sentenced to death and executed for conspiring with the Soviets.

In 1944, Boris III died unexpectedly shortly after a visit to Berlin. Soon after that, Stalin declared war on Bulgaria, when there was no longer a single German soldier present in the country. The Red Army crossed the Danube in September 1944. In the mean time the underground movement controlled by the Communists toppled the government in Sofia and sent the Bulgarian troops abroad to join the Allied forces in fighting the Nazis. Thousands of Bulgarians fell in Yugoslavia, Hungary, and Austria, alongside the advancing Soviet army.

Two atomic bombs were dropped on Japan to end the war. The splitting of the atom, a major event in the history of humankind, was not felt as such by our baby boom generation. We were just children without much sense of appreciation for fundamental breakthroughs in science. The Manhattan Project took place a years before I was born, and its scientific and technological data were kept secret for a long time after the war ended.

For us, World War II was something given, something from history. However, the reverberations of it were felt throughout my childhood, coinciding with the first years of the cold war. The media was full of slogans about how horrible, inhumane, and dangerous the imperialists were in the West and how peaceful all the nations of the socialist camp were here on this side. The propaganda sounded so convincing. When the first Soviet atomic bombs were tested, we did not pity ourselves but were assured that the "mighty Soviet science and technology" would protect us. We were caged behind the Iron Curtain, and the future for Bulgaria was to follow the world division agreed to in Potsdam.

The building of the wall in Berlin was very painful for the German people. For us in Bulgaria, a real Iron Curtain went with our western neighbour, Yugoslavia: an electrified fence. They were expected to be our brothers in Communism, and serious talks about creating a Balkan federation under the Communist model were under way. Back in 1934, a resolution of the Comintern in Moscow was taken, recognising Macedonian nation and language. After WW II, Bulgarian Communists, now in power, were instructed by Moscow to take a census and recognise two separate ethnic groups on the ID cards: Macedonians and Bulgarians. Most people felt it was rubbish because anyone was free to say, "I am a

Macedonian," and others were free to say, "I am Bulgarian," or even, "I am Macedonian and Bulgarian," at the same time, just as someone could say, "I am Varnian" (from Varna). But after that instruction, people were afraid to say anything at all in regard to their identity, anticipating troubles coming in the years ahead. For that reason, the Bulgarian Communists quite wisely dodged the order.

The Western allies, which supported Tito's underground resistance during the war and exerted a strong influence on him, were not in favour of a Balkan federation under Stalin's model. They supported the building of his Socialist Federative Republic of Yugoslavia. The bitter confrontation that followed between Stalin and Tito caused the Balkan federation project to be scrapped. Poor comrades in Bulgaria had trouble reversing their policy.

During the cold war, barbed wire and an electrified fence separated the two Communist countries: one under Tito, supported by the West, and the other one, under George Dimitrov, supported by Stalin. For us, that was the Iron Curtain to the West, which supported Tito in his opposition to Stalin. Behind the fence was a Western-style federation of Yugoslavia, where private enterprise was not entirely forbidden and where people could travel the world freely. We could apply for emigration to Australia in Belgrade but not in Sofia. To go to Belgrade, we needed some form of exit visa, like we would use to go to western Europe. Bulgarians were locked behind the Iron Curtain passing along our western border. People who managed to escape to Yugoslavia, if caught, would be extradited back for a certain number of sheep demanded by the authorities there. So it was not a very reliable escape and could lead to humiliation.

The totalitarian regime of Dimitrov was Stalin's solution for Bulgaria. Dimitrov, who lived beside Stalin for many years, was already old and ill. But upon his return to the country after the war, he lived long enough to execute all the former government ministers of the tsar and do away with Traycho Kostov, the existing local Communist leader during the underground Nazi resistance, who was standing in his way to seizing full power. Kostov was sentenced to death after a quick mock trial. A new constitution, which denounced the monarchy and introduced a republican dictatorship, was imposed after that, while the country was still under de facto Russian occupation. The royal family, including Simeon II, the underage son of Boris III, was forcibly exiled. Boris's brother, Prince Cyril, was executed.

We had lots of human rights under the new republican constitution. The right of free religious faith was one of them. However, the evangelical churches, which inherited the Protestant movement, were badly persecuted. The Orthodox church was not officially stopped but restricted and later infiltrated by the secret services. Young people could not go to church without coming under surveillance. One's education and career could be affected severely. Dimitrov died in 1949, and a mausoleum for his mummified body was erected in just three days. Stalin died four years later in 1953.

Several momentous events took place in the world that year.

The United States affirmed themselves as the most powerful nation in the world by harnessing the nuclear reaction and exploding the first hydrogen bomb (H-bomb). The mysterious source of the energy of the stars was finally unveiled and proved by experiment. Their supremacy in science and technology was sealed after developing and putting in real use the first electronic stored-program digital computer. This was to change life on earth like never before by mastering the power of information processing. The information age began. From that moment, processing information became essential in every human activity.

That same year, in a small lab in Cambridge, England, humanity also discovered the code of life, learning how information controlling terrestrial life was encoded in DNA. Ironically, in the same year, Stalin, who had previously pronounced genetics a pseudoscience, died in Russia.

Stalin's death was announced with the sound of a siren at the nearby factory. We were very scared because it was Sunday, and the siren never sounded on Sunday. Had World War III started, or what? Then the regular radio programme stopped, and an announcement was made that "the father of the working class" and, the "coryphaeus of science" had died. This announcement was repeated with a deep mourning voice on the radio almost every other hour. The kids were told not to play loudly, and the whole country was declared in deep mourning for a very long time. It was a beautiful winter with lots of snow and children sledging, which made that year brighter.

That same year in Britain, Queen Elizabeth II ascended to the throne to rule over a nation which had just won a long battle against an evil force, threatening the very existence of humankind. They won during the darkest hours with little hope, by standing firm and convincing others to join.

Apparently not everything looked dismal for us in the East in the years that followed. During demonstrations which took place in Sofia with the announcements of the new People's Republic of Bulgaria, poor Roma people were marching, shouting, "Няма вече цинга манга- епи си дургар!" ("No more gypsies; we are all comrades"). The minority Roma people were despised and treated with contempt in the past, and they sincerely believed in the declarations of freedom and equality.

The new system did bring significant advantages to poor people, including free education and jobs. It also changed the social climate by clamping down on contempt towards minority cultures, as well as uneducated and poor people in general. This of course was far from real freedom. Individual freedom was, in fact, reduced if not completely eliminated. The real policy towards minorities was to annihilate their culture.

It was not until the 1960s that the narrow repressive culture was replaced by the milder tyranny of Todor Jivkov. People still got locked in prisons or labour camps for what they believed, but mass trials and executions no longer took place. The regime entered a period of a moderate benevolence and stability. The notorious camp on the Danube island of Bellene was closed. Perhaps the only shadow in the beginning of Jivkov's reign was cast by the execution of Ivan-Asen Georgiev, a CIA agent who was the country's representative to the UN; he spied for the Americans. He was pardoned, but Moscow apparently blocked it.

2

The Race for Technology

2.1 A Time for War and a Time for Peace

A time for war and a time for peace. (Ecclesiastes 3:8)

Technology has been important to humankind in times of peace and in times of war since prehistoric times, when forging a sharp sword or a plough could determine the survival of a tribe in a hostile world. But in the twentieth century, timely advancements in technology became crucial. World War I was fought with big guns. Throughout all of World War II, the technology of big guns was even more important and crucial. Heavily fortified lines were difficult to take without breaking down fortifications with powerful shells. Shooting down airplanes was not an easy task, either, and now guns were in the air too. The key was accuracy. The precise aiming at targets, moving or stationary, was considered very important to the business of warfare, because guided missiles were not yet around (they came shortly before the war ended).

In the United States, a huge unseen army of human calculators were employed to compute firing tables for the artillery. The calculation of ballistic trajectories was not trivial and involved many variables: changing atmospheric conditions, the type of shell, the type of the gun, and its positioning on the terrain. The army needed high-calibre mathematicians and physicists to develop the formulas.

Before the war, the main tool for practical engineering calculation was still the good old slide rule (slipstick), which simplified multiplication and addition via logarithmic functions (hence the name logarithmic ruler). However, this was a low-precision tool, based on a mechanical slider, where the number was represented by a distance. It was an analogue tool, not a digital one. In analogue computing, the values are represented by physical entities like mechanical distance, voltage, and electric current. Hi-fi sound systems until recently were analogue. The sound was recorded on magnetic tape as a waveform of magnetic field, converted to voltage during playback. Nowadays, hi-fi is digital. The sound waveform values are represented by numbers, and these numbers are recorded on the media by miniature magnets. During playback, the magnets induce magnetic field jumps and the numbers are converted back to waveform voltage values, which drive the loudspeaker.

Simple mechanical analogue calculators were used for quick, on-the-spot evaluation of moving targets like aircraft. With later advancement in electronics, it became possible to engineer amplifiers and use their voltage or current to represent real-world values. These operational amplifiers could be interconnected to make modular circuits with designated inputs and outputs, simulating mathematical functions like addition, multiplication, and integration in respect of time and others. By interconnecting these modules in more complex circuits and propagating the signal back, it was possible to model any real-world process that could be represented mathematically, especially by differential equations.

The Boeing 29 aircraft, called the Superfortress, for example, had an analogue central fire control system. The

B-29 was the most expensive single project of the US military, exceeding even the Manhattan Project. For a short time, engineers believed that was the future of real-time process control, not only for guns but also in controlling industrial processes. However, very soon, they were taken over by the rapid advancement of digital computing technology.

The main disadvantage of analogue computing is its low precision because of noise and drift of the physical quantities, representing the numbers. In contrast, digital computing uses digits. The physical values representing a number have distinctive large boundaries, which are much more reliable. For example, a wheel with ten spring-held distinct positions can represent a single digit, and three of them can represent all numbers from 0 to 999. Their disadvantage was they were slow and cumbersome. Before the war, the standard digital computer machine was a ten-digit electromechanical calculator, weighing twenty kilograms and incorporating thousands of moving parts. It worked at thousands of revolutions per minute. That roughly corresponded to a thousand addition or subtraction functions per minute. These were basically tabulating machines used for sorting data on punched cards (Hollerith cards). Hundreds of these were commandeered from IBM during World War II for the Los Alamos Lab and other places for ballistic calculations. Thousands of individuals used them to calculate gun control tables.

The first practical digital electronic computer, ENIAC, joined ranks with the gunners at the end of the war when the first A-bombs were already on their way to Japan. It was built on electronic valves, used in radio and radar applications, which modelled ten-state switches, but unlike their mechanical brothers, they were incredibly fast. The A-bomb's design could not wait for the electronics. The Manhattan Project was initiated in 1942, before electronic computers were available. It meant that some of the IBM tabulating machines had to be used. However, ENIAC played a significant role in the design of the hydrogen bomb.

From a theoretical point of view, knowledge about neutron chain reactions was relatively advanced from the experiments with the first reactors, but the engineering task of designing a working military weapon was huge. The critical mass for a chain reaction to occur depended on the density of the material, and it was necessary to calculate a special encasing that could hold, allowing a sustained chain reaction to start building pressure and temperature and continue for a very short time before the material actually exploded. Shortly after the explosion, the chain reaction would stop because of the expansion and pressure fall. That involved calculating propagation of shock waves inside the encasing with the limitation of size required for a practical deployable weapon.

The fact that fission worked in practice did not make engineers entirely confident about the details of how the particles interacted. The forces involved were still riddled with mystery, even after the great achievements of quantum mechanics and particle physics at the time. But they knew the way the stars worked was fundamentally different. Results from spectral analysis and research on the sun showed that a great amount of energy was released from the sustained conversion of hydrogen to helium. Observations of the stars allowed scientists to realise that they evolved over billions of years, gradually changing the way energy is released, depending on their size. These observations confirmed the speculation about nuclear reactions on the sun. The conversion of hydrogen (one proton) to helium (two protons) meant that energy was released, not by splitting the element but by fusing two hydrogen nucleotides into one, which actually produced a new element- helium. From experiments performed in 1932, scientists already knew about fusion from fusing isotopes of hydrogen. The reaction was known to release energy.

Now, what was fundamentally so different between *fission* and *fusion* so that the former released energy when one atom was split in two and the latter did so when two atoms were combined into one? The answer was found in the binding energy of atoms, which increased as the size of an atom (its mass) increased, but at some critical point, when the mass became too big, the binding energy started to decrease. This was a phenomenon linked to the way attracting and repelling forces in the nucleus worked together.

In the years before World War II, scientists were fascinated with fusion. They wanted to experiment and see more by creating a small copy of the sun here on Earth. There was something magical in the plasma, which was drawing humanity to itself since they first captured fire from lightning and tamed it. Fire was crucial to the advancement of humankind, by helping preserve and sanitise food, as well as keeping warm in the freezing cold. No one who stayed close to a bonfire could escape that mystical sensation; something close to a supernatural happening occurred as flames reached to the sky, releasing thousands of sparkles and creating a twister of wind that can be heard from a distance. The chance to master the nuclear reaction of fusion was given to scientists by the US military at the end of the war.

At first, the government opposed the project as too expensive and unreasonable, without a prospect of creating a practical weapon. Moreover, the Russians did not have a nuclear bomb at all, not even a fission bomb at the time, so no one was threatening them to justify the project. The Russians, led by Kurchatov, created very good theoretical nuclear physics, but they were missing the technology for uranium enrichment and apparently were not aware of the very advanced stages of the design of a nuclear weapon in America. They were not quite sure which uranium isotope was best for fission and did not have a clue of how to make an explosive device out of uranium, even if they had the quantities required. But they were very good at spying.

Things in the Soviet Russia quickly changed course after the Americans used their first nuclear weapons in Asia. The boss of the KGB was put in charge of all nuclear projects in Russia. Having obtained crucial information about the US designs, they were able to advance rapidly and tested their first A-bomb just in four years. Crucial to their success was the information gathered from physicists in Los Alamos and Oak Ridge National Labs, which was passed to the Russians by Julius and Ethel Rosenberg. At the height of the Korean War and the hysterical fear of the rising power of Communism that followed, Americans found it impossible to show mercy to the Rosenberg couple, and they were both executed in 1953.

Most of the US nuclear scientists and engineers were split on moral grounds about the creation of the fusion bomb. For the majority of them, the temptation was far too strong to resist. But when the Soviet Union detonated their first fission bomb in 1949 the devil went in. The American politicians saw that creating a more powerful new type of nuclear bomb, based on fusion, would create a deterrent in the coming cold war. The project was initiated, and the arms race started.

2.2 In the Beginning Was the Calculus

A lot of energy has been wasted in arguing who invented the first computer. John V. Atanasoff, an American of Bulgarian descent, had a patent dispute with John Mauchly and Presper Eckert, the creators of ENIAC, for his invention, the ABC, which was operational in 1942. He won the case, although many argue that his invention, the first electronic digital computer was not a truly programmable, general-purpose computer. A remarkable feature, however, was that it used binary digits to represent data: a feature of all modern computers that appeared later. Electromechanical digital computing devices were built using relays before that time, but they were not practical to use. Colossus was an electronic device based on vacuum tubes that was used in England for deciphering encrypted Nazi messages during the war. It was operational by 1943 but was not a general-purpose computer, either.

Innovations usually come after many years of hard work, trials, and errors. It's important to establish priority, protect intellectual property of companies and individuals, which compete in a free market, and come up with the solution to a problem. It would be unfair if others could use someone's invention without spending any money to develop it. So it does matter to be recognised when you are the first. The other attraction of being first is, of course, fame. People like to be famous and there is nothing wrong with the passion to be first, to strive and compete for ingenuity and excellence. But fame also carries the danger of becoming complacent, arrogant, and envious, aiming at superiority over others. Science and engineering are full of examples of acrimonious rivalries between otherwise good and capable individuals.

In the seventeenth century, Isaac Newton and Gottfried Leibnitz had an acrimonious dispute, including accusations of plagiarism. This debate was about who invented calculus. Historians now credit the invention to both scientists, recognising the fact that they both independently came to the concept at the same time. However, this was only because both were known for their wholehearted and passionate commitment to maths and science; their credibility was upheld because they used their invention in their other works. Newton used it in his studies of the laws of nature, the foundation of modern mechanics.

From days of old, engineers have been desperate to find methods to calculate different values, such as the forces an arch of a bridge would experience before it was built. Some calculating tasks were not simple and straightforward; they required multiple steps. At some steps, decisions needed to be made on how to proceed further, depending not only on the input values but also on some intermediate values that were produced. If you could describe the solution of a problem as a clear and unambiguous stepwise specification, then you could use it many times with different input values and produce different output values. Such specifications are called algorithms. In the old times, having an algorithm for a particular mathematical task meant to have an algebraic formula for its calculation. For example, the Pythagorean theorem gave a formula for calculating the hypotenuse of a right triangle given the other two sides. The Euclid geometry gave other useful construction calculations. But how could formulas be found for the complex tasks physics was facing in the seventeenth century?

Newton and Leibnitz's calculus was a great mathematical invention which studied in detail the nature of how values, dependant on other values, changed. In other words, how would a function output (result) change, depending on its input (argument) values. For example distance equals velocity multiplied by time. Here distance is a function of two arguments: velocity and time. If the velocity is constant it is easy to find the distance over time, but if the velocity changes arbitrarily it would be difficult. One could make it by chopping the whole time of the journey in smaller intervals so that the speed could not change much during any small interval and could be assumed constant. One then could sum up the distances travelled during the small intervals to find out the distance of the journey. Calculus uses this idea to do the job by introducing the concept of infinitesimal. A ratio of infinitely small numbers, then is called derivative and their summation called, integral. Formulas for other physical entities like volume, work, and power, describing more complex processes, can be devised this way. Calculus is considered the starting point of modern applied mathematics and a method on which all modern engineering fundamentally rested. It was truly the mathematical powerhouse of the Industrial Revolution in the nineteenth century. It helped reduce all calculations to a very limited number of simple basic functions: addition, subtraction, multiplication, sine and cosine, square root, and a few others.

Yet the basic functions still had to be calculated by hand in order to produce the final results in the form of numbers. For this reason, engineers created mathematical tables, which showed the results of these functions for a set of argument values that varied. The tables defined, as it were, those simple basic functions. They became essential for navigation, astronomy, engineering, and other fields because they guaranteed accuracy. The problem was that human errors to calculate them were difficult to eliminate.

In 1822, Charles Babbage came up with an idea to build a mechanical device, able to compute such tabulating functions automatically. His Difference Engine was intended for calculating polynomial functions, which were used for interpolating (approximating). A function which was difficult to calculate could be approximated (replaced with certain known precision) with a polynomial function for which a simpler formula existed to calculate the values. He had generous funding for this job, but before finishing the project, he diverted his attention to the design of a more general-purpose device called the Analytical Engine. This new design had all the essential characteristics of a modern general-purpose computer, except that the components were mechanical wheels and levers, and the program was created on a punch tape from a Jacquard loom. However, he failed to secure funding for this larger project because the donors lost confidence in him.

All projects have to fight for funding through the support of other people, but this also requires networking and marketing skills. Babbage had few friends and many personality clashes, so his project ended before he could build a prototype. Parts of the Difference Engine survive today and can be seen in the Museum of the History of Science in Oxford. The beautiful design diagrams are almost completely preserved. A reconstructed machine based on that documentation is now on display in the London Science Museum and remains an inspiration for all who embark on careers in computer science.

Mauchly and Eckert, the ENIAC creators, also argued about priority with John von Neumann, but the invention of the computer, as we know it today, was obviously a gradual process, independently taking place in more than one country and achieved by more than just a few individuals. The British had a significant contribution with Turing's work on the principles of computation and the people in Manchester who built the so called Small Scale Experimental Machine (SSEM), but establishing priority in it for some other purpose than fame now is useless. The invention took place during the war with the Nazis, when our humanity, with its ethical values, was put to the test. Like soldiers on the front line, scientists and engineers within the countries allied against the evil worked hard and shared their ideas and achievements. The funding was also centrally provided by their governments in a way to best serve the common cause.

The physical basis of the computation is important because of the speed. If the calculation is too slow, the machine may not be used in practice at all, even though the principles of computation and the precision of calculation are correct. For example, a numerical algorithm for weather prediction uses the current data for the atmosphere to forecast the weather for tomorrow and the future days. The algorithm and the machine would be useless if they couldn't produce a forecast for two or more days. During the war, electronic vacuum tubes, used in radio transmitters, were known to be able to switch current very fast, in the range of microseconds. That meant an electronic computing device could work a thousand or even a million times faster than a mechanical one.

On the other hand, the principles of computation, regardless of the speed, were of primary importance for a general-purpose computing device, because if they were wrong, the machine could not be able to compute the task at all, never mind the speed. The principles of computation focus on questions like "What kind of calculations is the machine able to perform? Can all mathematical functions be computed? What is the precision of the calculation? Can it resolve other types of data processing, which cannot be expressed with calculating numerical functions? How is the calculation task requested from the machine (in other words, how is it programmed)? How many intermediate results can the machine store without running out of resources for large computational tasks which cannot be broken in parts?"

All these questions relate to the modern concept of computing architecture, which is one of the main areas of computer science now. At the time ENIAC was being designed, answers to these questions were mostly unknown to the designers, despite the fact that most of them were fundamentally solved as early as in 1936, when Alan Turing proposed an abstract machine (the Turing machine). His device was not intended to be physically built but instead used as a model to produce an answer to those questions. In other words, the speed of calculation was not an objective. Turing proved that his model could solve all problems that could be expressed as lambda calculus (λ-calculus), another purely mathematical model proposed by Alonzo Church six years earlier. In other words, he showed that both models were equivalent. The scope included vast areas of numerical algorithms, virtually all known information processing areas.

However, unlike the λ-calculus, Turing's model of computation was very simple and powerful: a finite-state machine (FSM), connected to a tape. A turnstile for example is an FSM with two states: locked and unlocked. When a customer inserts a coin the machine transitions from locked to unlocked state. When the customer pushes to pass the turnstile transitions back to locked state. In this case the FSM receives two types of signals: 'coin inserted' and 'push'. It only needs to recognise the right pattern of signals. If it is pushed before the signal for coin insertion it will not unlock. Turing's FSM needed to perform a very limited number of operations. It could read a symbol from a tape, attached to it, write a symbol to the tape, erase and move one space in a particular direction. The device needed to have a limited number of states, but an unlimited supply of tape. The beauty of this simplicity was that it could be understood not only as an abstract tool by mathematicians, but also as a design hint by engineers, although the model was not intended for practical calculations. The whole power of the Turing machine was actually hidden in what was initially written on the tape; that was, in effect, its program or its software, as it were.

There were a few key moments to it. First, it was a universal machine able to perform all sorts of calculations, with only a very restricted set of instructions. Secondly, for the first time, it introduced the concept of a stored program; in this case, written on tape. Thirdly, it introduced the concept of hardware and software, although these terms were not articulated in the literature until later. Separating hardware from software was a crucial moment in the invention of the general-purpose computer.

Turing's abstract machine defined the fundamental principles of computing and opened a possibility for the engineers to build architectures for realistic high-speed machines, guaranteed to solve a large class of problems and, while doing so, to focus their attention on the physical implementation and the speed, rather than on fundamental principles. Any machine to be built could be assessed in features against Turing's, and if it could prove to be able to emulate it, in other words, to compute anything it could, it was said to be Turing-complete. In other words, loosely speaking, universal.

In 1943, an entirely nonnumeric approach to information processing was put forward by Warren McCulloch and Walter Pitts in their seminal work on neural networks. They tried to simulate the neural structure of the brain by creating a mathematical model of a human neuron cell. By interconnecting artificial neurons, modelled programmatically, they studied the class of tasks these networks could solve without bothering with exactly how the human brain actually worked. Researchers found that such circuits can do a good job in pattern recognition and in identifying images of different objects. However, learning and cognitive tasks were impossible without propagating signals backwards, which would allow the network to register different stages of the learning process (in other words, to memorise past experiences). Studies in this area were hampered at the time by the fact that simulating such networks on purely digital devices required an excessive amount of memory and processing power, which the early computers did not possess.

In the 1990s, when I was investigating simple neural network models for my degree in medical physics, I was faced with the same problem, even though computer technology had advanced enormously by this time. Despite powerful desktop computers in use, our models were limited by the larger number of neurons we could realistically have on the network without slowing down the simulator to an unreasonable degree. So my models could not compare with the digital algorithms directly applied to similar tasks.

These experiments convinced me that indeed cognitive and behavioural power was directly dependant on the number of neuron cells and the number of connections between them. But they also suggested that the way the brain worked was fundamentally different.

2.3 Computers Go General

> And I saw that all labour and all achievement spring from
> man's envy of his neighbour. This too is meaningless,
> a chasing after the wind. (Ecclesiastes 4:4)

At the end of the war in 1945, scientists and engineers were planning to build fast electronic general-purpose computers and were already talking about business computing, not just weapons. The only available fast computer built on electronics (vacuum tubes), ENIAC, was not truly general purpose at the time, rather "general bombers": It was used by US generals to calculate artillery tables and develop the first H-bomb. Developed at the University of Pennsylvania by Eckert and Mauchly, it was originally designed as a large collection of arithmetic units, which resembled the logical structure of tabulating machines. From an architectural point of view, ENIAC was a gigantic electronic accounting machine. To reprogram it for a particular task required setting hundreds of manual switches as well as reconnecting cables. That could take days and even weeks of preparation work. To run a particular computing task, the intermediate results had to be output on hundreds of punched cards and then fed as input for the next run, over and over again, until the final result was produced. This method was taken from the way the IBM tabulating machines worked. One particular computation for the H-bomb required over a million punched cards to be used. Until 1953, when an external memory on magnetic core was installed, there was no internal memory to store the intermediate results or the program information. The intermediate results were exported on cards and loaded in again for the next run.

The characteristics of the modern computer, as we know it today, emerged in a report written by John von Neumann in 1945 after a series of discussions with people involved in the design of previous devices. Von Neumann, who was familiar with Turing's work, analysed the current status from his point of view as the top applied mathematician of the day. He married that expertise with his feasibility study coming from knowledge in the fields of physics and electronics as well. This approach allowed him to have a vision for the technological advance ahead in the future.

The new architecture was a fundamental breakthrough in computing machines for a variety of reasons. The concept of a program crystallised in the form of a coded sequence of instructions, stored before execution in the computer, just like the data to be processed. Mathematicians could write their calculations in the form of a program without the need to go to engineers to reprogram the machine via cables for a new task, like on ENIAC. This separated 'software' from 'hardware', a terminology that came later. To write their program, mathematicians only needed to know a limited number of operations, forming the instruction set of the computer. The instruction set was carefully chosen so that each instruction type corresponded to a unit of hardware implementing the needed calculation and also large enough to allow for programming a large variety of computations, making the machine general purpose. The architecture had to take special care of the way data was inputted and outputted from the machine so that the restricted size of the internal memory did not limit the ability of the device to process larger tasks. It meant that lower speed devices could be attached externally and used as an extension of the internal memory, thus expanding the power of the machine. In this way, the memory of the machine could be extended infinitely, just like the tape of the Turing machine. It was Turing complete, in that sense.

This new architecture was not just another theoretical computational model, able to simulate the Turing machine, but designed to be built in practice on available components. In fact, the report assessed the feasibility and defined a framework in which to pursue effective calculation in terms of memory size, speed, and ease of programming.

Von Neumann was passionate about implementing the principles outlined in the report. When he tried to collaborate with Eckert and Mauchly on building a new machine, they declined; they were already planning to build the successor of ENIAC: EDVAC and UNIVAC. They felt that the laurel was theirs already and did not want to share it with him. In order to avoid further disputes on priority, John left the laboratory at the University of Pennsylvania and found an umbrella in the Institute of Advanced Studies (IAS) in Princeton, where many other scientists (emigrants, like him, from Hungary) had already found shelter from Nazi-ruled Europe.

IAS was a great place to work. Founders like Abraham Flexner had the clear understanding that the return on investment in fundamental science usually comes after many years of research and sometimes without a positive outcome. However negative outcomes also had a value by marking directions with a dead end so that wasting effort and resources in that direction in the future could be avoided. Also great new ideas often come as a by-product of something else. All this meant that funding of fundamental research could not be provided in the usual way, with a proven market demand and return of investment. IAS was founded to provide the right environment to pursue knowledge for its own sake. This principle would not work without the generosity of those making it happen and for the basis on which American society was built. Only love can liberate human creativity, protecting it from the pressure of market conditions, politics, or any ideology. Moreover people were content with the moral side of the war, and enthusiasm and a generous spirit were the norm.

During the war, the computer development was also a strategic high-security business funded and strictly controlled by the army, like the design of the nuclear bomb. For this reason, all claims on intellectual property were suspended. However, by 1945, the war was over, and although the development of the H-bomb was still a secret, the development of new computers was relaxed in the public domain, only their use was controlled. Von Neumann quickly secured funding and built a team of enthusiastic engineers so that by 1951, a new machine was operational. It used binary arithmetic and an architecture which now can be recognised in every laptop or smart phone today.

The design contained internal random access memory (later called RAM), which could read or write from any location at random by being given an address of that location. It was to be used to store two types of information: data and program. A control unit connected to the memory was able to fetch one instruction of the program from the memory. The instruction would identify which memory locations (cells) the data operands were in, what the operation was (the instruction type), and where the result would need to go. The control unit then would kick the corresponding operational unit, also connected to the memory, to execute that operation with those operands. After that, the control unit would go to fetch the next instruction from the memory and continue in this manner until the final instruction of the program was reached. The architecture also contained input and output units, which would allow it to connect with the outside world to initially load the data and the program in the internal memory, and to output the results.

One can see that the key to the new invention was the cyclic way the control unit operated. One can also see that having a device with enough capacity to memorise numbers (in other words, to store binary digits reliably) and fetch them back at random was crucial. It was not a futuristic dream, but the electronic industry was simply not ready to deliver that quickly because there had never been the need before. The so called selectron was a static electricity device, patented and promised to come soon, but it delayed the project and jeopardised the outcome with yet another claim to its intellectual property. Then the team was surprised by a generous offer for help from Manchester University in Britain, where Tom Kilburn and Fred Williams had already built an experimental stored program machine called the Small-Scale Experimental Machine (SSEM), based on reengineered oscilloscope tubes (cathode ray tubes, or CRTs). CRTs were used at the time for signal display in the emerging electronics, radar, and TV industries. Seeing the SSEM working on the Williams tube gave confidence to American engineers. Greatly encouraged, wizards in electronics, they engineered their own RAM device based on Williams tubes. The von Neumann machine went operational in 1951.

The first bomb based on fusion, the H-bomb, was designed by a team led by Edward Teller, another Hungarian émigré at Los Alamos Lab. It was tested successfully in 1952. The Russians, led by Andrei Sakharov, followed with a series of prototypes until in 1961 they detonated the largest thermonuclear explosion ever seen on earth. The military hawks were now controlling the state in both the West and the East. Finally, a nuclear proliferation treaty brought the military back to senses.

Big in size and limited in power (compared to what we have today), the IAS machine had just 5 kilobytes of memory (1,024 cells, each containing a "word" of 5 bytes (40 bits); it offered no floating-point operations and no indexing. Writing software presented a challenge to the first programmers, including the most famous scientists and engineers of the time. Yet they were fascinated by what they could do, compared to their manual calculators.

And this was just a beginning. They sensed they were witnessing the birth of something extraordinary, which could change all aspects of human life. Scientists realised that the power of the electronic computer went beyond fast calculations of analytical formulas. The numerical algorithms could model real-world objects and processes with accuracy and precision. They could simulate, test, and experiment new designs without the need to actually build anything physically. There were vast number of areas of human activity which could be automated to improve life. They were witnessing the beginning of the information age.

The architecture was rightly named after John von Neumann. It was copied in a very short time in implementations across the United States and around the world. A copy was quickly made in Los Alamos, where the mainstream feasibility work on the H-bomb was performed. Illinois University created the ILLIAC I, which soon evolved into a multiprocessor supercomputer. It was first used in 1957 to calculate the orbits and the appearances of Sputnik 1. In 1952, IBM hired von Neumann to build their first commercial computers, the 701/702; the IBM 650 was introduced in 1955, using slightly more advanced components. The Russians also built their БЭСМ later, strongly influenced by this design, which was in academic public domain in the United States.

Being a world-leading authority in many areas of applied mathematics and physics, with his likeable personality and generous character, von Neumann influenced thousands of people and inspired them to develop new methods, algorithms, and solutions to practical problems based on the new invention, the computer. The emergence of information technology (IT), of which the computer was the cornerstone, changed the whole world around us, permeating areas like accurate weather prediction, space exploration, graphic design, economics, and many others.

2.4 Man in Space

Non-academic people today do not see a great difference between fiction and reality, as far as space is concerned, because space explorations are so common. It was not like that when I was a child. No human-made object had ever escaped the Earth's gravitational field. We loved reading about Jules Verne's voyage to the moon with sentiments of romanticism, even though we knew shooting the moon with a gun was not the way to go. Sci-fi books on space voyages, based on the credible science of the day, proliferated. Humanity always likes living in a world of fantasies.

In the 1950s, space beyond the Earth's atmosphere was spooky, a dangerous area scientists knew little about. Our generation was the last with this Earth-based mentality. The moon had only been seen from one side, the near one that is always turned to Earth due to the gravitational lock as it orbits our planet. Blurred pictures of Mars from ground-based telescopes had such a poor resolution that the giant Valles Marineris, running along the Martian equator, and other dry canyons on its surface (then called canals) continued speculation that civilisations similar to ours might be living there. Knowledge about the outer planets of the solar system was primitive.

At the end of nineteenth century, K. E. Tsiolkovsky calculated the minimum horizontal speed required for an artificial object to go into orbit (escape velocity) at approximately eight kilometres per second, also called first cosmic speed. He is credited to be the first to calculate it in the context of rocket technology, because he suggested for the first time the use of multistage rockets fuelled with liquid oxygen and hydrogen to achieve escape velocity. It looked so simple in theory, but it took the engineers more than half a century to master the technology of the materials needed for such a breakthrough as well as the vast resources to spend on such project. This was the point when the term "rocket science" was coined. The Soviet constructor-in-chief Sergey Korolev and his counterpart, the German/American Von Braun, were both inspired by the works of Tsiolkovsky when they were making their first steps in space technology. In the end, it was determination and inspiration that made it happen.

After World War II, the Americans transported to the United States a significant number of V-2 rockets, manufactured in Germany. They also employed a significant number of German engineers who had worked for the Nazis. After cleaning out all their past history, they were employed to test, analyse and further develop the design for the US military in a race with the Russians.

But so did the Russians, though they did not have the cream of the German staff, people like Werner von Braun, the chief architect, Kurt Debus, and Georg von Tiesenhausen. However, as good as ever in discipline, they used the captured V-2 documentation and, with Korolev in charge of the project, modified and turned the rocket into an intercontinental ballistic missile very quickly. Yet the first picture from space was taken in 1946 by the Americans from a V-2 modified for stratospheric flight.

In Stalin's time, Korolev was sent to a Gulag-type concentration camp for over five years. His transgression was not political but criminal: diverting state money and materials to play with building rockets. It was a time when jet propulsion and rockets were still considered fantasies in Soviet Russia, where the communist dictators were the only ones defining what was right and what was not. "Yes, you were not told to make these things, so why are you doing them with such a passion? For fun? Come on, there must be some profiteering here." When Khrushchev came into power and denounced the cult to Stalin, Korolev was called to build his rockets for the party. While the American system was to find money and then the people to do it, the Soviet system was to first send people to prison and then to call them back to do it without money.

Korolev's genius was not so much in technical matters as in skilful management and organisation suitable for the Soviet system. The first rocket built under his leadership was the so-called *semyorka* (the seventh), which was an intercontinental ballistic missile for the military. That one was magnified into the iconic Vostok with four boosters round the bottom and the spacecraft, with the spherical capsule for a person, on the top. The key to the success was the fuel. It was kerosene based but specially refined with a top-secret formula. While engineers knew that liquid hydrogen was the best for its energy/weight ratio, kerosene was much safer; it was stable at room temperature and did not need a sophisticated cooling system. Vostok was later modified to Voshod and then to Soyuz, which was later employed for the international space stations. It is acknowledged as the safest rocket for space travel, even today.

There are not that many truly fundamental technology breakthroughs in the history of humankind. Going into space was one of them. It was very exciting for all of us, living inside the Iron Curtain, to see the first breakthrough coming from our side of the divided world. With the new political climate after Stalin's death, the first fruits of the Soviets space programme came in 1957 when Sputnik 1 became the first human-made object to go into orbit around the Earth. As schoolboys, we gathered with our teachers in the evening to watch the satellite pass over. It was moving fast, like an aircraft, in the night sky. Later, we understood that what we were seeing was in fact part of the carrier rocket remnants, left flying deliberately slightly behind. The satellite itself was just half a meter in diameter and naturally could not be seen, even with reflected sunlight. I also remember the sound of its transmitter: "b-i-i-p b-i-i-p" which was played time and again in the radio programmes praising the "great Soviet science and engineering." It was a time of national pride and inspiration in technology for us ten-year-old kids. At the time, the Americans were working on intermediate range ballistic missiles and designed the Jupiter-C launcher, which sent their first satellite, Explorer 1, into orbit in 1958, just months after the Russians.

At the time, the Soviet system was demonstrated on the world's political arena in a very convincing way, not only in terms of scientific and technological advancements. From a moral standpoint, in view of the environment in which our young generation was growing up, it did not always look as malicious as one might think. It had a human face too, despite the fact that space programmes, of course, were all driven by potential military applications. The Russians were ahead of the Americans in rocket technology and already had surface-to-air defence missiles, which they kept secret. Both sides were now presenting themselves as ethically moral and peaceful. The Americans were defending the world of freedom, while Khrushchev was preaching "mutual peaceful co-existence" of capitalism and socialism, alongside competition between them. He actually managed to raise the morality and ethics of his empire on the international arena by carefully crafted responses on issues of defence.

In 1960, an American spy aircraft, a U-2, took off from a base in Pakistan and flew across almost all the vast Russian territory to the north. The Russians could detect the aircraft on radar but did not have any aircraft which could fly at such a high altitude. However, they already had air defence rocket systems. They shot down the aircraft with a missile for the first time in history and captured the pilot, Gary Powers, who managed to eject, alive. They kept silent for some time, tricking the Americans into lying about the incident in the UN Security Council. It was a big embarrassment on the world political arena, when the Russians unveiled their information. Powers was later exchanged for Rudolf Abel, a Russian spy.

In 1961, when I was thirteen, the first stage of the race for conquering space came to an end. After two successful tests with dogs, Yuri Gagarin flew into space on Vostok; he made one full orbit and returned safely on the ground inside the spherical capsule, which was parachuted from an altitude of seven kilometres. The whole country and all the Eastern Bloc were euphoric. The propaganda was, of course, combined with reports of the continuing failures in the US space programme, which was falling behind.

The Russians had a disadvantage in that they had to launch their spacecrafts from Kazakhstan, the most southern point on the globe available to them. This needed a bit more energy to launch into the desired orbit. However, their biggest challenge was with landing on hard ground. Russia did not have appropriate water basin for landing, and the parachutes had to be stronger. The Americans launched from Florida, gaining more speed from the Earth's rotation. They landed in the ocean, east of Florida.

The following year, the Russians made a contract with Cuba's leader, Fidel Castro, to create their own military base on the island and started to install ballistic missiles there. They justified it with the fact that the United States had bases in Pakistan and Turkey, near the Russian border, and they violated Russian space on many occasions. It triggered a world crisis, which nearly brought about World War III. The Americans were panicking. They felt very vulnerable. Not only did the Russians send a man into space, they also had the H-bomb and could shoot aircraft at high altitude with their rockets. Presumably, one day they could carry the bombs into space and launch them from there. No longer would spy aircrafts like the U-2 be needed. The Russians could watch and monitor from space as well as attack from space. The proud US military was on its knees.

The Cuban crisis was resolved when the United States promised to quietly remove a base in Turkey in six months' time, while the Russians withdrew their weapons from Cuba. This probably was the culmination of the cold war. Added to the pressure on the Americans was the war in Vietnam, which was not a cold war. Many young Americans were dying in battle every day. The American government was facing opposition and protests from its own people and from other countries, questioning the rationale and the ethics of the war. The Berlin Wall was erected at the same time, presenting another crisis that had to be handled. After it was finished, it sealed the divide between the world of equality and the world of freedom.

One month after Gagarin flew, President John F. Kennedy pleaded to the Congress for more money to catch up with the Russian advances in space technology. In October 1961, all he asked for was given to him. In a historical speech in Houston, he announced the moon programme:

> For the eyes of the world now look into space, to the moon and to the planets beyond, and we have vowed that we shall not see it governed by a hostile flag of conquest, but by a banner of freedom and peace.... We choose to go to the moon in this decade ... and, therefore, as we set sail we ask God's blessing on the most hazardous and dangerous and greatest adventure on which man has ever embarked.

This was a golden time for Werner von Braun, who had already moved with his team to NASA in 1960 as director of the Marshall Space Flight Center, hoping to make his dream come true: sending a man to the moon. For some time after becoming a naturalised American citizen, he obviously did not have peace with himself, despite being a nominal Lutheran, and his past tormented him until he experienced a remarkable conversion to evangelical Christianity. Later in his life, he said, "Through science man strives to learn more about the mysteries of creation. Through religion he seeks to know the Creator." His life is a great example of how human passion for knowledge and ingenuity can be trapped to serve an evil purpose and how God can change all that to work for good.

2.5 Mere Bulgarian

Dryanovo was a nice, quiet provincial town after the war; in the 1950s, it joined the industrialisation which was sweeping over Bulgaria. With a central decision, the workshop for repairing railway coaches was transformed into a larger factory for manufacturing all new passenger coaches for the country. The town had started to grow, mainly by migration from the surrounding villages but also from other towns. For a short time, beautiful lively villages gradually turned into desolate places, with just a few pensioners. Working people still loved to come back to their family nest over the weekend and work the land, but they now found farming could not sustain their growing families. With their new professions, their mentality changed over time. After their old grandparents and parents at the villages died, the country houses turned uninhabitable and desolate.

The town, however, was bustling. The prosperous factory was even able to support musicians and had its own brass band. They led the parades in town, which took place three times a year: on May 1, the labourers' day, May 24, the commemoration for St Cyril and Methodius, also known as Literacy Day, and September 9, the socialist revolution.

The school was full of children hungry for modern technical knowledge. However, most of us were still linked to country life and nature, based on our family upbringing and national culture. In literature, we read Botev, Ivan Vazov, and Petko Slaveykov. Botev was a talented poet and a revolutionary against the Ottomans. Vazov's *Under the Yoke* was a historic novel about the national uprising for independence. Everything in the curriculum was focused on patriotic pride, revolutions, and the uprising, very much in unison with the ideological foundations of the totalitarian regime. Literacy Day celebrated the Bulgarian alphabet, but nothing was mentioned about the Bible or the work of Christian missionaries. Petko Slaveykov, a literary publicist and scholar, one of the pillars of the national revival, was also on the curriculum, but little was mentioned about his Christian education work and the enormous effort he put in translating the Bible to modern Bulgarian during the Turkish rule.

Elin Pelin and Yordan Yovkov were prominent authors before World War II, representing the "hardship of the peasant under capitalism." Only the poet Yavorov depicted the town culture, still influenced by the rural mindset of ordinary Bulgarians. Debelianov and Liliev were "poets of the soul" yet badly influenced by the decadent nature of European modernism. Understandably, they were loved by the teenage generation. We had a literary circle, organised by our teacher in literature, and Smirnoff, a celebrated local poet, was trying to deviate from socialist realism to modernism. It was a good influence for youngsters like us, overwhelmingly technically oriented to absorb some bits of a wider general culture.

The first black-and-white TV programmes started in the early 1960s, but TV sets were still expensive, and my family, as many others, could not afford it. We gathered in the evenings to watch news and films in the community room of the nearby factory hostel. The most popular evening programmes were the news: *Around the World and at Home,* followed by *Good Night, Children.* Foreign programmes were exclusively Soviet re-transmissions, which were meant to fully immerse the society in Soviet culture. Yet with it was also good stuff like *War and Peace* (Tolstoy), *Crime and Punishment* (Dostoevsky), and other Russian classics. *Hamlet* was filmed with a Russian cast, including the actor Innokentiy Smoktunovsky. Over a dozen people would gather in the hostel; the magic blue screen was so small, with a snowy picture, yet we loved it. Few programmes were live, perhaps just the news and the football matches. It was also a form of social event where neighbours felt we were all together, especially for sporting events and popular films.

In my last year at school, I was very influenced by my older brother, who studied engineering in Poland. There he picked up a libertarian spirit and did not have much appreciation for the Russians. He was quite a dissident and heavily influenced by the West. He loved the philosophy of reasoning and was a fan of Descartes. He translated for me from Polish some pieces from Descartes's tractate, which I gobbled like a hungry chick. It was my first introduction to the discipline of reasoning and thinking. The little seed my brother sowed with Descartes later grew into a useful gift when I became a student and had to master difficult subjects on my own. I did not bother to open the suggested literature first but would have a bash on the problem myself. Only after that would I read what the others had done, after I felt helpless or had my own primitive solution. That approach awoke me to the most important things which were driving the subject, and this proved rewarding to my studies and later to my professional life. It opened my taste for self-study and research.

Naturally, I spent my spare time as a young schoolboy studying the laws of physics, machines, and engineering. I read some popular science books about Einstein's theory of relativity and enjoyed it, even though I only grasped a little of it. I also learned about radios and some simple electronics.

In our little provincial town, new technology was predominantly seen by consumer electronics and clothes. The first clothes made from nylon (shirts, underwear, raincoats) looked fancy and fabulous but soon were found to be less comfortable than the cotton ones. This was also the time when the zip was introduced in clothing (everything before was only buttoned. I remember wearing my brother's clothes from Poland, which looked high tech and fashionable. I wore them and prided myself among the other lads. It was also the beginning of miniskirts and the swing, but they were seen as a dangerous invasion of Western capitalist culture, and a nationwide campaign was declared against them. My brother had a very bad conflict with Dad about wearing swing and shoes with pointed front. I think the last hopes for a deep bond between Dad and brother died then. I longed for school to be finished so I would be set free from Dad's supervision by going to study away in Sofia.

Students who were leaving had a party in the local restaurant, which looked more like an American saloon but with a stench of plum whisky (*rakia*), *mastika* (a strong spirit like Uzo), kebabs, and burgers. We spent the day before the party cleaning and decorating it. I wore my first suit and tie. We did not wear ties at school; our uniforms were like military clothes, and every boy was required to have a crew cut. We were allowed to grow a bit of hair on our heads before school finished.

To get a place in the university, I had to sit entry exams in Sofia on mathematics and physics. I still remember the excitement and joy we had with my sister and brother, who came specially for the day of the results. "I made it," I said when I saw my name on the list. "I made it!" Looking back to it now, I realise the upturn of the old political system and the coming of the new one, with free education and upholding the underprivileged young people, the poor, definitely gave people like me a chance. But I was without any great privilege at all, just an opportunity to study and follow my heart.

I left the little town of my upbringing at eighteen and went to study engineering in Sofia. The technical university, my alma mater, was then called the Higher Institute of Mechanical and Electrical Engineering Vladimir Lenin. In 1964, it had just opened a new discipline: electronic computing machines. Four years earlier, the government made an ambitious plan for industrialisation of the country in agreement with the Council for Mutual Economic Assistance (COMECON). It was created after the war to counteract the European Common Market and was the main coordinator for economic planning in the Eastern Bloc. Computers and electronics were at the heart of the new plan.

A new wave of thinking sought to promote more people on the merits of professionalism rather than on political background and party allegiance. Ivan Popov, a Communist who studied in France and later made an engineering career in Germany and Hungary, was called to serve his own country. He became instrumental in creating a multitude of new strategic institutions and organisations. The key to it was a new division of Scientific and Technological Intelligence in the Committee for State Security (CSS: the Bulgarian analogue of the KGB) to engage in industrial espionage.

At the time, the country did not have much experience in building or even using computers. They were new to the whole world, just twenty years after ENIAC. There were just three computers imported earlier: Minsk 2 from the Soviet Union in the Bulgarian Academy of Sciences (BAS), a French Gamma 30, and a British ICL 2900. An IBM 1460 was imported in 1966. Yet Bulgarians were very ambitious to design new models. An experimental computer was designed and in BAS in the sixties, but it never got to working stage. However, a very advanced electronic calculator was in production, and many were exported to the Soviet Union.

Based on these achievements, Bulgarians tried to persuade COMECON to allow them specialise in computer design and manufacturing. Ivan Popov was the lead and inspiring figure in these negotiations. Eventually, the country received a mandate to design and manufacture large scale computers, magnetic disk and tape memory devices, as well as magnetic memory media. Many people thought of this a joke and laughed at it. The cynics labelled it with the traditional saying: "На гол тумбак- чифте пищови" (two guns on a bare belly).

2.6 The Making of an Engineer

By the time I arrived in Sofia for my study, my sister had already been studying dentistry in the Medical Academy for two years. Initially, I shared a room with her. Our parents both worked, but it was still very tough to support us because private renting in the capital was very expensive. The Medical Academy was very reputable. Students had to study five years to become doctors. The tuition was very high. Many students came from abroad, mainly from North African countries. During the early sixties, the dental school, my sister's specialty, included students from East Germany. This was the time when the Berlin Wall was just being raised, and they were all very upset about it. That was how I first heard it. There was nothing about it in our media in the beginning.

We knew we were living in an odd system, but when you're young, you tend to look at it with the Orwellian humour of *Animal Farm*. We did not have to bend our conscience too much because we were just first-year students. I was self-confident, full of energy and optimism, looking forward to a career as a successful engineer and scientist. Most young people were in favour of the government policy of investing in modern technologies, allowing poor lads like me to become educated in modern science and engineering. I was very naive to think that it was only science that I had to master. During the second year of my five years of higher education, the wings of our politics-free attitude were trimmed when we had to respond to issues of moral and politics.

Actually, we were harnessed into politics while we were still children. The junior school had the Pioneers organisation; we wore red ties and had moral obligations of faithfulness to the Fatherland and the party. Everyone was a Pioneer. After entering high school, Pioneers were automatically converted into Komsomol members after a special ceremony. The Communist Youth Union (Комунистический Союз Молодежи), under the model from the Soviet Union, had a patriotic Communist youth agenda. Every student was a Komsomol member, which followed automatically from school, because otherwise one would be in trouble.

One of our colleagues was seeking reference for the Courts for her boyfriend at another college, who was allegedly involved in a serious crime. Her action was considered a serious error since she was standing in the capacity of secretary for our group. The committee decided to expel her for this. However, when it came to the general meeting, the majority of us followed our emotions and voted against this proposal because it was obvious she acted out of love.

The result of this rebellion was that everyone in the group was expelled by a higher authority, the Faculty Committee, after a series of interrogations and trials, where our personal characters and ethics were exposed. However, this did not sit very well with the university reports up the ladder, since our group was one of the best performing in study. The lecturer on mathematics was often teasing us saying that we were the "cream of the cream". So all of us were restored well before the final year by an even higher authority. The penalty was to be sent to summer brigade in the ditches, a building site where we had to do all sorts of work, including digging for pipes and communications and levelling the ground. We spent most of the time flirting, gossiping, smoking, and babbling about pop music, cinema, philosophy, and science. There we got to know each other better.

The key subjects during the first two years of study were differential integration calculus and electrodynamics, which were taught by two competent and inspiring lecturers. These subjects were the threshold to the engineer's diploma. As a rule of thumb, everyone in the faculty said that if you passed these two exams, nothing could stop you from graduating in the following three years. There were also one-year courses in physics and chemistry, which were weaker, but there were plenty of other sources on these subjects one could read from. Books were relatively cheap in those days, translated from English to Russian, which we used fluently on a technical level. The Russians also had a very good school in physics, mathematics, and engineering, and some authors like Landau, Kapitsa, Kolmogorov, and Kotelnikov were world-famous scientists who put their names in the field.

Electrodynamics was a fundamental subject for our degree in electro-engineering, and I really liked it. I had a reasonably good understanding of Maxwell's equations and marvelled in the beautiful way electricity and magnetism worked in harmony. I adored Einstein and read lots of popular books about him and on relativity. I tried his actual papers, but my mind could not click easily to the ideas behind it. However, I delighted in his writings on popular science and metaphysics. His pacifist initiatives and his involvement in the Manhattan Project to develop the atomic bomb were a model of how scientists should relate to society.

The following two years included more specialised stuff like semiconductors, electronics, pulse techniques, arithmetic and logic of computing machines, computer programming, digital and analogue computing, electronics hardware, safety, and measurements. The thrill were Boolean logic and Finite-State Machines, which were the basics of digital automation at the time. Components we played with were electromechanical relays, vacuum tubes and semiconductors, produced by consumer electronics for radio and TV.

It was only twenty years since engineers actually learned how to measure information they were trying to process with computers. Claude Shannon's theory of communication proposed to measure the quantity of information by the uncertainty it removed on the receiving channel. He linked this idea to the concept of entropy, earlier devised in thermodynamics. He also suggested Boolean algebra could be used to design logical circuits that process numerical information.

Our course on programming in the 1960-ies included simple numerical algorithms to code in machine language and Algol, a high-level language, but there were no computers available to play with for some time. After all, it was just fifteen years after the first commercial computers were available in the United States. In the last year of study, we had a Russian computer in the college and I wrote my first "Hello World" program.

Theoretical computing was experiencing its golden age. Stephen Kleene, an American mathematician, invented regular expressions which could be calculated by machines with a finite number of states. With his models, one could clearly see the power of the computer, not only in numerical computations but also in other areas like text processing, lexical analysis, and building compilers. However, finite state machines have a limitation on the size of the tasks they could process, which ultimately was the problem of ENIAC. Long before that, in the 30-ies, Turing proposed his model, a FSM connected to tape, which gave engineers a clue on how to architect their machines. In that sense it was a fundamental break-through in computer science.

Another inspiration for computer science students was Edsger W. Dijkstra, whose book, *The Discipline of Programming*, provided methodologies for writing well-structured programs. These programs would not go into infinite loops or deadlock, especially when common computer resources had to be accessed by multiple programs at the same time. He advised not using GOTO statements in a computer program. In von Neumann's machines, programs are executed sequentially, one statement at a time, but a GOTO statement causes the control to jump from one place of the sequential code to an arbitrary one elsewhere in the program. This allowed mistakes which could lead to disastrous consequences during the difficult debugging process before a software application was released. He elaborated on the concept of concurrent computing, which also helped solve networking problems. As a result, a series of new programming languages emerged, including Pascal, C, and Ada. He was the principal founder of software engineering as we know it today.

I have a book from 1966, when I was a second-year student. It contains two popular papers, one from Alan Turing, "Can Machine Think?", and another from John von Neumann, "On General and Logical Theory of Automata." They were a great inspiration for us, and I realise how blessed we were to have them translated into our own language, not Russian, so soon after they were published in America. There was a good school of mathematicians in Bulgaria at the time, who were pioneering information technology in our country.

In this paper, Turing was considering how smart machines can be. Could a robot be made as smart as its creator and, in a sense, be undistinguishable from a human? He firmly believed that machines could be made as smart as humans and even smarter when the tape storing the program and the intermediate results was infinitely large. I took delight in Turing's theorem affirming that a machine with just a few states and an infinitely long memory tape could resolve larger and more complex tasks than any finite state machine.

Turing put forward a thesis, based on hypothetical experiments with his machine, claiming a robot could be undistinguishable from a person. This of course assumed there were no time constrains and the tape was infinite. A new direction in computing, called artificial intelligence (AI), was born.

While on summer brigade in the ditches in Sofia, the second-year students who were being punished for our rebellious behaviour often started philosophical discussions. What are we, actually: just biological robots or something more? If our brains had a finite number of brain cells, then we were no better than a machine with only a few states and a long tape. We intuitively thought that the more neuron cells the human brain had and the more complex the network between them, the higher the intelligence. But what is intelligence and thinking? Turing actually defined thinking to be what his machine does and assumed that number crunching was all that humans were able to do, in addition to their physiology and mechanics. We are opened to the outside world, which is infinite, but does that automatically make us smarter, like Turing's machine with an infinite tape? After all, there has to be someone to write the program on the tape: a human or another machine. Where would that knowledge come from? It could be rubbish or something dangerous, causing destruction. The idea of learning machines was building momentum at the time.

A question remained: How do brain states relate to subjective mental states? Could an engineer formalise and measure these things? If we ever did, would that fully explain consciousness? This valid question remained unanswered. Are there degrees of self-awareness? Humanity was not aware of the existence of harmful radiation before it was discovered. Now we are more aware of it. By analogy, is there a limit to mental awareness? Does it include awareness of the existence of a Creator of all things? And ultimately, what is the meaning of our existence? Does life has meaning? What about the moral dimension in life? Can it be modelled by computation as well?

Thoughts about moral at the time among young people were inflamed by Isaac Asimov's science fiction book 'I, Robot', where he defined three laws for a robot: 1. A robot may not injure a human being or, through inaction, allow a human being to come to harm; 2. A robot must obey orders given to it by human beings except where such orders would conflict with the First Law; 3. A robot must protect its own existence, as long as such protection does not conflict with the First or Second Law. These laws were very net and simple but when we started to think how they can be programmed in a machine it turned quite complicated. It could possibly work if no human being acted against each other to cause harm. But when countries send their soldiers to obey orders and kill, that is the very opposite of Asimov's laws. Which human lives should the robot protect? How do you define the enemy? Yet sending robots could save human lives on one side of the conflict. And surely there are different human beings with different moral mindsets. Who defines what is right and what is wrong? These were irresolvable questions for young lads studying computers.

As an engineer-to-be then, I believed all knowledge about the world we live in came from observation and that rational thinking revealed knowledge which could be hidden. But nothing could happen that was not based on matter, I thought. This was essentially the belief of a materialist. The beauty of science for me then was in its methods of reducing the complexity of the real world by postulating as few as possible axioms, which can be tested empirically. By creating a mathematical model then it is possible to deduce knowledge and create other models by logical evaluation and calculation or rational thinking. The role of the engineer then was to apply that knowledge to create 'stuff' for living. But there ought to be other ways of knowing about the world we live in, apart from rationalising. I was convinced humankind was limited by nature in the sense that life had no meaning other than to improve its ways of living or to know more and more about its material self. I believed we could never understand the world in its fullness so I had a feeling we were all hopelessly abandoned. I believed in a god who was perhaps nature itself or who created it, but who was not interested in his creation anymore. He did not have a moral agenda, anyway. God was not personal to me then, and in that sense, I did not know him.

Is our being actually simply an expression of biochemical processes of our body, just a movement of matter? That was what was affirmed by Marxist philosophy. It was based on German philosophers Georg Hegel and Ludwig Feuerbach, proclaiming the proletariat was a messianic people, but religion-'opium for the nations'. However I noticed the concepts behind it were not too far from religion. Trying to read Hegel I did not make much progress because his so called 'absolute idea' was a very convoluted concept. An inanimate, impersonal kind of thought emanating from the material world, but so abstract that one could think of it as a pantheistic god. There was a lot of resemblance with the Greek philosophical concept of 'logos', the force of reasoning that animates the universe and the Aristotelian 'First Cause'. But it helped me later understand Jesus Christ as the Logos of the universe. I struggled then to understand if there is perhaps something exceptionally different in man that makes him unique from other creatures and from machines? Thoughts about soul and spirit and the divinity of humans were faint but sincere among young lads but they were later dampened as we got fully engrossed in our engineering studies.

Our education was at the bachelor's of science and engineering level, but it was taught over five years with a practical project, a written thesis, and an oral examination. There was also lots of philosophical and political rubbish too, and we had to be examined on it: dialectical and historical materialism (Lenin), political economics (Marx), Scientific Communism (the philosophy of Plato, Hegel, Socrates, and Thomas More's *Utopia*), the history of the Bulgarian Communist Party. They were on the curriculum to feed our spiritual hunger and keep us busy, so that we could not go 'astray' too much in our own thinking.

However, philosophy was not one of my ongoing interests then because of the natural repulsion we had towards the brainwashing imposed upon us. But I liked the subject of ethics and read a lot more than required. Erasmus was one of the thinkers I tried to read. Some of his works were published and allowed to be discussed because they acknowledged the notion of free will. He was also critical of some of the doctrines of the church during the Reformation period, which matched well with our atheist materialist culture.

Tuition in our universities was free. However, we had to pay for our books. Transportation was not very expensive, and students were given discounts. Food in the shops was not too expensive, but there were few choices: two types of cheese and a few types of salami; the meat was bad quality and very expensive. Frozen fish from the world's oceans was good and not very expensive. Bananas were only available at New Year's, with long queues to get them. There were a couple of specialty fruit shops in the capital which sold oranges throughout the year.

We rarely saw times of abundance, even during relatively prosperous years. Everything could suddenly go on shortage, even basic things like toilet paper. The country was self-sufficient on forestry and timber, and we had relatively stable production of paper. However, at some point, perhaps due to major problems in the factory, toilet paper almost disappeared from the shops. People were queuing for it, and it was rationed at two rolls per person to avoid stockpiling. It was at that time when this joke went out: "Why is there shortage of toilet paper? Because the economists in the Central Planning Commission planned per capita and not per bottom."

Later, I moved to the very fringe of the town, closer to the Technical University, and shared a room in the attic with a former schoolmate who studied maths in Sofia University. The ceiling on one side was so low that we had to bend over when going to our beds; otherwise, we risked crashing into the tiles of the roof with our heads. There was room just for two tables serving as desks and a gramophone my brother gave me. On it, I played classical music, mainly Beethoven, Bach, Brahms, Tchaikovsky, Gershwin, and of course Chopin, which was always the best background while studying at my 'desk'.

Our music education at school was not very good. When I was a child, my parents sent us with my sister to private violin lessons. Apparently, I did not show much talent, and soon they had me off it. I cannot read music even today. However, listening to just a few classical composers over and over again on my brother's gramophone as a schoolboy and later awakened me to a love of music. I enjoyed classical music and the rich cultural inheritance available in the world.

Music had no censorship or boundaries. We just had to reach out for it and afford it, financially. Vinyl disks with classical music were affordable and quite rich in variety, but there were no Beatles or Elvis. The only disks I remember were those of Charles Aznavour and local pop singers like Lilli Ivanova. The more lively Western pop was only available copied on tape from vinyl discs smuggled from the West. Pop music records were very precious, and no one would lend them to anyone to be played away from home. Tape recorders were expensive, and cassettes did not exist yet. So we only listened to Elvis and the Beatles at parties where someone had a tape recorder. I loved to listen to pop music, but I was more in favour of sentimental performers like Nat King Cole.

I was poor but happy, very happy with life, anticipating brighter future ahead. I quickly became immersed in the life of the capital, which of course looked very rich compared to what I knew from the little provincial town of my past. Some film critics in Sofia organised Filmoteque, which was a non-commercial institute, like a closed club; they showed censored, restricted films from the West: Fellini, Bergman, and Russian films like the iconic Eisenstein, Tarkovsky's *Stalker*, and others. The only catch was a half an hour lecture from a film critique beforehand, which we had to endure. In fact even the lectures were quite interesting. Students loved going there, as it was one of the little things away from materialism that spiced life by opening a window to Western art and culture. We naturally adored the sex idols of the time: Anita Ekberg, Sofia Loren, Liz Taylor, Marcello Mastroianni, and others, but ironically it was also about the message there, exploring decadence and existentialism, different from the dull mainstream 'socialistic realism' controlling all cultural life in our country, which was meant to bring optimism yet seldom it did.

In leisure time, under the influence of my brother, more serious stuff was available from his book shelves like Ernest Hemingway (*The Old Man and the Sea, A Farewell to Arms, To Have and Have Not*), John Steinbeck (*Of Mice and Men, The Grapes of Wrath, Cannery Row*) and other American authors which were published because they showed how 'bad' capitalism was. I enjoyed finding out more about the life of ordinary people portrayed in them though the spirit of hope was quite darkened in most of them. America was different now, we believed, a land of prosperity and freedom. We read lots of other more humorous or entertaining stuff like Jerome K. Jerome and Robert Burns. We had Shakespeare's *Hamlet* as part of the curriculum at school, but I never managed to tune in to the spirit of it then, although it was translated very well, something I appreciated later in life. I read science fiction a lot then, including contemporary writers like Ray Bradbury, Stanislaw Lem, Isaac Asimov, Arkady and Boris Strugatsky, as well as past authors like H. G. Wells (*The Invisible Man*). Most of the other literature was dull socialist realism, which praised the 'socially liberated' man and condemned religion and everything that did not promote the party. There were just a few contemporary Bulgarian authors who did not follow the crowd, like Yordan Radichkov. They were very popular.

2.7 Men on the Moon

> The race is not to the swift or the battle
> to the strong. (Ecclesiastes 9:11)

There was a tremendous opportunity there to be taken by our generation. The world was divided into two big, polarising powers: the Soviet Union (USSR- Union of Soviet Socialist Republics) versus the United States of America, and each one was competing for superiority. The race for domination in space was crucial to this, and the key parts were rockets and computers. Things were advancing very quickly. The time was coming when computers would soon enter the office and assist in manufacturing, transportation, and communications, but not yet. In Bulgaria, technocrats who had Communist and socialist backgrounds and Western education were previously kept in the shadows, but they were now promoted to high ranks of the government to draw plans for technical advancement. We, the graduates in electronics and computing, were riding the wave of the computer revolution.

In the late 1960s, we were enjoying the relative freedom of the post-Stalin era, when the governments of the Eastern Bloc had to employ the best and most talented and energised people to rise to the challenge of the West. People with determination and zeal to win the technological advancement race were on demand. In Bulgaria, specifically, unlike in the Soviet Union, that battle for people's talent and energy could not be won just by propaganda or patriotism. Although a close ally, Bulgaria was culturally different from Russia. The Bulgarian mind, being pragmatic in nature, has always resisted brainwashing and influence from ideology; we are stubborn, insubordinate people. The new political elite realised that they needed more than just dictatorship and commandeering to sell their policies and motivate people. The time of the crude police state seemed to have gone, and intellectuals were allowed some space to think and express their views in relative safety, at least in science and technology.

The days of resentment were replaced with a new era of dissent. The influx of scientific and technical information from the West was virtually unrestricted and even encouraged with translated books and access to magazines. The restrictions on media, travel, and speech were no longer so severe. Travel to Western countries for trade and business began to take place, but it was strictly controlled and only for the few who met the criteria. Because of that, lots from pop culture and art sneaked in as well. Elvis and the Beatles were at the height of their popularity, and our student parties were naturally immersed in that culture. We hoped the system would eventually transform into another one, more democratic, and this spirit had taken over almost all of the Eastern Bloc, except perhaps for the Soviets. In Czechoslovakia, the Prague Spring movement went even further by relaxing the political system and the media.

In the meantime, the newly born computer industry worldwide was advancing with hurricane speed, producing more powerful computers not only for the military but also for the economies across the world. The next generation of computers came into being when two crucial innovations in electronics occurred: Vacuum tubes were replaced with transistors, and the internal memory, which used CRT or other unreliable media had rested on magnetic core technology. That one used tiny little magnetic rings to store the information bits. These innovations dramatically reduced the size and the power consumption of the hardware, while speed and reliability increased.

At the same time, new ideas augmented the von Neumann architecture. The Manchester University Atlas computer project, for example, released in 1962, for the first time introduced pipelining, where the next instruction was being fetched and decoded while the previous was still in execution in the arithmetic unit. The machine could also proceed with fetching the operands (arguments) if there were no conflict with the memory location where the result from the previous instruction was to go. This technique increased the performance dramatically. At the time, the Atlas computer was one of the fastest in the world.

Another improvement was virtual memory, similar to caching. This allowed the application to use a memory space several times larger than the actual RAM physically present. The areas in the memory accessed by a program usually are not fully random but exhibit some locality throughout the execution process, because of the sequential nature of the algorithms, the existence of loops, and so on. So the memory available to the program was divided into pages, and only those pages which were actively used at the moment were made present in the RAM. The rest were on the external memory (disk or drum) and were automatically swapped with inactive ones when needed, as the program was running and executing portions of the code.

The concept of interrupts was also introduced where the device controlling the input/output would interrupt the main process and update it when it finished. This new mechanism was first used for printing and was called spooling. At the same time new more powerful application level languages for programming and operating systems were designed, which were better able to bridge the gap between the machine and the programmer, reducing the human effort of coding.

Large scale integration electronics had allowed for reducing the size of computers and increasing their speed. Smaller computing machines, no longer requiring strict environment conditions, started to be introduced in the factories, office, and on board of military equipment. These were called 'mini' and 'micro' computers while the more powerful ones in the data centres retained the name 'mainframes'.

In America, after Kennedy's speech to Congress, the Apollo programme was stepping up. The government poured out resources into space exploration, creating numerous agencies and centres, military as well as civil, competing with each other and often duplicating each other's work. The American approach did not consider such competition between numerous lavishly funded organisations a waste.

The technical challenges of the moon mission were numerous: Three men, including equipment for landing and leaving the moon, had to be lifted and accelerated to second cosmic speed, which compared to Gagarin's was not eight but eleven kilometres per second. It meant over ten tons had to be sent into orbit and then over five tons of them had to be further accelerated to escape velocity: the speed needed to completely leave Earth's gravity.

After considering many options of staging multiple existing rockets, the team led by Werner von Braun proposed a completely new design, with a much larger diameter and three stages. Liquid hydrogen was the choice of fuel because the military already had experience with safely handling it, except for the first stage, which burned kerosene-based fuel. Hydrogen provided more energy per weight, but with less density, it was more bulky as well; hence it was the choice for the second and the third stages. The rocket became over one hundred metres tall. That was how the famous Saturn V came into being.

In addition to the challenges to rocket science and engineering, mission control had entered unchartered territories. The moon was three hundred thousand miles away. This was called deep space, as opposed to low Earth orbit, where spacecraft orbited our planet at just hundreds of kilometres in height. The trajectory to the moon had to be carefully chosen and calculated to minimise fuel and the need for corrections by firing the engines, the most unreliable and critical parts of the mission.

More reliable communication facilities had to be built. Large computing centres were needed on the ground at different locations on Earth for orbit control; they needed larger antennas, new data communication methods, faster computers, and new programs for information processing. These developments gave birth to new concepts and ideas which went beyond the direct requirements for the space mission. Between 1967 and 1973, ARPANET was born, consisting of many geographically dispersed nodes with computers, employing store-and-forward packet switching, instead of circuit switching, typical for the telephone networks. The new method allowed data and voice to travel equally fast and reliably. Data was chopped into small chunks which travelled separately and then reassembled at the other end. To send and receive data from one end of the network to another, a layered architecture was devised, allowing the control information to be processed separately from the real data, the payload, similar to the postal service. This allowed maintenance and upgrades to be performed in the future with minimum interference to live systems. The TCP/IP protocol suite was born, which became the cornerstone of the internet.

The advances in computer networking were paralleled with advances in operating systems. MULTICS was one of the first operating systems with time sharing, providing remote access for multiple users and employing dynamic hierarchical memory with multiprocessing and dynamic reconfiguration. A stripped-down version of it became a prototype later for UNIX and other operating systems.

But computers also had to become smaller. Crucial parts of NASA's mission to the moon could not be fulfilled without a reliable on-board computer for guidance and navigation control. While the Command Module was orbiting the moon, the Lunar Module, with two astronauts, had to perform the landing on the side of the moon visible from Earth. The Apollo spacecraft had two on-board computers for orientation and manoeuvring which had to work even when the spacecraft went behind the moon and the Earth was not visible. At these times, no communication with Earth was possible. These on-board computers had the power of a smartphone today. To minimise electronics and power consumption and to increase the speed of calculation, they used lower precision arithmetic and had to be updated frequently with data received remotely from Earth-based computers. Otherwise the errors coming from low precision could accumulate over time beyond the limit allowable for precise orientation.

The mission could not possibly succeed without a more accurate space and time coordinate system on which to anchor all movements in space during the voyage. It may come as a surprise to learn that although Newton's law of gravity looks simple when two bodies are involved, no exact formulas are known for the movement of three or more celestial bodies in general, even today. Such cases need to use approximations or computer simulations. In this mission, only two large bodies were involved: Earth and the moon, as disturbance from the sun and the giant planets like Jupiter and Saturn was expected to be minimal for the short time period of the journey. The navigation was facilitated by the fact that Earth and the moon had very stable motions. Yet no human had travelled that way before. It was a truly Magellan-type of mission. It needed accurate tools for anchoring all spacecraft position measurements and movements during the journey and the landing. The transit system created in the early 1960s for the mission became the precursor of the global positioning system (GPS) in use for satellite navigation on Earth today.

In December 1968, Apollo 8, lifted by Saturn V, became the first spacecraft with people on board to leave planet Earth. The three astronauts were the first people to see and photograph the planet from distance, showing it as a whole disc. Before that moment in history, astronauts orbiting the Earth could see its curvature, but never as a whole disk. The journey from Earth to the moon lasted three days, after which men entered the gravitational space of another cosmic body for the first time.

While orbiting the moon many times, the crew read the first verse of the story of Creation from the Bible on Christmas Eve of 1968. They returned safely back home. The following year, with two more flights, the Americans tested the equipment in Earth and lunar orbits while the whole world was holding breath, thinking it would be another year or two until they actually land. In fact, it happened in midsummer.

In Sofia, pictures and technical information of the Apollo mission were regularly displayed on the windows of the US embassy in large colourful photos. I remember staying hours on end, looking at every little detail that was on display. The colour pictures of the Earth from that distance were mind blowing. For the first time, people realised our planet was blue. Images of Saturn V, the Command Module, and the Lunar Module were also on the window. The pavement in front of the embassy and the whole street were always filled with crowds. I stood there in awe, almost worshipping man's achievements in the cosmos. The door of the embassy was half-open, and one could see the library in soft cosy light with shelves full of books, just beckoning. The desire to step in and reach for a book was hard to resist. I would have loved to read more about the technical details of the mission and learn more about that distant world of freedom. I knew the entrance was strictly monitored by the secret intelligence. One often heard stories of people who entered and were later called to be questioned. I was afraid this would jeopardise my career in computing. Those were moments of immense sadness, bringing me almost to tears. This brought about the first thoughts in my mind about how I could possibly escape to that land of freedom.

In July 1969, news about the flight of Apollo 11 was in the air, but very little got through the state-controlled media; the reports were always short and cold. Regular TV transmission had been in operation in the country for over ten years, and quite a large proportion of the people already had TV sets at home. As NASA was preparing for the moon landing, the computing students in Sofia, were very excited about it. We were wondering if the landing would be transmitted live on TV.

Can you believe it? It was not.

The expectation among the students that it would was high, but the majority of the country did not even notice when Armstrong and Aldrin stepped on the moon's surface. There was a short report later in the news, with videos of Armstrong's first step on the moon, which I watched holding my breath. Later, we heard that our country was one of the only ones in the world not to show the moon landing live. The Russians did. This was a shame. My heart was filled with bitterness about the world we lived in.

The Apollo mission was an extraordinary risky leap into the unknown, unique in its achievements. Today's generations, sunk in a world of computerisation, robotics and virtual reality, cannot truly appreciate the wonder and its place in the history of the human race. We hear some of them saying "it was not a big deal" or others saying "it was faked", a sci-fi computer generated movie. Yet the steps of the astronauts on the moon are still there, a silent witness of the "giant step of mankind". They were the first steps of humans on another celestial body. A manned mission to Mars would not eclipse it even with the enormous challenges presented by the greater distance to that planet.

I found it difficult to forgive the people who governed our country at the time for not showing the landing on the moon live on TV. But it was not the only disappointment that month. On July 21, Russian tanks entered Czechoslovakia and crashed the reformist movement. With them were their allies from the Eastern Bloc, including Bulgarians. I think there was no better way to undermine the trust in those who governed.

3

The Golden Age

3.1 A Time to Love

A time to love and a time to hate. (Ecclesiastes 3:8)

My first year as a student started by working in a fruit-picking camp in a village near Plovdiv. Most first-year students started their university experience with an autumn brigade in agriculture. First- and second-year students were also summoned for some activity during the summer.

It was a gorgeous, golden, sunny autumn in the warm Thracian Valley, with tree branches bowing under the heavy fruit harvest. We picked plums and apples and then, later, corn. That was when I spotted her: a slim blonde girl with reddish freckled cheeks and beaming, large bright eyes. One could easily sink in such eyes; they were close to blue but with a touch of other colours, which made them warm and even more attractive. Her thin wrists, obviously not intended for corn picking, were bandaged to prevent tendon inflammation. She had a fair complexion, not typical for Bulgaria, more like Scandinavian. I liked her from my first sight, but she did not respond in the same way. I was not the only one who liked her.

Our romance developed later. In the last year of study, women were naturally seeking the attention of men for the specific purpose to marry. I realised I was a target too. She was an only child and liked being independent and in control, not very easy to achieve in a culture still ruled by the Eastern subjugation of women. Raised in a more liberal family where the traditional patriarchal form of marriage was not seen as important, she did not much value the institution of marriage. Her grandparents did not officially marry when they got together and lived in fidelity and unreserved trust for a long time, till their jobs required them to have a paper. Married life was exclusively for the upbringing of children, and the man was sacrificed on that altar. Cooking supper for the husband was not the house rule, even if he was the sole provider of the family. It was more like practical advice; if you didn't, the man may leave you. But I shared these views since I always did the chores anyway, raised in a family of three siblings and a working mother.

One way or another, we married because we liked each other, and we were in love, although I was too young, not fully mature in matters of love and family. I was not aware that there were different categories of love: friendship, affection, erotic, love-love (sacrificial). For a young couple in their twenties, love was more about feeling, not so much about a relationship. Being fellow students, we had common interests in cultural and professional matters and agreed on most values in life, including honesty and openness. For me, still an unbeliever, the most important commitment in marriage was to be faithful to your partner, and that was honestly shared. I was not a family man at the time, and having children was a bit scary and not my priority, but I did not mind as long as there was someone to engage with them. Family matters looked too complicated to me and the responsibilities, too heavy. I could not imagine how I could possibly afford to have our own home in the city of

Sofia with the salary of a starting engineer, much less than the average earnings of other professions in the country. Besides, because of the shortage of housing in the capital, it was not the money that was the actual deterrent. Availability and access to it were the major problems, usually resolved via strong networking and quite often bribing.

At our wedding, we had dinner with a very closed circle: our parents and two friends, who acted as witnesses on the signing in the Wedding Hall of the town beforehand. There were no bridesmaids or wedding cake or any noise at all. I was happy but did not have a big sense of a celebration. My wife aspired to the freedom and equality of women and did not take my name, but that was not an issue.

The few implicit lessons I learned about marriage and parenthood came from my grandma and parents; I came from a patriarchal system in a Christian tradition, where marriage and fidelity were for life. Granny used to say, "If you get cross with your spouse in a heated argument and shut the door in a mood to leave, just stop for a moment, go around the house once to cool your head, and then come back home before you decide on anything serious."

However, my generation naively considered this morality outdated or irrelevant to the present age. We did not believe it. In fact, it was one of the pillars that were still holding the country. The government, which silenced the church from public space on the subject of marriage, realised the vacuum and later adopted the Family Code. It was a legalistic text full of ideological rubbish which no young person would ever think of reading or practising. In real life, the tune in society was still played by ex-revolutionaries who often preached freedom in relationships and sacrifice of family for the party, and who in their private life were mere adulterers. This early revolutionary attitude was later banished by strengthening the morality and discipline, at least for those in leading positions. It was not very successful.

The West at the same time was overtaken by the sexual revolution, and although the party was waging war on everything that was coming from Western culture, it was too little, too late. There were lots of channels of influence eroding the system from within. Living in the revolutionary traditions of our history, Bulgaria's ruling elite imitated leaders in countries like France, for example, where adultery was okay, as long as it was kept in private. This dichotomy of morality meant hypocrisy in public life was accepted as normal, and in reality, that became the highest standard in Bulgaria.

The generation of my father was still well influenced by the old Christian family morality. However, it was not upheld and practiced by any institution and gradually eroded over time. When their children started having marriage problems, parents did not know how to address them and provide guidance. The examples I had from my brother's and sister's marriages, both divorced, were not encouraging; they provided no clues or models at the time, with my little life experience. I did not have confidence in relationships with women; I was scared, really, and if it was not for nature, I probably would never have married.

Marriage, guided by Christian ethics, requires "discipline" (Matthew 19:4-11). The Bible says that we should marry one spouse, because we are created that way, but then we are required not to divorce. The husband carries authority and higher responsibility; he is ultimately responsible if relationship breaks. He must be able to manage well with his other half. However, this is through loving each other, through trusting, caring, and protecting, not by subjugation or domination (Ephesians 5:25).

I had no problem with all that, but it was also in the old tradition for a man to marry after he built a house. So I did not believe that could happen. Thank goodness, I was warmly welcomed by my wife's parents, who let us live in their house until a better solution was found. Men who lived with their wife's parents were ridiculed in our country and called "заврян зет" ("tucked-in son-in-law"). But I did not pay much attention to that. I felt I could ignore it because I had no other option. Moreover, I was well cared for there and loved. It was indeed a very gracious act.

Despite the horrible life experience family had in Communist Russia before the war, my mother-in-law had a strong appreciation for the Russian culture and the people she was brought up with. She possessed an extraordinary memory, which allowed her to recite for hours from Pushkin's *Eugene Onegin* and other poetry, referencing Leo Tolstoy, Dostoevsky, Chekhov, and other writers, and sang beautifully. She also sang lullabies to her daughter during childhood, I was told.

Having grandparents who lived abroad in the distant past, the whole family was sunk in an interesting mixture of Russian and German culture. They firmly believed that Joseph Stalin was exclusively to blame for the distortion of morality and horrible persecutions. They thought that had Lenin lived a bit longer, Russia would have turned into an idyllic socialist system of brotherhood, fraternity, and material abundance, as foreseen by the theories of Marx and followed by the labour movement of the past. Yet views changed over time. Students, who lived in the West while they studied there, they picked up some appreciation for the personal freedom of the capitalist system, especially when socialist governments were in power there. They would joke, "Capitalism is rotten, but why does it smell nice?" and "Lenin did not know how to enjoy life, and he did not want to let others enjoy it either." The flat was very often a place where their friends would come and discuss for hours the history of politics, like for example the similarity between the French and the Russian revolutions, both having led to terror.

Space was tight in the two-bedroom flat where we lived with my wife's grandmother: five people altogether and even six later, after our daughter was born. To this very day, it is difficult to comprehend the sacrifices this wonderful woman, my grandmother-in-law, had to make all her life for her family. It was a privilege to live under one roof with such an extraordinary person. She shared a lot of her experience in family life and tactfully guided the first years of our marriage. I heard a lot of interesting stories from her life in Soviet Russia and the underground anti-Nazi movement in Bulgaria. With Stalin already gone and dethroned as a cult idol, she was more relaxed and willing to talk about their ordeals during the horror of the past.

A contemporary of two world wars, her husband was a lawyer by profession who studied in Austria; he was an international trade union activist. When the headquarters of the trade unions moved to Moscow, he became a representative from Bulgaria in Soviet Russia during Stalin's regime.

In those years, as many times in history, people's imagination was captured by the promises of a fairer society without God, in which man was in the centre of their belief system. They were struggling to understand why the democratic society they had in their vision was now degenerating into an autocratic evil empire, filled with corruption. Some continued to honestly and naively believe it was possible to openly campaign for a multiparty political system and a more open society. Others, finding themselves threatened by this opposition, declared their opponents 'enemies of the people'. My wife's grandfather opposed Dimitrov, who lived in exile there after the process in Leipzig and was Stalin's right hand on Bulgarian matters. Both men often engaged in bitter arguments about politics, policies, and strategies. His wife considered the actions of her husband naive and irresponsible to his children and family. After the assassination of Sergey Kirov in 1934, she became firmly convinced that a time of terror was coming; she begged her husband, "Please, please shut up and keep quiet. Don't get into open political quarrels anymore."

Apparently, a serious row erupted between the couple, and it never healed. One night, her husband was arrested and taken away in a black cab from their flat in Moscow. While he was leaving, he told his family, "Don't worry; this is some mistake. I will be back tomorrow." He never returned, falsely accused of spying for the West, and was executed during Stalin's purges in 1937. On his dossier was Dimitrov's endorsement "Враг народа" ("People's enemy"). His wife was given a few days to leave the Soviet Union with her two children, my wife's mum and her uncle.

They returned to Bulgaria, an independent kingdom with Western-style capitalism at the time, and were interned in a little town near Varna as "dangerous people" coming from Soviet Russia. She had to sign in to the police every now and then. But the real hardship was to feed two children with no job and just a patch of ancestral land from her father. They only survived with the help of relatives and friends. She could not do well in a country increasingly under pressure from the Nazis to surrender its neutrality. Eventually, the country came under Nazi domination. Her son-in-law (my father-in-law) joined the underground Nazi resistance but was arrested after a conspiracy failure. He was put on death row, and only the rapid advancement of the Allies in 1944 saved his life.

The first years after the war were not favourable to the family in Stalin-occupied Bulgaria either. After Stalin and Dimitrov died, the political system in Eastern Europe relaxed under Khrushchev. However, the suppressive spirit still dominated. For far too long, the family had lived under constant fear from prosecution; they did live according to the rules but they felt guilty and unsecure for their dissident beliefs and thoughts. Those of us in the younger generation also feared to say what we thought, but it was different when this spirit persisted over generations.

My wife's mum, a teenager then, had developed a stammer, and after her father was arrested, constantly expected that something bad could happen every day. Now they had a few friends in Bulgaria who had opposed the tyranny of Stalin, and paid a heavy price. They were persecuted but then restored and promoted during Khrushchev's short-lived escape to freedom, which was followed in Bulgaria with a new party line called 'April Line'. With their independent characters, they were never raised very high, just enough for the establishment to portray a change of direction to the public. The new policies were called real socialism. Then the spooky years of Brezhnev began in Russia.

For some time, we were four generations squashed in a small flat in Sofia, but there was a very peaceful, loving atmosphere. A long time ago, while the grandparents studied in Austria, they picked up quite a bit of Western European culture. We celebrated Easter and a German-style Christmas with 'O Tannenbaum' (Oh Christmas Tree) and 'Stille Naht' (Silent Night). German was quite often spoken too, especially to my kid. Close friends of theirs lived next door in the same block, and they often spent time together, especially on Christmas. They had a little daughter, but the father had defected to the West. The law in Bulgaria at the time was such that if anyone defected to the West and then returned, they would be put in prison.

One night at Christmas, all of them were having tea when there was a knock, the door opened, and Santa Claus walked in. He handed out luxurious presents that looked like imports from the West. He sat the little girl on his knees and told her fairy tales and blessings while his eyes gradually filled with tears. Everyone suddenly recognised his voice and realised it was the girl's father, who had been missing for years. Everyone was deeply moved but kept silent, even though they recognised him. He stayed until late in the evening and then left. This story was kept confidential for quite some time. A long time passed, and after the fall of the system, the father returned from Germany and told them that it was he who came to Bulgaria on a false passport, disguised as Santa. Sadly, the girl's mum never forgave her husband for leaving her and did not want to reunite.

Back to those years when I married, the family of my wife arranged for us to take a late honeymoon trip to Austria, which was behind the Iron Curtain. The restrictions on travel to the West were no longer so severe, but in reality, it was all arranged by networking. What happened next with our honeymoon was quite a shame. I asked for a week's leave from work but was refused. It was a critical time for the project, indeed, but I had a colleague or two who could provide a cover. So it was above all a matter of envy. But it also was part of the game up the pyramids of power. The check, I suppose, was not so much about who was behind this, but testing how high he was in the pyramid. Tourism to the West had just been open to "mere mortals", but it was all taken over by protégés of those in power, and the checks were always thorough. Being one of the lucky ones was in fact a matter of trust, allegiance, and privilege. I did not feel strongly about fighting for it.

The holiday refusal was certainly an attack on my marriage, but I felt uncomfortable being in the position of privilege anyway. Both my wife and I felt very strongly against privilege. Some ridiculed me and asked why I didn't escalate my case up the ladder. Everyone hated the system just like me, but other people's mentality allowed them to take every opportunity for their own advantage. I was afraid escalation might cause new problems to our sponsors, former dissidents, now pardoned yet still not quite secure. I felt that I had to play fair too, but what fair meant in those circumstances was not clear to me. When you know your moral ground, you know your enemy and your friends. You know your opposition, and you take the challenge to stick to a principle. But I did not know my ground. How could I? How could one live by embracing double standards?

3.2 Fatherhood

When late in life I became Christian, I found it very difficult to forgive myself the mistakes I made as a parent. I didn't have the right parental model to learn from. But finding excuses did not help. My experience in adolescence was that a father should be strict and enforce discipline. Love was somewhat secondary. Fathers should not show their love with hugs, kisses, or even a smile. Understandably, according to the role model I saw in my Dad, I viewed my responsibility predominantly as providing for my children, educating them, and building a strong character so they could make their way through life.

However, I thought teaching would start when they were able to understand, not when they were still in the cradle. Besides, I was not naturally at ease with babies or little children. Until my daughter was born, I found infants very annoying and a waste of time for a man. It took some time before I developed fatherhood instincts. My father never hugged me or showed his love in any other form understandable to a child. I never felt true love emanating from him, although he took responsibility and provided for his family. I lived with the feeling that I was an intruder in his life. It could be because I knew from Granny that he did not want a third child: me. But he was strict and disciplined all his children. We all feared him and were very careful not to do or say something that may provoke his anger.

I forgave my Dad because he did not have a role model, either. His father was killed in World War I when he most needed him in adolescence. So the way he related to me was the way he was actually taught by his mother, who fulfilled both roles, mother and father at the same time. I heard her say, "A father should behave so that his children fear him." Later, when I learned about the "stiff upper lip" maxim in Britain, I understood that strictness, discipline, and not showing emotion were not a special feature of just our family or even of the culture of the East. It was more or less the culture of the time, when children were supposed to be seen but not heard. It was not until late in life, after my father had died, that I was reconciled in my mind with this and acknowledged how much he actually did care and loved all of us, according to the morality and ethics of his generation.

But why should morality and ethics have a generational attribute? Should they not be the same over time, regardless of what happens in the political and social space? Should they not influence the society with values that last beyond a generation? As a nation which far too often resorted to resolving problems by fighting and revolutions, Bulgarians had their morality and ethics redefined at each major shakeup. The young lads like me were naturally repugnant to what was preached in public by the regime. Any literature on the subject of family life was riddled with political rubbish; we despised it.

At the same time, teaching in church was not existent, not in the faintly glowing Orthodox church, where lighting candles, burning frankincense, and kissing icons were perhaps the most important activities. Only the evangelical churches, though under suppression, had some teachings, but I did not know them at the time. The only direction could come from family, which was it should be, anyway. Few parents found it possible to spend time with their children, as both parents had to work to provide basic needs. The model of two working parents was deliberately promoted and encouraged as a high virtue of emancipating women, giving themselves for the sake of the people and party. The party did have an interest in creating and supporting a model that would allow the young generation to be brainwashed and taught in every aspect of their life by the media, school, and work. However, the failures in parenting of many like me came not from allowing that kind of brainwashing. The key to fatherhood was love, which we did not express and share. My generation inherited a culture in which adults felt embarrassed to show emotions and affection in public as well as behind doors.

Yet love is built into our nature. As a kid, I naturally loved everybody and could not understand why everyone didn't respond with the same feeling. I sincerely wished everyone happiness and success, often to the extent of denying myself the same things. However, my life experience was telling me indirectly that unlimited generosity was only possible in a society that believed in it. Since true love is one way, unconditional, and sacrificial, and indeed defines the very meaning of life (1 Corinthians 13), a loving kid must learn how to avoid insecurity in a world that extols selfishness and competition over generosity. In such a world, one would need to fight fiercely for recognition. As a child, I often fell in the trap of trying to constantly please others in order to reassure myself of that recognition.

Perhaps subconsciously, I passed the same behavioural patterns to my child. I always insisted on honesty and integrity, but in Bulgaria at that time, these words meant little because they were not defined. The only place they were defined was in the Bible, and we despised it. We no longer had the patriarchal system of our grandparents, which allowed them to pass wisdom to their children. I never saw that happening in the families of anyone I knew. Parents complained about their children being difficult, and children complained about their parents being annoying.

It was easy for a father like me to fall in the trap of doing things. I had precious moments of teaching my daughter to cycle, roller-skate, and ski. But when she went through school, checking her workbooks was a disaster. I concentrated too much on her errors, the negative, without allowing myself time to praise her achievements and build her self-esteem. I was also easily caught up in a vicious circle of doing my things and forgetting that sometimes, loving my child just meant being there with her, sharing moments of rest and goodness. At such moments, my daughter would open herself to share things that were important to her, even if they looked stupid to me. But I did not have time to think and respond in the right way, to empathise. I would just say something to fill a sentence. But kids are clever. They have something built into them that judges the right way. Such talk would mean to her, "I am not important to you."

I realise now that my involvement was crucial for creating a bond, an attachment that would make her feel secure and comfortable with me. Without that, children become selfish but without self-esteem and confidence. At some point, doing the chores at home together was no longer possible; it was not fun for her, and there was little in sharing communication anyway. So it gradually became a duty, something that my daughter had to do in her own time, as it suited her. It was really like a punishment, another broken relationship.

Yet eventually, we got blessed with a new flat, a home of our own. Money was never enough, but we no longer struggled to make ends meet. I was saving for a car. Cars were bought after making a deposit and waiting on a queue for up to ten years. After we moved to a new place, we decided that our daughter could stay for a little bit with her Granny while she finished year seven and then changed schools. It suited me well, as I was just beginning to finish my PhD and needed more time on my own. This year obliterated the remaining bits of attachment she had with us, her parents. Later in life, I understood how important that age was for her. It was the time she started to think about how she should relate to people outside family, what they think and do, and how she should place herself in the social space. After she was a grown-up, I realised she was very vulnerable and found it difficult to discuss problems without being emotionally engaged; she generally lacked self-esteem. In many ways, she was just like me at that age. I was not gifted with eloquence. As soon as I started to speak, someone would raise their voice and take over, so I had to shut up because I could not be heard, and I did not like shouting. In our culture, one had to use one's elbows to get through in every aspect of life.

We cannot blame it all on the system we lived in. We were inexperienced young parents, that is for sure, but we also knew we behaved selfishly in many of our parenting decisions and chose to turn back, deluding ourselves that it was in the best interest of the child. At least we were not like many others, we thought. Examples of bad family life were everywhere: bosses at work and high-ranking officials with mistresses and children who behaved like hooligans in public. That was the environment which was trying to shape us. I am glad we managed to resist it.

3.3 From Plums to Computers

When you are born in a prison, you do not realise it until you know freedom. We knew we lived in a country that was like a prison, but nevertheless, we were full of optimism. The last fruit-picking student brigade I remember was in an orchard with gorgeous, large, dark blue plums. It must have been a very good year for plums; I had never tasted such mellow sweet fruit. With many people now engaged in the industrialisation programme, the farms were lacking hands to pick the glorious fruit the land had produced.

At the time, students leaving the university had to work where they were assigned, according to the Central Planning Commission. A residence in Sofia, the capital, was only a dream for most graduates. A special degree for computer technology was soon approved by the Politburo to resolve funding and resource problems and to resolve various restrictions, including residence. So I had a dream from childhood, and it was fulfilled. I was very proud of my diploma in computing machines. Just in time. What a blessing. The world was awakening to the dawn of the computer revolution. We were valued and needed. I started my first job with a large group of other graduates who were earmarked to work in the new Institute for Computing Technologies in Sofia.

The Soviet Union was a leading power in computer technology for the Eastern Bloc. They had a good theoretical school with original architecture, especially for use in real-time control, which helped build the computers that flew Gagarin into space and promoted other advancements of Russian science, design, and technology. However, they did not have advanced general-purpose computers able to facilitate scalability and compatibility when used outside the army in economics, accounting, and design. Those had just begun to emerge in the United States, but the Soviet Union was falling behind, mainly because of the incompetent control of computer science and cybernetics by the politicians during Stalin's era.

The design of software applications across the vast empire to the East also lacked strategy, and lots of teams wasted their effort in implementing the same algorithms for a variety of incompatible machines even in the centrally planned economy. Applications were not portable across machines with various performances, big and small, something the Americans seemed to have managed to do, even in the world of free market and competition.

In 1970, when I started my career, a small factory in Sofia had been assembling general-purpose computers with a Japanese license since 1967. This line was stopped after a political decision in COMECON to start working on cloning the IBM System 360. The 360 was the next generation, after the invention of the modern computer in IAS, and featured many great new ideas. It was designed as a family of machines with different performance levels yet compatible between each other; a program could run on the smallest model as well as on a bigger one without reprogramming, something termed scalability. But how could we copy it without having something tangible to look at?

The Coordinating Committee for Multilateral Export Control (CoCom) was created just after the war by Western countries to counteract the Eastern Bloc's technological advancement. Due to CoCom restrictions, our country could only buy US mainframe computers for general use in computing centres, but they were strictly controlled, and the hardware could not be disassembled for copying. So we had to reverse-engineer them by revealing the connections between the components visually or with a circuit checker or from whatever user documentation was available. More documentation was made available through secret business intelligence abroad, which we knew very little about then, but it was not very much. Moreover, our components did not always match the US design, so we had to replace them by knowing exactly how the prototype logical circuits worked. As a result, the hardware design we produced was quite original.

In contrast, much of the system software, the operating system, was based on a slightly modified IBM code, produced with software disassembling. Knowing well the code was essential when subtle errors in the hardware implementation caused program errors that needed fixing. Also the cost of writing application software was becoming higher and higher in proportion to the overall cost of any engineering business solution. The design of new algorithms for data processing engaged lots of brain power, and it was important to minimise the cost. That was the whole idea behind taking the reverse-engineering approach. The existing applications, in general, were supposed to work unchanged, just pirated and rebranded.

But there was still a lot of work needed in user manuals and documentation as well as getting rid of branding and copyright messages and embarrassing, unexpected outputs well hidden in low-level routines.

The CoCom restrictions for Bulgaria, however, looked lax compared to those for the Soviet Union. At the height of the cold war and the competition for space, Russians could get virtually nothing. This was one of the reasons they were interested in having us on the project. However, they had their own restrictions against working with foreigners. Almost all high-tech centres there worked for the military and were closed to foreigners, even foreigners from the Eastern Bloc. The solution taken from our leaders was found in Minsk, the capital of Belarus.

In 1970, Minsk had an established institute for civil (not military) applications; a manufacturing plant was already producing Minsk 22, modern low- and middle-range-performance computers based on discrete transistor components. The new Minsk-Sofia project envisioned the design and implementation in serial production of a hybrid of the smallest models of the IBM 360 family. We were sent there almost immediately after we joined the Institute in Sofia and spent some time working with our Belorussian colleagues.

Our background and culture at home were academic romanticism. We had neither training nor experience in quality management, configuration and version control or any design and manufacturing standard apart from safety. The country was manufacturing consumer electronics: radios and TVs, but those standards were inadequate for the newborn computer industry. With no experience in industrial electronic design, certainly not on that scale, we gladly embraced the Soviet system for free. Their electronic industry was based on rigorous military standards, which after all had sent Gagarin into space successfully just a decade ago. In Minsk, I saw for the first time a strict and disciplined approach to hardware documentation, version control, technological discipline, and acceptance testing.

There were many engineering design challenges. This was the first computer built on integrated circuits (ICs) of medium- and large-scale integration, which encapsulated a few gates or a whole logical circuit, like a binary register, on one chip. This was also the first computer family with microprogramming, which allowed the instruction set to be partly programmed instead of implemented through hardware circuits. Replacing part of the hardware computer control with programs inevitably slowed down the computations, but when fast read-only memory components were used to store the microinstructions of the program control, the slowdown was not very significant. Microprogramming lowered the cost and was used for smaller machines.

Following the IBM 360, the architecture was allowing for building a family of compatible computers. In addition to that, most of the fundamental concepts in computer science, on which all modern computers were to be built, had just evolved from academic and military projects and were being implemented commercially for the first time: multiprogramming (allowing the computer to perform multiple tasks concurrently), time sharing (allowing multiple users to use one machine concurrently), and teleprocessing, as opposed to batch processing, allowing for tasks to be performed remotely.

Fast external memory on magnetic discs was a key component for creating virtual memory. Without that the creation of a unified system with scalable performance was practically impossible. The running of large computing algorithms required lots of randomly accessed internal memory. To make that possible on smaller models, having only a little memory the application program had to continuously exchange large chunks of data between the core memory and the external memory on disks. In order to free the application programmer from taking care of it, the operating system was designed so that it took over control of this process of memory management. The solution was called 'virtual memory' since the application programmers no longer had to write programmes accessing real physical memory but an imaginary one, virtually unlimited. The computer operating system did the rest for them transparently. This functionality was also crucial for computer systems shared between many users concurrently.

The machine we were designing was the smallest in the family. It had 64 kilobytes of core memory, extendible to 256 kilobytes, external disk memory on several 5-megabyte devices, and was connected to the central processor via an input-output system with an exchange rate of up to 300 kilobytes per second. It could perform tens of thousands operations per second, later augmented ten folds. Higher performance models were being designed in the Soviet Union and East Germany. These performance parameters naturally look miserable compared to the current technological levels, where even a smart phone is more powerful in every respect. But they were high achievements at the time, even globally. What a blessed time for young engineers like us.

Our colleagues in Minsk were mainly Belarusians, but many of them were educated and trained in Russian universities. They were very amicable and friendly chaps. Despite the fact that we had a lot to learn from them, they did not patronise us. They let us work within their group as if we were one of them. There was a lot to share. The Bulgarian team had an excellent understanding of the System 360 architecture and its specification details so we made sense of the electrical diagrams of the archetype very quickly. That complemented well their experience in middle-scale electronics design, according to their superior engineering standards.

Socialising was always enjoyable, except when the supply of vodka was a bit over the top. Russians told similar kinds of jokes, and those of political nature were not held back. There was a wonderful spirit of solidarity and trust on a human, personal level. They hated the authoritarian system just like we did and obviously wanted to get rid of it. Nevertheless, they were disciplined, more than we were with our disorganised academic style.

Similar in language and culture, we were quite different at the same time. In general, our Soviet colleagues were more open to collective work and teaming. They were more heartfelt as well than we were with our analytical individualist style of work. It was a good influence on us to open up and be more collaborative. Only occasional outbursts of snobbery and pride, as members of a great nation could overshadow the respect we had for them. However, those with pride were not the most confident otherwise, at work or in their families. That made me think that the Soviet system actually undermined their confidence. Those with real confidence were from families linked to Russia's Christian past. Despite all the evil attributed to the Russian empire some seventy years earlier, it did promote Christian values in the public space. Christian values permeated the fabric of Russian rural society, thanks to the church and writers like Tolstoy and Dostoevsky. The remnants of the fruits of these values obviously passed through generations and survived to our time.

3.4 Apogee

If Communism in Bulgaria had a golden age, that was it. Despite the oppression over personal freedom and the evil of corruption, the industrialisation programme in the 1970s, especially in the electronic and computer industry, was successful. Agriculture was not badly affected by the drainage of subsidies for other sectors, and perhaps in proportion with industry, it succeeded with an increase in tourism. In the high ranks, one could see new personalities which had less of the old bravado style and fewer sycophants around them in servitude.

Technology was at the heart of the Communist government; they had seen they could not only animate the whole nation but also solve pressing economic needs of the country, in a world driven by technology. Computerisation was one of the major factors.

Back home, we were surprised by moving into a new purpose-built office. All departments involved in the mainframe computer project were gathered together in the open space of a huge hall on one floor. Bye-bye, academics, and hello, engineers. A new interior design with cubicles made of light portable walls was introduced to facilitate team building and better communication. All this was copied from French electronic design institutions. Ivan Popov, a French graduate, was now the top boss in the Politburo, the sponsor of the computer programme; he came a couple of times to see us at the onset of the project.

We had to start building our own prototype, the smallest in the family of compatible machines, with IBM System 360 models 30 and 40 as archetypes. People in the factory where manufacturing had to start were not very happy; their Japanese-licensed assembly business was suppressed, and they were forced into the new product from the top. At the same time, a whole constellation of factories and smaller design labs were launched elsewhere in the country for printed circuit boards, disc and tape memory devices, and other products.

There were problems of all sorts: unreliable components, staff shortages in manufacturing, training programmes behind schedule, and so on. But we were very enthusiastic and worked hard, literally day and night on shifts, logging the progress in a diary for the next shift. The first prototype, called Baba Anna, served as a master copy and was growing day and night. Our team, responsible for the design of the input-output system, worked passionately, building all sorts of simulators of devices that were not available to test the implementation during the construction.

The machine went operational very quickly, to the surprise of all the bosses. In 1971, it was displayed at an international show in Plovdiv, with many fixes on the printed circuits boards made by hand and soldering iron at the last moment. We had to demonstrate the flexibility of the architecture by connecting to a German printer. However, the connection did not plug and play as expected. There was a problem in the printer, which we were able to pin down for them, and they fixed it. Bottles of German beer were opened on the show stand when that huge spreadsheet printer started pouring out paper like a river. Having a great respect for German technology, we Bulgarians were very proud that we could design and build machines on the same level as them. In fact, the German chaps at the exhibition respected us, having helped them to successfully diagnose and fix their problem. It was good teamwork.

This show raised the profile of our research and development (R&D) with the group in Minsk, where the project had not reached implementation stage yet. By showing a working prototype so early, our new computer industry also won the confidence of the huge Soviet market and opened the doors for favourable trade contracts.

However there were troubles ahead. The assembling of a new machine in serial production was usually followed by a long process of 'tuning' before release. There was nothing to tune in the design, but hardware manufacturing errors were difficult to troubleshoot, and the machine usually failed when initially powered on. The first machines had their wiring done manually by technicians. There were thousands of wires, and just one wire placed on the wrong pin was enough to mess up the machine. Not all production engineers were experienced enough to fix that sort of bug, and they called the design team on a daily basis. In fact, during the first year, we almost permanently stayed in the factory, 'tuning' machines and training people on the right methods. The Russian standard required a limited time to fix a single fault. So during reliability acceptance testing, we had to work the night shift. With no trained production staff available, design engineers had beds mounted in rooms next to the test rooms, and we were awakened each time a problem occurred to help fix it. There was not much sleep then, just some comfort to get horizontal and relax if you could. The reliability problems were mainly associated with bad contacts of the printed circuit boards in the casing. The work was arduous.

It was like during a war. In fact, it was the cold war, a war for supremacy in space, technology, and now, the economy. The pressure from the top was very high. There was a lot at stake at a national level. Many countries from the Eastern Bloc were bidding for portions in the whole computer advancement programme, and the green light would be given only to successful participants in the first stages. Political careers on the top were at stake, but we knew that our own professionalism and future depended on this success too. In the beginning there was a good internal collaborative attitude between individuals right across the whole organisation, which brought down any barriers if low-level bosses acted out of reasons of rivalry.

At the time, we also respected our political sponsors. They were sensitive to our needs. We worked with discipline and enthusiasm, and enjoyed what we were doing. Unfortunately, we were lagging behind schedule, and the management pushed ahead for factory release by cutting corners. So the first machines were sold with manual wiring and untested couplings. They were commissioned for East Germany and

Hungary, where we did not yet have a maintenance network developed. Germany and Hungary were countries with traditions in engineering and machine building, and their leaders proudly looked down on Bulgarian computers anyway. The problems associated with bad sockets were fixed later on in Hungary, but it was very difficult for our tradesmen to enthuse Germany in buying them anymore. After the manufacturing problems were fixed, huge numbers were sold in the Soviet Union and other countries. The Russians had a very good maintenance and support network, and for years, they had good experience in maintaining computing centres. They did not rely on us for maintenance. However, their production capacity was insufficient for the vast economy that was under modernisation. The Soviets were hungry for computers.

At the Plovdiv International Show, we had the chance to test our 'plug and play' implementations against other devices produced in the Eastern Bloc. The stand was later visited by the top boss, the first secretary, accompanied by a large cohort of high-ranking officials. I had an amateur camcorder and shot on film the visit. After the delegation had gone, the state security chief approached my boss and asked for the film. Since the atmosphere got very heated, he wisely took his leave, but our manager, knowing what would follow, did not go away until he saw me destroy all the footage. This incident badly affected our team's spirit, but it was quickly forgotten in the hype of the media that followed.

It was a blessed time for me and my colleagues, most of whom were people with a humble upbringing. Few of us had ever travelled abroad. My first flight abroad was to Minsk in Belarus. There was a lot of design work as well as standardisation, which required regular meetings in Moscow to coordinate the activities on the whole programme. We often travelled to Moscow and helped support installations in Germany and Hungary too.

Life in Russia, even in the capital Moscow, looked grim and poor at the time. The food shops had clear shelves. Meat and other essential food seemed completely off the table. We were told they got most of their supplies by orders at work on a system similar to rationing. Many of our younger colleagues lived in communal flats and their life shuttled between home and work. The underground in Moscow was the only lustrous place in marble and light. The streets and boulevards were wide but without green trees, a townscape full of multilane high traffic and monuments.

In East Berlin, which had one of our first installations, I saw for the first time the Berlin Wall, which just had been raised. The Brandenburg Gate was blocked, and the parliament building was all in scars from the street battles between the Russians and the Nazis. The German colleagues were very friendly but people on the streets looked grim, visibly shaken by the recent past of dictatorship and horrendous warfare.

This was a time to meet with other people and see other countries and cultures. Our product was also displayed at a show in the West, at an industrial exhibition in Cologne, West Germany. This was more of a political show than a trade presence. However, the country did manage to export some floppy disks and memory devices to the West.

As the project was drawing to a close, our group continued to hold together. We were bored and wanted to get away from cloning the IBM System 360. So the team switched from mainframes to minicomputers, which were being designed in another division. They had implemented the first 12-bit and 16-bit minicomputers in the country by cloning DEC PDP-8 and PDP-11 machines. The team was engaged in designing the more powerful 32-bit DEC VAX line. We joined their effort by designing control units for telecommunications and later developed our first original design: test systems for disk memory units based on minis. Working on minicomputers gave me first experience with computer networks and protocols. ARPA, the West's military network, was becoming an archetype for distributed systems; eventually, it turned into the Internet.

A large factory for manufacturing disk drives was built in the town of Stara Zagora, and a facility for manufacturing magnetic disk media was put in Pazardzhik. They later became the largest producers of magnetic memory devices and media in the Eastern Bloc. The disk acceptance testing system in Stara Zagora had an expensive Western machine, and it always overloaded. Our experience in mainframes allowed us to build a simulator of an IBM 360 channel, controlled by a lower cost minicomputer which was already in production in another factory in Sofia. Our software developers then wrote test programs under the same specification and in effect reproduced their expensive test system. It was a completely original engineering project with a significant economic effect. Hundreds computing centres in Eastern Europe and the Soviet Union were running on Bulgarian disks- the most reliable fast external memory in the Eastern Block.

This was a glorious time for the country's computer industry, perhaps the highest in its technological history so far. In those years, Bulgaria had a revenue of several billion roubles from exporting electronics and computer products to Russia and Eastern Bloc countries. In 1977, the American trade journal *Electronics* noted that Bulgaria was second in the world (after Japan) in exporting computing machinery, per capita. Naturally, most of it was sold in the COMECON countries, mainly the Soviet Union. However, a significant part of it was paid for by the Russians in oil, so it was equivalent to hard currency. The country did not have domestic oil and gas production, so that was our lot, but when there was a surplus in oil, it was re-exported to other countries.

Almost all of the initial investment in the computer industry was paid off. At the same time, Bulgaria was also an exporter of energy, due to the nuclear power stations on the Danube. So it was fair to say that in the 1970s, the technological programme was a good investment for the country.

However, this progress was based to a great extent on stealing. We used intellectual property belonging to others without permission. People in all countries practice industrial espionage. While this could be forgiven in the beginning, when our poor country needed to modernise its economy, it could not be justified later, when the technology was put in the hands of partners with evil regimes, supporting the dark world of tyranny, oppression, and genocide. That did not set the right attitude in the minds of those who came to govern the country after the system changed. I do not believe it helped their children to reach their potential either, though they became the privileged of the day.

But the real malevolence of our corrupt Communist system was the betrayal of innocent, low-paid, highly qualified people, who worked like slaves behind the Iron Curtain yet with loyalty, professionalism, and a sense of duty. It was a time of trust and selfless belief in the benevolence of the system. When the whole world was split in two during the cold war, our little country was caught in the middle. So the government went boldly for technological advancement, and that was right. Such unknown soldiers were sacrificed without even being noted by history. However, their own country turned its back on them after the unleashing of free enterprise and privatisation later.

Hundreds of thousands of people were employed in the computer industry during the golden age. In Sofia, there were more than two thousand employees involved in R&D. The company was already established in the computer industry, an attractive place for graduates and young engineers. We had many protégés parachuted to work in our department before being sent to privileged jobs as sales representatives abroad. A year or two with us was acknowledged throughout the country as a good mark on one's CV

3.5 Leisure when You Can

It would be untrue to say that under Communism, we only worked and did not have entertainment. Drinking parties took place quite often and lifted team morale. They were a vital mental pressure valve while we worked on the computerisation programme, which imposed a strict, military-like culture upon us.

We were often called to work on weekends, especially during equipment testing for certification and release. But there was a compensation scheme to record all our extra working time, and we used it later. That allowed us to enjoy flexible work time, even though we ended up with days that often were neither paid nor given for a holiday.

None of us had cars when we started our careers, but now, quite a few did. Sometimes, when we felt unproductive, we would just take got on the car and go out to eat or ski on Vitosha, a mountain just above Sofia with stunning views down to the valleys and the town. Sometimes, we managed to escape for a few days in the snowy mountains of Rilla, farther away. One colleague had his father's house available to us from time to time in Samokov, a town just an hour and a half drive from Sofia, near the ski resort of Borovets. Samokov played an important role in the national revival and had old churches, monasteries, and historic buildings. The panoramic views of the mountains up in the blue sky made it divine. There we would gather, a small bunch of colleagues, having tea together and socialising in good spirit. This was when the exhilarating Abba were at their peak, and watching them on TV, exhausted from all the fun on the snow up the hills, remained a sweet memory.

I personally liked having time off to mountaineer and ski, but my wife was not sporty. She was not keen on skiing and usually only came when our little daughter came as well. Our kid quickly became an advanced skier and was good company, but after she grew up, she no longer liked coming with me and preferred to go with friends from her school.

The Black Sea was another attractive holiday site for me and my daughter, but my wife did not like the sun though she adored Varna, the town of her birth and childhood. When I was a schoolboy, I often went on summer camps to Obzor, where the Old Mountain chain dips into the sea. I have divine memories of the low mountains with beautiful oak trees. I do not know how the name *Black* came for this beautiful sea. The Greek name Евксински Понт (Póntos Áxeinos) is possibly associated with the Old Persian *axšaina*, the colour of turquoise. The Bulgarian coast looks east, and the sun always rises from the sea, creating incredibly beautiful dawns. Before midday, the horizon looks dark or silver because of the angle of the sun. However, in the afternoon, when the sun goes west behind your back and the sky is clear, the waters turn into blissful turquoise.

Once, my family had visitors from East Germany. We had met them while on a beach holiday. They had a daughter the same age as ours, and I organised a camping trip for both families in the Rhodope Mountains. The Rhodopes are unusual. They are like a sea of hills stretching for miles and miles in all directions. In the summer, large fields with swaying grass and wildflowers made you feel like you're walking on a plateau. We intended to drive up to some of the charming artificial lakes and camp there for a couple of days. Quaint picturesque villages and little towns are home to beautiful rural architecture, weaving craft and styles of folk singing, unique in the world. No wonder one song made it into space on board of

Voyager 1 and Voyager 2 probes in 1977 as a sample of music, a message to other possible civilisations in the universe.

When we were near the town of Dospat in the River Mesta Valley, the road passed close to the border with Greece, and the police stopped us at a checkpoint. They did not want to let the German car pass because so many holidaymakers from East Germany crossed the border to escape to the West. The Iron Curtain on our border with Greece was very weak. We wondered what to do, and then it occurred to me to just show them my ID. Since our corporation had a factory nearby on the southern border, I had a special stamp for visiting border regions. After they put all of it on record, they asked me to confirm that our friends would not abscond to Greece and let us go.

My wife liked having chats with German friends on a holiday even though she did not like wild camping in tents near mountain lakes, where bears were all around. She spoke German. But with all my busyness at work and little leisure time to share, I realised she was becoming unhappy and depressed. She liked town architecture, going to new places, socialising, attending parties, and going to cultural events like concerts, cinema, and the theatre. There were not that many culture places to visit in our little country, and travelling abroad was restricted. I found parties very boring. There was little there I could share. Too much booze and flirting till midnight made me feel sick, and so did the forthright vulgarism when matters of love and sex were discussed. I once got too passionate about the subject of love and what it meant to me; I realised I was behaving like a geek in that environment, but I did not care. That characteristic of me was truthful, anyway. But to me, these parties only served for gossiping, intrigue, and brewing extramarital affairs. It was a very cynical age.

We loved music and art. Engineers, economists, scientists, and artists who grew professionally during the industrialisation programme of the 1950s to 1970s were now forming some sort of lower middle class, which increased demand in the city for entertainment in music, literature, and theatre. Many artists defected to the West, but some made a career without doing so. Our two famous musicians, Boris Christov and Nikolai Giaurov, Nicola Ghiuselev were internationally recognised. These bassists lived abroad but gave local performances from time to time. I liked pieces from famous operas but did not enjoy an entire opera, which could last over two hours. So my wife and I eventually found common interests in classical music. Our country's classical performers were very talented. We sometimes had visits from world-class conductors, who made their performances even more special. A modern building, the National Palace of Culture, hosted Claudio Abbado with Verdi's *Requiem* and Tchaikovsky's *1812 Overture*, truly stunning performances. LP records by Sviatoslav Richter, David Oystrakh, and others, playing German and Russian composers, were our favourite and were very affordable.

We also enjoyed good jazz. Dixieland was a popular style in the sixties, played by the big bands of Bulgarian radio and TV, directed by Vili Kazasian, but Milcho Leviev managed to create an original style. He later emigrated to America.

Some theatre performances were very good. One of the plays that moved me most was *Life Is a Dream*, written by Pedro Calderon de la Barca, the Spanish Shakespeare. In it, Prince Segismundo was imprisoned by his father, King Basilio, in an attempt to prevent his destiny from unfolding in an evil way. It clicked my mind for the first time to the topic of exercising free will with destiny. The outstanding performance of Naum Shopov, who was perhaps the best Bulgarian actor ever, certainly contributed a lot to the success of this piece. He also played the Bulgarian tsar Boris III in *Tsar and General*, a film which showed Boris for the first time as a real human being, taking to his heart an old friend of his, the general who spied for the Russians. He was a tsar torn apart in the difficult decisions he had to make for country, family, and friends in the coming World War II. He truly wore a crown of thorns as, depicted later in a book written by Stephane Groueff.

Writing good humour during the gloomy years of Communism was a real challenge, but one man, Jordan Radichkov, made it on the level of a world master. His play Суматоха (*Turmoil*) made me laugh like I had never done before. I loved reading his short stories, something like *Winnie the Pooh* for adults. Simple, humble, and set in Bulgaria's picturesque rural countryside, their message went beyond the national folklore into the broader world of human wisdom. His parodying style of expressing human relationships of love, compassion, jealousy, and envy is uniquely genuine, free from any foreign influence. The power of his works can only be measured by international standards, but in our small and insignificant country, nothing could travel far. I believe one day, he will get the recognition he deserves.

3.6 Missiles and Bread

The civil service was mandatory for every man in Bulgaria. Men were normally called after their last year of secondary education and served for two years. Those who were accepted in higher education, however, were suspended from duty for the duration of their study. As a very valuable resource, after taking our computer engineer diplomas, we were immediately assigned to build the country's computer industrialisation. But after four years, the army got us. I was terrified by the time ahead because we heard thousands of stories of young people being bullied and abused in the army. However, we were nine years older than the majority of people who served as regulars. With five years of study behind and another four working afterwards, we were ridiculed as 'pensioners' by the youngsters but otherwise respected. Quite a few men from the university and colleagues from my place of work were summoned at the same time made a good company.

In the spring we were sent to a military academy for the artillery, hosting a school for reservist officers. The difference between us, the reservist and the cadets could be seen clearly when we were lined up in ranks. The majority of us looked hunchbacked and visually impaired behind glasses.

There was nothing horrible to start. We got up early in the morning and ran for at least half an hour, washed, and lined up for morning round check. Keeping to a tight time schedule was a bit of a challenge, but not too difficult, even enjoyable; everything was planned, everything was timed for you. There was nothing to worry about: no management meetings, no bosses to harass you, no technical problems to solve, no family responsibilities or shopping or anything else. Just do the simple things you are told: a perfect rest for the mind. With lots of physical exercise, the training was very refreshing for our rotten old bones. It helped a lot to restore our fitness.

Our major task was to study a Soviet surface-to-air missile control system and maintain it for the engineering force. In technical terms, it was a real-time control system based on lamp electronics; although over fifteen years old, it was great fun. The lecturers, officers from the air defence forces, were very proud of this 'super high-tech' stuff they were teaching. Systems like these were able to shoot down American flights over Soviet Russia in the past, while the Americans were still struggling with their air defence technology.

Apart from that, we had to master basic skills in handling Kalashnikov rifles and other guns for the artillery, but we were seldom given loaded weapons because we were "absent-minded professors." We did have real-life firing training on the ranges, after which we had to stand guard with live ammunition loaded in the guns. We were called to serve for the summer, so it was not too difficult, but I liked my sleep and disliked the night guards. Quite often, to prevent myself from falling asleep, I watched the stars. Bulgarian summer nights are usually very starry. It led me to romantic thoughts away from a soldier's duty. Crickets sang as I watched the Great Bear and the Milky Way, turning slowly round the Polar Star on each shift. My hearing was very sharp at the time, and I could always hear the guard commander coming with the next shift or even a mouse rustle in the bushes.

After six months, we were given the rank of junior lieutenant and were supposed to be sent out for active service in the field for another year. Instead, they sent us back to Sofia to work at designing and manufacturing computers. So we kept our jobs, but the difference was, we were not paid any money while in military service. This was a law no one disputed. Thankfully, I got some extra work, teaching support engineers. My family survived those eighteen months with my wife working, while her mother looked after our daughter. This was the plight of many of my colleagues with children.

The success of the computer industry programme over a relatively short period of just ten years was a great achievement indeed. It was made possible with the extraordinary enthusiasm of young lads who came in their multitudes after five years of college. They provided a vital supply of fresh blood to the enterprise, which above all was relying on enthusiasm and inspiration. They were indeed 'the essence of the blossom' of bright people in the faculty, according to one of the lecturers in maths. Many of them dreamed of becoming famous scientists, engineers, or inventors.

Later in life, I noted how quickly after university graduates in England embarked on trying to make a fortune from every bit of knowledge they had. Making money was instilled in every fibre of their nature, perhaps from adolescence. For us in the East, making money was impossible and even deemed unethical. Becoming famous and great: yes. Rich: no. This was preached by the partocracy, which did not know anything but revolutions and commandeering. Some of us were more pragmatic and career oriented, but the majority were dreamers. Yet those dreamers were the ones who made everything happen, working hard over many years, sacrificing personal life and family. It was heartbreaking to see these young lads, born in a small, insignificant, and unknown country, taking pride that they were all together on the global scene of high technology.

At that time in the US the patent claim by John Atanasoff, an engineer and inventor of Bulgarian descent, was recognised as a co-inventor of the first computer. Events like these helped keep the morale high.

3.7 Super Supercomputers

After the army, I wanted to take a break from industry and embark on academic research and theoretical work. By research, our management always meant looking into what the West had done and replicating it. Talking about theoretical work did not resonate in our industry-oriented culture and only provoked scorn. The modus operandi here was "steal, copy, and live." Our realm of industrial R&D had just been shaken by moving our business from the State Department for Science and Technology to the Ministry of Electronics and Electro Techniques. In the high ranks of the Politburo, the aging Ivan Popov, the father of computer technology, was made redundant. He was replaced by Ognian Doinov, a technocrat. Many thought it was just the routine game of pawns, played by the dictator, Todor Jivkov. In fact, it made sense. The maturing computer industry was handling billions in revenue and had to start focusing more on trade and services than on original development. The rivals in the Politburo had no vision for continuity and original design in computing anyway. They did not think about serving the national interest. Those who did were apparently suppressed by orders from Moscow. They wanted to make their own marks in their own way in their fields. The changes in the Politburo signalled a major shift in policy, which needed new people. Professor Popov had had his day and was ruthlessly thrown out of the elite, to become a mere civil servant. A party that demanded love and respect from every citizen used people like handkerchiefs.

For some time, the lure of a career in informatics, a newly emerging field, drew me to publish a paper for the Congress of Balkan Mathematicians. There I encountered different professional atmosphere and like-minded souls resonating with my heart. In 1977, the sixth congress was opened with a classical music performance and academic ceremonies. For a moment, it looked credible to find a full-time job in the Academy. Our group leader had been trying to gain a foothold there for a long time. With my support he managed to launch a project in the computing centre of the Institute of Mathematics.

However, all my attempts to take a more active role there failed. It took me a long time to realise that he was deliberately pushing away his associates with an aptitude for theoretical work and research, feeling jealous for his own aspirations in the Academy of Sciences. When frustrated, his people sought to take new jobs away from him in other departments and institutions; he was not happy with that either, always trying to contest and damp down the new openings. Most leaders in science had that attitude. They did not show that gracious spirit of the teachers happy to see their chicks flying away and doing well elsewhere. Instead, they were cunning in making the system work just for them. They complained about the system, yet in the end, they actually embodied and represented it in full.

My zeal to pursue a job in the BAS started to fade away because the little glimpse of the culture there from my part-time work allowed me to see that working among mathematicians as an engineer would be a big challenge, just as it was for John von Neumann's engineering team in IAS. The theoreticians were afraid that engineers may try changing the culture, turning it utilitarian, driven by needs of the economy, instead of the goals of pure mathematics for its own sake. Computer science and informatics were just beginning to be developed as mathematical disciplines in their own right, and the rivalry was high, even internally. The other thing was the pride of some of the mathematicians, who looked down on engineers as second-class people. They would probably see me as someone who would try to change the connections in their brains with a soldering iron.

I could understand the anxiety and the concerns of several like-minded chaps, true and humble mathematicians who loved the peace and quiet away from the pressure of ambitious administrators and politicians, who by contrast completely owned our engineering organisation. Just like in IAS in America, being independent from commercially and politically driven minds, trying to destroy creativity and the humble effort to make pure science, was feared. That was what I was looking for too. But I did not find even a hint of being welcomed there by a person in authority. If there was any future for doing theoretical computer science, it would be in my current workplace, I concluded. Perhaps I could make it alone, without money or anybody else. That would solve the problem of rivalry and sabotage from above.

In science, moreso than in engineering, there is a tremendous scope for individualism. In fact, the greatest scientists of the past were individualists who did not follow the established authority in the body of knowledge or administration of science. Instead, they exercised creativity and innovation, breaking with traditions and conventions, shaking things up, and spearheading according to their judgement, reasoning, and vision for change. But at the end of the day, you either led or followed. Rivalry and competition, selfishness (to put it bluntly), are motors of innovation in capitalism, but here, in my country, I could see only pyramids of power, where rivalry was a silent killer of all creativity. The higher you went, the less knowledge and professionalism you needed to have, less you loved what you were responsible for, and less you loved the people up and down the ladder. Where was the leader I could follow or emulate? I was like a lost sheep in the wilderness.

In the meantime, the world went madly computer-hungry. High-performance computers were in high demand worldwide. There were lots of areas which demanded faster processing: simulation of the Earth's atmosphere for weather prediction, oil exploration, fluid dynamics and modelling for aerospace design, analysis of satellite imagery, manufacturing control.

One way to speed up computing was to make the data paths wider. Lower range computers only had hardware to add 8 bits at once. Larger numbers were handled by 8-bit additions, one after another, controlled programmatically starting from the lowest ranks. This is similar to the way hand calculations are performed by adding first the lower ranking digits from right to left. Most scientific calculations required 32 and even 64 bits, which powerful computers now performed with fast electronic circuits, not programmatically. But for most application areas, enlarging the data width beyond 64 bits did not make sense because few applications required such data precision.

Another way to increase power was to invent faster components, and yet another one was to make multiple processors work on a single task in parallel. The industry in the West and the Soviets had secret military programmes which took the first route as more conservative but realistic. Moore's law in microelectronics proposed that the number of transistors on a chip doubled every two years. The increase in density made it possible for the electric signals to travel between components faster. As a result, computers quickly became faster and faster, doubling the processing power every two years, with the price dropping and at the same time becoming an order of magnitude smaller in size. But in effect, the power was increased mainly by increasing the clock speed. Moore's law stopped being valid when the structural limits of the semiconductors were approached. Other methods for boosting power had to be explored.

Matching what one loves to do with the need to earn one's living has been a problem for many scientists. To resolve this problem facing many others like me, with an aptitude for research, our management opened part-time postgraduate places in conjunction with the academy, where people could earn a PhD while working. Quite a few of us were PhD students already, but except for the exams, which were taken externally, not much progress on real scientific work was made by anyone.

Paradoxically, in this elite institution, the supervisors were not happy with part-time postgraduates working on practical problems related to the need of the company or even the country in general. Linking such work to a government programme or a long-term project was far too dangerous for the well-being of those in key managing positions. Anyone having a fresh degree in some field could become a potential torpedo for blasting someone's job in the higher ranks. PhD supervisors who were line managers always preferred their part-time postgraduates to work on some vague problems, sometimes far away from what was going on as planned R&D. There was obviously a conflict of interest there, but nobody from the high ranks was aware of it, and no one was prepared to fix it.

The part-time PhD programme was just a way to keep you there, but no one was interested in the results of it and sometimes, in effect, even sabotaged. Our supervisors in the capacity of line managers would load their students with plenty of routine work, up to the point to nearly block their postgraduate work. Time off for a holiday was seldom given for more than a week or two per year, with special permission, even those who were officially registered as a postgraduate. We piled days and weeks of holiday entitlement on compensation, which rolled over from year to year and eventually was lost, not even paid. There was always something important: troubleshooting, reliability testing of a new product that went wrong, and manufacturing problems in the factory of a product due for export.

The country employed the Soviet standard for postgraduate and academic recognition, with "Candidate of Sciences" (equivalent to a PhD) and "Doctor of Sciences" as a higher doctorate with significant contribution (corresponding to a doctorate of science). The Candidate degree was meant to be awarded for original contributions in some specific field of knowledge. Naturally, it involved independent monitoring by a public body where the dissertations would be submitted, followed by a public oral defence in front of a specialised scientific council. The council had representatives from the university, the research institutes of BAS, and industry, accredited for scientific work and supervision. During the course (three years for full time and four years for part-time), students had to pass four exams: Philosophy, Russian Language, Western Language, and Specialty. The Specialty included a mixture of subjects depending on the field of postgraduate work.

I had a passion for high-performance computer systems based on employing multiple machines or processors to work on a single task: a parallel computing system. I started the state-of-the-art survey by looking in our own library and found a Russian translation of a book about the ILLIAC IV computer, the successor of ILLIAC I, which was used by students in IAS and later was installed in NASA. It had up to 256 processing units to work in parallel on data that was intrinsically parallel.

Pictures from space or radar images could contain thousands of rows, each with thousands of pixels. These large arrays of data, representing mathematical matrices, very often needed the same operation: addition, multiplication, and so on, to be applied between all their scalar components. These operations could be executed hundreds and thousands of times faster if enough operational units were available.

Machines like ILLIAC IV still operated according to von Neumann's principles: one sequence of instructions, but in this case, each instruction was applied to a multitude of operands. For that reason, they were called Single Instruction, Multiple Data (SIMD) devices. But what about data that was not organised in vectors? A significant number of numerical algorithms contained multiple different formulas and operations on loosely coupled, randomly organised data, which could also be executed in a parallel fashion. What if, unlike in the von Neumann computer, we did not prescribe the order of computation in the program at all and left the machine to work it out?

If we took that approach, the program would only need to prescribe the formulas (in other words, the operations and their interdependence). In that case, the program would look like a network or graph, with nodes representing the operations and the links- the data dependences. The links would represent the paths along which the results would 'travel' and turn into operands for other operations. Consequently, the computer control unit would need to track the availability of the input operands and, when they arrived, execute the relevant operators. According to that idea, the machine could itself find the most effective order of computation according to availability of instructions ready for execution and available computer resources (idle operational units). This was what I could propose and develop for dissertation. The new architecture could be simulated on existing machines I had access to through mainstream projects. All I needed to do was hide from routine work by going to the library during a quiet day and, little by little, make progress on whatever crazy idea would come into my head. The library was my sanctuary.

There was, however, no other sources like the one about ILLIAC IV available, and the internet wasn't around yet. There was a large institute for searching scientific and technical information, created at the time, but computer science was not well covered there. We had to generate topics for searching and submit them to their staff, after which we would get the results printed on paper. The search could catch most Western university papers and reports in the public domain. We could request copies of some of them, but they required paying hard currency for the printing and postage, which no boss would bother to authorise unless under pressure from an existing 'government' project. I personally could not afford them. Alternatively, we could ask colleagues who travelled to the West on other jobs to get them, but that was a very long process. There was no time for theoretical research, anyway, and no support from superiors. We were an engineering institute working in a narrowly defined application area, and the bosses were unwilling to see subordinates becoming more educated and knowledgeable than them.

Nevertheless, after a couple of years, things were going well. I had the outlines of the new design and decided how to build a program that would simulate it. I honestly believed this was an idea that would make me famous.

One day, to my amazement, I finally got the academic paper reprints I had requested via a friend. It turned out that scientists in the free world had been working in this area for some time now. Generous funding for research programmes in the West had given computer scientists the ability to work on crazy, radically new parallel architectures for multiprocessing. There was a US project led by Jack. B. Dennis and another one in the UK by John Gurd. They called the graph control mechanism I devised independently "data flow." However, my method of firing the operations was different. Their machine designs were better developed mathematically and supported with theoretical models. I decided that their solutions were more practical and feasible for the current hardware technology. That situation crashed my spirit, and I threw the papers on the highest, dustiest shelf.

At the same time, the interest in new architectures for super fast computers had risen around the world. Almost every university on the West had one or more projects to address that. New programming paradigms in computer science had arisen from these new ideas. So-called functional languages would suit the new data flow machines. A new approach in the area of logic and knowledge management, related to artificial intelligence, produced declarative languages in addition to classical procedural languages. They were intended to allow application programmers to create knowledge base (intelligent database) machines much easier and faster.

I dreamed of joining one of those projects in the West, but could not see how it could happen while both sides of the Iron Curtain were engaged in a bitter cold war. Thoughts about emigration came along again. Could I keep my family together, or should I leave them behind?

A couple of years later, an audit from the board for academic qualifications found that most part-time postgraduates in the institute were far behind schedule with their studies, which was a bad mark for our supervisors. One of the problems was that students had no time to work on their dissertations, but a crucial concern was that there were no original ideas for PhD work. Students just felt lost, without a sense of direction. This turned to be the right time for my work on parallel machines, as my survey contained all key authors and publications in the field. In effect, it also contained new directions for research and work. I was told I had done enough and just had to introduce my colleagues to what I had done, finalise the work, and submit a dissertation.

4

The Imprisonment of the Mind

4.1 A Hole in the Soul

Even after I lived and worked in Sofia for over a decade, I was still attached to the peace of my little hometown where my father, in good health, had retired and worked a small patch of vineyard. I usually went by train across the Balkan, which I loved. After I stepped off the train, it was a very short walk to my father's home, a walk that went up a hill and overlooked the green forest on the slopes across the valley of the river, with the railway bridge farther on. I walked this way hundreds of times as a child in summer, and we sledged down it in winter. Every single bit of it called for nostalgia.

Mum and Dad's flat was on the upper floor of a block on the top of the hill, with even more beautiful scenery below. They would take me up another hill on the northern side of the town to the vineyard; in the late summer, plums and apples bent down the tree branches. My Dad grafted them himself with his beloved local Balkan varieties and tended them all year. It was on a southern slope, well exposed to the sun, with a charming view towards the Tryavna mountains. This was the highest place in the hills where vines could be grown successfully. The grapes were just beginning to ripen in preparation for a late September harvest. I always came back for that. Mum, sadly, was finding it difficult to climb the hill and there was no road access nearby, so she often preferred to stay home.

My sister lived not too far away, in a larger town some twenty miles up the road to the Shipka Pass across the Balkan. She worked there as a dentist, serving workers in a large factory. She was a tender and loving person who grew up with two brothers and a strict father. There was very little there for mentoring and support of a girl; it was all entirely provided by mum. She, my brother, and I, though different by temper, had traits in common: straightforward, candid, nonconformist, and acting on principles. I had the advantage of learning from the mistakes my older siblings made in life; I tried to become more diplomatic yet assertive, but confidence was always difficult to master.

My sister was a lovely girl, dedicated and selfless. I had a great affection for her, and so did her many friends, but after her marriage broke down, she lived with her little daughter as a single mum. It was very tough. She needed support from her close relatives, but Sofia, where I lived, was not so close. I realised that each time I went to visit her, I was just using her dental services, always in a hurry back to work. She was trying to start a new relationship for marriage, but it probably did not go well. She did not share much in this area with me. I was not aware my sister was experiencing severe loneliness and had a personal breakdown, which eventually led her to committing suicide.

Nothing in my life had shaken me so much as the time when she passed away. For a very long time after that, I struggled to understand what happened and refused to accept the fact. I battled the emptiness created by her absence. I felt guilty that we, two brothers could not do enough to protect our sister from emotional breakdown. I personally did very little to give her the support she needed in a difficult period of her life.

We often don't realise how little is needed to make those we love feel better: just be there in their space, spend time with them, say a word of love and encouragement, empathise with them, hug them, and hold their hand. Instead, we don't know what to say; we think the silence is shouting, "Do something," and because we don't know what, we run to seek refuge in our business. No! The silence is not shouting; it is our hearts of stone that are longing to soften, but we don't let them. Instead, we feel embarrassed to let our love come out.

One tragic day, I was told about my sister and rushed there. When I arrived, my brother, who lived in the same town, seemed to had disappeared, and my mind began to freeze. One horrendous task was loaded on my shoulders: to tell Mum about her daughter. I just did not know what to do. When I arrived at my father's home, I felt as if I had a stone in my throat. I told the plain truth, directly and without much gentleness. Mum started wailing and weeping for some time and then stopped. She was more courageous than both of her sons.

Not long after that, Mum's condition worsened. Despite lengthy examinations in the hospitals in Sofia, doctors could not find an effective treatment for her. She died after a debilitating illness. It was a horrendous time. I only started to realise the void in my life after she and my sister were gone. It all happened in a very short period of time like in a film of horror. I wished we had them back, but in vain. Something crushed me after those events, and I realised life was never going to be the same again.

The loss of our sister was something I thought we could have prevented, and this was the most painful of all. Deep in my heart, I loved her so much and always liked seeing her, although having lived away, we lost touch over years. This was an excuse I easily made for myself, but it did not make me feel better. Then, without saying anything out loud but in my heart, I started blaming my brother for letting this happen. My affection for him disappeared and never returned. He lived in the same town and lectured at the technical university there.

I realise I was very selfish then. Compared to my siblings, I was much better off; we had our own home and a car. I had a good job; what more could I want? The philosophy of existentialism was still remote in my mind. Yet I was still looking for something and was unsatisfied with my career. I was not up to facing the challenges in my personal life: a disillusioned and lonely wife, an alienated child, a divorced and lonely sister longing for a true friend in life, and an older brother who also faced divorce, abused alcohol, had conflicts at work, and struggled to make ends meet in a family with two children. He, like me, found it difficult to collaborate at a higher level at work. Yet he was a brilliant engineer, a lecturer to hundreds of students, passionate about fluid dynamics.

As a naval country, Bulgaria had interest in technology for shipbuilding, engineering, and navigation. A department of hydrodynamics was opened in Varna, and my brother later found his niche in development. An ambitious PhD work was perhaps his only meaning in life for some time. He designed, engineered, and actually built a simulator for experiments in cavitation: the mysterious phenomenon that cause ship propellers to erode at high speed. Research had found the main reason was the bubbles in the water created as it was moved by the screw. They rapidly collapsed and produced mini shock waves, damaging the propeller's moving parts. However, the exact calculations were computationally intensive, and this hampered attempts of engineers to design high-speed moving parts.

The problem required powerful computers as well as experimental models to account for imperfect boundary conditions. Apart from his work on mechanics and fluid dynamics, he embarked on writing computer programs for these calculations, envisioning very practical applications, not only for ships but also for advanced fast-revolving concrete mixers. He also designed and built a small super-cavitations ring for his students to play with. What he did, the Western researchers were doing by spending thousands of dollars for similar hi-tech projects.

At the time, our computers at work could only work in batch mode, one user at a time, monopolising the machine for a given time slot. They usually only read data given to them in the form of punched holes: paper tapes or punched cards. Punched card machines were only available at computing centres, which were still scarce. One could often arrange to run a program on a computer, but time on punch machines was usually a bottleneck. Debugging a program was a pain and a good test in patience. To fix a bug could require making just a single punch hole in one card of the program entry pack, but you could have to wait a week or so for that hole to be made. Debugging time was a large proportion of the whole lifetime of a program. Naturally, my brother came to me at our institute, where we had plenty of capacity on punch machines, since we were not engaged in creating application software.

His calculations were my first encounter with application programming. At the time, I was only involved in hardware electronics design and system programming: the design of operating systems and low-level code of device drivers, which controlled the hardware electronics. I was surprised and very excited to learn that a lot of the fluid dynamics problems my brother's team were trying to solve had to do with Maxwell's equations, the same ones that governed radio waves and the flow of electricity in the grid. We marvelled at that mystery. What was that common, fundamental thing in nature that caused liquid and gas to behave in a similar way as electromagnetic waves which travel through a vacuum? The models used in these two areas were disjoint, incompatible, but there was something fundamental in nature that suggested they could be unified. He was dealing with an application problem but had something from the bug of theoretical scientists, whose imagination was easily captured by the beauty and wonders of nature.

He came to me for help with the punch holes, but it seemed like he was also looking for a more intimate collaborator in the application area. It was an opportunity for me to switch from system programming to an application programming, which from the perspective I have now could have been a very successful career move. But I did not dare to move. I was mad about supercomputer architectures and had my own passions.

There was another reason: I felt detached from him and was scared by his personal problems. Perhaps he also needed someone to lean on at the time, to support him, at least with a tap on the shoulder, putting an arm around him, and not much more. No, I did not respond to it, but I now regret my cold-hearted decision. I now know the diagnoses of this: a hole in my heart which I was trying to fill with the wrong things: selfish ambition and pride. Both of us were raised in that Stoic culture, making it difficult to engage emotionally with each other. We are all created with deeper feelings that are often choked by the world around us.

4.2 Managers and Leaders

> The good shepherd lays down his life
> for the sheep. (John 10:11)

Being unfamiliar with the Bible till late in my life, I read that verse for the first time, despising it. Many leaders today are ignorant of it too. In the early 1980s, in our cynical citadel of technology, we, the mature professionals eager to manage and lead, would laugh at it too.

There is a misconception that to be a leader, you need to be placed in a position of power. In fact, anyone with professional achievements is a leader by the mere fact that people admire them and try to copy them. Celebrities also find themselves in the category of people who influence others strongly, although they might not choose to lead in good faith.

Without that sort of natural recognition and authority, it is difficult to lead even when we are placed in a job that gives us some form of power. But it is when we have to make decisions affecting other people that the most important qualities of a leader are revealed: their sense of judgement about the behaviour of others, the ability to motivate and inspire people to give beyond their natural abilities, the ability to evaluate the situation they were in, and the courage to pursue an objective, not from self-serving ambitions but from a principle, in good faith. That is the kind of leader who is able to transform multitudes and even a generation, who changes the narrative of their time for better, who loves those they lead. Not that leading with fear is completely ruled out from the toolbox of a successful leader. In fact, that might be necessary to the success of an enterprise that employs people who are not good team players and who do not have a sense of responsibility. To add fear to the instruments of governing can still be an expression of love.

At the time, my ambition was in high-performance computing and multiprocessing. When I mentioned "multiprocessing" to my bosses, they felt it was not realistic unless we had a prototype. Soon, I was managing a design project for a device to connect both type of systems: mainframes and minicomputers. It was required to closely follow the design of an existing Western prototype, so that we could use all the available software on the market. More cloning. But it turned out to be a great fun. For the first time, I had a group of people and was learning new skills: planning, coordination, leadership. I divided the design work with clear boundaries and interfaces between the team members. After they had done the designs, I went through their diagrams one by one, meticulously checking their solutions in detail, correcting and making suggestions for improvement. They had just come from the student bench and had no experience. I did not know them. I could not think of relying on them without control in a strictly timed project that I myself was tasked for the first time.

The poor chaps did not much like such tight scrutiny, and some of them even felt offended. I heard them ridiculing me sneering and teasing one another behind my back: "Have you passed the exam, mate?" My management style obviously curbed their professional pride. They were right; my manner showed I did not trust them, and that is one of the most offensive actions in a relationship. But I did not regret taking a disciplined approach. It was the only way I could guarantee avoiding major problems later. In the end, they liked me and respected me because we succeeded as a team. Everybody likes to be a winner, even if the leader is not very inspirational.

Managing a project is an art, always unique, even when the team and the tasks are the same. The circumstances change and create a different sequence of events. The only invariants are the patterns of human behaviour and relationships: trust, friendship, cooperation, perseverance, courage, generosity, egocentrism, jealousy, envy. The way these patterns express themselves are well explained through the characters in the Bible. And the types of solutions are there too. But I did not know that wisdom yet, and neither did our top managers. The higher they were, the less wisdom they practiced. In our system, there was not much space for advice or debate. It was mostly telling from above and not selling. We were like the army: deliver or die. To mention love in this process was ridiculous. I realise I probably never said, "Thank you for the work and support," to anyone on the team. That went by example down the ladder from the top. Managers seldom personally thanked their subordinates for the work. On no occasion did I ever hear a word of thank, encouragement or support from my own boss.

My first project was successful, and the prototype passed all testing, including reliability. It went beyond engineering of just one keystone device. Customers in the largest car plants in Russia immediately wanted a large integrated system of mainframes and minis for manufacturing control. A respected Western company was a subcontractor for the control system. We successfully installed a prototype, and everyone liked it: the Russians and the contractors. The next steps were to replicate it across the multisite corporation. The main contractor also wanted to sell it to its other customers. They wanted to talk in confidence directly to me, ignoring the 'bureaucrats' in Sofia. This was a great opportunity for us, a team of three colleagues, to work abroad in a Western country, but I did not know how to play that game. I still believed I had to be loyal to the organisation, the monster that was, in fact, trying to crush us. Eventually, the customer's enthusiasm dried up, and it was all over. A significant number of devices were sold in Russia later without my involvement in system engineering so I missed the opportunity to move in the application area as well.

Back home from Russia, I slumped in the same depressing environment. I felt an urgency to decide which way I was going: scientist or engineering manager? My apprehension perhaps did not go unnoticed, and management sensed I might seek a new job in the academy. After our line manager was promoted to lead a division, new low-level managers were hatched. I was one of them and was given a group to work on small computers. Personal computing had just been born, and we endeavoured cloning the first IBM PC.

But I began to realise I had no confidence in managing people and caring for them under this crazy system. How can you care for people when no one cares for you? I could not overcome the challenges of conforming and playing the rules of the pyramids of power. Courses in senior management were only available to reliable staffers, to whom the doors to the high ranks were already half-opened. They would not let you in those courses unless they were sure you were committed to it. The real life was practicing Machiavellian governance, and courses were not helpful with practical skills anyway serving just as an acknowledgment and endorsement.

In the early 1980s, the atmosphere at my workplace gradually started to deteriorate further. We knew the system was corrupt in its roots because it was based on command and control being exercised from the top, while responsibility for the outcome was being pushed down. But the effect of this did not demonstrate itself negatively at the beginning, when the computer modernisation programme started and there was plenty of demand for development. Team spirit used to dominate our workplace, as long as our leaders cooperated honestly without dirty tricks and hypocrisy and without resorting to destructive internal competition.

After the 1973 war between Israel and the Arab countries, the oil crisis that followed caused the whole world to go into a recession. The countries from the EEC felt they had to protect their economies from the rapid technological advancement of the COMECON countries. They made a coordinated effort to break successful trade relations with important Bulgarian trade partners like Austria and Japan. At the same time, the United States issued a new embargo list, which included key technology components and machinery they knew Russia used in military programmes. There was also a deliberate and orchestrated attempt to discredit and expose Bulgaria as a terrorist state. This period was the second cold war, when the West targeted the ethical grounds of the Eastern Bloc. There was no defence against that sort of attack, because we were now standing entirely on stealing and deceit.

The economy of our country was approaching a point of stagnation, and the budget for developing new hardware started to dry up. Cloning was becoming more and more difficult because the technological gap with the West was deepening, and the available domestic and Russian components were not adequate. With increasingly narrowing product lines and market demand, managers who previously cooperated with each other to some extent were now in the position of bitter rivals. Despite artificially introducing a hierarchy to accommodate promotions, the directors could not think of a way out. Ordinary developers felt they hit the ceiling for promotion because few of them had an aptitude for management and administration. At the same time, they were tired of working on projects without significant financial reward.

Work in IT elsewhere in the country was scarce, and job changes were not encouraged. In effect, there was no job market. Whatever you tried to do through your network of friends, managers were afraid to take the risk of employing you in fear of creating conflict with rival pyramids of power. Because of the job stagnation, old teams found themselves in stormy conditions, and performance dropped. Bureaucracy started to erode the team spirit.

Few of us were good leaders because we were self-centred and quite often conformists. Some of the older guys, established professionals in their own field, who liked the work they were doing, led very small teams and were not looking for more. They were respected by their people. But others gradually turned from leaders and good planners into fire-fighters. Many of them had long ago stopped being professionals and were only engaged in finding loopholes for milking the system for themselves. Some were busy on other jobs in other organisations and had loyal deputies to monitor all the ongoing work at their base location. When they did turn up, they could not engage quickly. Most of the problems they were resolving would not have been there in the first place if they had been more attentive. Surprisingly, these kind of managers were admired for their craftiness. Whoever was cunning and could outwit the system to work for them personally, even at the expense of others, was respected. After all, it was okay to look after your own interests, wasn't it?

In a free-market economy, the organisation would have had to shrink by letting some people go and restructuring accordingly. But we had a socialist system of central planning. Restructuring in a modern technology sector needed reshuffling in the high ranks, which they did, but too late. This alleviated the condition, but only temporarily. All countries in the Eastern Bloc were continuing to slump into a deep political and economic crisis.

People generally do not like to be managed, especially in a totalitarian way. After I finished my first project, I was officially offered the job of head of a section. Our organisation was structured functionally, and projects were not supposed to employ people across sections. The new unit was formed without any discussion. I was simply told who my team was to be, and that was it. During restructuring, it was okay for management to cross-pollinate the skills of old teams across a larger division in the organisation. And we had to be thankful for what we had. Some of our colleagues, being in the position of rivals, were not so fortunate (or were they not actually the fortunate ones?).

That was the style of leadership in all departments in general, as I could see it. Inexperienced and egocentric myself, I had to move on. In the end, I realised working with a completely new team was not a bad idea. But I naively thought that all people from below liked me and wanted to work for me. I was excited with the time ahead, without realising that many of the new team were just moles for the bosses above me and would not be loyal or honest with me. Team building was not going to be easy in this new position of power. For the first time, I realised I was not perceived as the person I thought I was. Was it my personality? Was that how they perceived me truly in their hearts? How could I manage in this belligerent environment without having at least one person on my team I could trust?

I realised the change of feelings was because of the change of my position. Now I was seen as just another crafty boss who would not trust his people but manipulate them. This was how it was going to be in my managing career, and I tried to focus realistically on my new role without naivety. No doubt one had to work hard to woo friends and supporters, yet not from below but from my level and above. This was difficult too. The bureaucrats were so crafty and manipulative that they watched you and could turn people against each other if they saw a new alliance building. I decided it was not worth the effort. Building an alliance after many years of horrendous effort would not lead to anything other than creating a new branch of an existing mafia. That culture was repulsive to me. I had authority among the people on the project team, but now my managers shook this authority and almost killed it by giving me a position with elusive power. Enthusiasm for the job suddenly drained off because I saw what the future held. I did not expect anyone to love me, but I obviously did not have the skills to work with people, though I had a strong desire to learn. There was no one to learn from. All role models were repulsive.

Paradoxically, the key to success as a functional manager was perhaps to always overpromise and very often under-deliver. I could not understand it. In my family upbringing, not to keep a promise was a grave sin. In our Spartan task-oriented culture, one should die if necessary to keep one's word. In our management system, that virtue was preached but not practiced. In real life, prudency had a different dimension; to succeed, one always had to overpromise. One may think that was a modern, "can-do" attitude. Far from it. Subordination was a very strong driving force. Bosses expected mid- and low-level managers under them to be potential rivals for their jobs. They were not looking for deputies who were able to stand on their own strength. Instead, they were looking for flattering and servile characters who would always depend on them. Those were the ones who would be pulled up when the time came for them to go up the ladder.

I should have had no problems with loyalty and queuing for the ladder. To be disloyal for me was another grave sin. But loyalty means you are with that person, even when they are wrong. However, if you cannot help them get it right, what is the point of staying loyal? There are limits to your loyalty. Beyond those limits, you no longer know the ground you are standing on. Besides, bosses usually found I was useless in conspiracy and independent, usually knowing too much about pure technical matters to feel dependent on someone else.

Things worked well in the beginning; we had a fairly flat management structure, and the team spirit led to good performance, with cooperation and a generous sharing of knowledge. But when the organisation grew older, the structure became hierarchical; the mid-level managers were in effect redundant but kept their roles just to justify more power, larger dominion, and higher pay. I only saw this phenomenon in the West later, in large global corporations. However, the macroeconomics there allowed for periodical restructuring through redundancy, an effective social security system, and a mature job market. Communist Bulgaria did not have those things, since everything was supposed to be centrally planned in advance and managed in the closed economy of the Eastern Bloc. Unemployment was the gravedigger of capitalism, we were taught.

There was something far more destructive to team performance than that. The majority of us came from a humble, rural upbringing and were completely unprepared for the industry's highly competitive environment. Under pressure, some people were rude and cruel, often reacting by trying to put others down. The root cause was not so much envy and hatred as fear of rejection. Those people often felt just like pawns in the schemes of the managers, rather than team members with a common goal. Quite often, people were not motivated but commanded and rushed like cattle.

There was a general sentiment among high-ranking managers that putting others down was a "typical Bulgarian trait." I never accepted that. I could see it coming from team members who lacked self-confidence and self-esteem; they did not always realise they were working in an authoritarian culture, where it was inevitable for the leaders to be hypocritical and evade their responsibility by pushing it down unfairly on the people they managed. They required a high level of commitment and expected sacrifices from their people, but they didn't offer the same upward to their own bosses. Quite often, they did not demonstrate their own commitment to a common goal. This degraded morality was typical for the Communist system, which postulated utopian principles of equality and duty, just like George Orwell's *Animal Farm*.

If there was some sort of typical trait we needed to deal with, it was a lack of discipline and team spirit with commitment. One may think that Communism should have sorted that out. In fact, it exacerbated it. There was no incentive for working hard because the system favoured a flat pay. Since they were not in charge of their own lives, people practiced a 'quiet rebellion'. It consisted of finding inoffensive excuses for not doing the job. As the joke about socialist workers went, "They cannot pay me less than what I will work for."

In that respect, Bulgarians also invented their own wisdom: "Бог високо, цар далеко" ("God is too high, and the tsar is too far away"). It meant, "There is no one here to either watch me or protect me, so I will do as it suits me." We came to this not because of our past of slavery or because too much freedom had been given to us. It was because we lacked faith. We lost our trust in authority in general and our faith in justice.

Did this come from our ancestors or from the centuries under foreign powers? I don't know. Maybe over time, we turned insubordinate and stubborn. We are not easily motivated by material gains or inspired by a cause. In a team environment, we would listen and sort of agree to a common goal and our responsibility in it, but then, we would go and do our own thing instead.

4.3 A Time to Be Silent

A time to be silent and a time to speak. (Ecclesiastes 3:7)

We were feeling suffocated by the spiritual emptiness, but not only at work; the whole nation craved for something beyond material technological advancement. During this time, I got a reference book on astronomy and found the ephemerides of Jupiter in it; one night, I turned my binocular towards it. For the first time, I saw its moons like little dots on both sides of the disk. I was very excited. I bought a more powerful device from Russia, a monocular, since there were no telescopes available at the time. I remember spending time looking at the craters of the moon and the shadows from the mountains through just eight times magnifying optics. I knew that Galileo, the father of modern science, first discovered the moons of Jupiter at the turn of the seventeenth century, using a very primitive instrument.

I suggested to my closest friends that we gather on a regular basis, not for drinking, but to just relax and share knowledge outside our direct professional interests. I wanted to share more on astronomy (not astrology), alongside the evolution of stars and extraterrestrial communication. This also generated some thoughts on metaphysics. It was far from any serious philosophical endeavour. Yet when news about it was heard at my workplace, everyone from the group fled. They stopped coming, fearing they might be prosecuted for gathering and discussing forbidden topics or plotting something bigger. The gathering of groups at home for any other reason than useless social drinking was carefully monitored. Later on, when I was reading Orwell's *1984*, I thought the author must have experienced the thought police in my country before he wrote that novel.

Feeling tiny and useless in a culture that only recognised materialism and rivalry as the main motives of life apparently is not unique. People were oppressed for their convictions in various ways, even in the theistic world of Western Europe, at a time when religion exclusively owned the scientific enterprise, and there was no freedom of expression. Galileo came under ideological pressure from the religious establishment when, based on his observations, he started publicising the heliocentric system of Copernicus. He was using a new invention, the printing press, to disseminate scientific papers and books, some of which were affirming that the sun was *not* orbiting the Earth, but the other way round. While his works deflated the grand pretensions of the clerics to be the sole interpreters of the Bible, they did not undermine the message contained therein. However, when that stirred up debates on a scale unseen before, the church was very alarmed because the existing doctrines were wrong in mistakenly interpreting some allegorical texts and poetry in their literal meaning. This was in conflict with the scientific evidence of the day. The church made a big mistake by accusing him of heresy. Although he backed down, silenced and threatened by the Inquisition, the clash with the clerics shook not only the religious establishment; Christianity as a whole was put to test. That moment of weakness provoked the rising of atheism so that it took ground and has continued since. Even though the Reformation later put the human-made doctrines and the wrong interpretations of the Bible right, atheism continued to grow stronger because of the mistakes of the church.

Yet the freedom to express myself and feel valuable to others was not the only reason for my loneliness and depression. I was reflecting on what I was missing. My sister and my mum recently died, and it was a terrible blow to my spirit. I felt very lonely and without a soul mate. But on the other hand, I finished my doctorate and had a group to work with. That should have been positive and motivating.

However, I found it increasingly difficult to work with my boss. He was not interested in me anymore because, despite my loyalty, I looked too dangerous for him with my new qualification. He had my department in his division, just as a tool enabling him to have more people under his wing. But he did not keep me in the plans of what he was doing with people in my department. So I officially had the group, but in effect, I was not in charge at all. My people had me as a bureaucrat, lurking in the corner and annoying them every now and then with something they knew would not be blessed from above. I realised it was not personal; I was not alone. It was the plight of so many other low-level managers. They found the vertical managing line dysfunctional and the horizontal links between low-level departments redundant and useless. Years ago, when I joined the small group my boss was leading, we were all united in a kind of dissident spirit against the system, fighting for our place in the technological advancement of the country. But now, we were turning into the epitomes of the same system.

Another major source of depression was that my relationship with one of my best friends had soured. He was also given a group of people to lead, and I was very optimistic about collaborating with him. I offered sincere and unreserved support to him. However, all my attempts to woo him were unsuccessful. I could not understand the reason. It looked like someone was manipulating him for their own benefit, but at the time, I took it personally. The feeling of rejection was increasing when more and more people started keeping away from me. Had I done something wrong? Were they afraid of me? Why? After many years, it dawned on me that the divide-and-conquer method was secretly in operation behind the scenes to keep everything stable. Most low-level managers were manipulated against each other. Otherwise, an alliance against the upper ranks and ultimately against the system would have grown very quickly.

At the same time, supercomputing had become quite an attractive area for new PhD students, but I was again deliberately taken off from owning the research area I pioneered with such love and hard work, against the tide at the time. I was not officially allowed to supervise students, though I was habilitated, a procedure for certification equivalent to associate professorship. Nevertheless, I was magnanimous at the time, trying to be at least friendly and helpful to new students. But most people did not like being helped; they were restricted by their supervisors and wanted to do it themselves. All they wanted was my survey and the key papers I managed to pinpoint and collect over the years.

I was approaching a career level where few could go further up without becoming affiliated with the totalitarian government's structure. Some time ago, I was gently encouraged to become a party member. At some point, I was tempted into believing that if I took up a higher level position, I would have more freedom to work the way I wanted or, at least, to travel abroad and then defect with my family. This was a delusion.

We were under pressure to become something we were not, squeezed into a mould that did not fit our original design. I was feeling like an alien in this world, to adopt the Communist philosophy, offer allegiance to the party, submit to corrupt work practices, work hard, and shut my mouth. What was the meaning of it? I could not see my efforts bearing fruit anymore. Many like me were feeling that we were following the wrong ethics, but what precisely the ethics were, and where it was supposed to come from, was a blurred image.

I wrote letter after letter to universities abroad, asking for their papers and reports, and also begging to visit them to work on specific projects. These were sent by post, but none of them got a reply, apparently intercepted on the way out by the censors. In the meantime, the management of the institute gave a green light to a group in another division to clone a supercomputer for satellite data processing and oil exploration. The prototype had a SIMD architecture, similar to ILLIAC IV, and was specialised for data arrays and matrix calculations. The project was successful, and many of these computers were sold in the Soviet Union, China, and Vietnam.

There were also rumours going around that top officials in the government had made a secret deal with Western tycoons to support some people from our country to work on joint academic projects. One could imagine that the selection of people would represent a tremendous challenge. It was a challenge for me personally, as I was responsible for some ten people carrying on routine development tasks, and they obviously could not all work on computer science theories. There was no publicly available official route.

A relative of my wife who worked in an Arab country on a government contract was travelling via London, and I decided to send yet another application for research work to British universities. I gave her the letter at the airport, which might have been noticed by the agents of CSS. A day or two later, my wife and I were called in and questioned by the police about the relative's alleged attempt to flee the country. Apparently, my letter had nothing to do with it. She was arrested but then released on guarantee from me and my wife.

After this incident, I was completely overtaken with more bitterness and depression. I took a firm resolution to do something that would set me free from this country. There were one or two opportunities of travelling behind the curtain in the past, but I was reluctant to go alone because I knew if I left my family and relatives behind, it would be very difficult or impossible to reunite with them afterwards, and they would be persecuted. At that time, I was reading a smuggled copy of Boris Pasternak's *Doctor Zhivago*; there was a long queue waiting after me. In the final scene, Zhivago died, suffocated in a tram. No change for the better since the Russian revolution. People like him were still suffocating on this side of the curtain.

In 1984, after some disturbances in the areas with minority Turks, the government decided to adopt a policy of forceful assimilation called "the Regeneration Process." The Turkish language was banned from public life. Shopkeepers were instructed to sell only if a customer spoke Bulgarian. It was forbidden to wear traditional clothes and observe their rituals and celebrations. There were nearly a million Bulgarian Turks, and in many ways, they were different from their Asian compatriots. Officials forced them all to change their names from Turkish to Bulgarian and started a campaign to forcefully exile those who would not agree.

In our company, one would think this only affected the regions with more compact ethnic population, in predominantly rural areas. To my surprise, it came in our division, a place with highly educated, proud people, where there was perhaps just one person with such a name. In a briefing with management, we were told that from then on, the person's name was no longer "this" but "that," and we were obliged to address him that way in any form of communication. Of course, no one paid attention and continued to call the person the name by which we knew him. But none of us stood up and said, "I am sorry, but this is wrong." Instead, some nationalists silently approved it in their hearts; others just kept their mouths shut in fear, because they knew opposing this in public was not like telling a political joke. It could have had serious effects on the dissenter.

At that time, some people in the organisation developed mentally illness. There was also one suicide I became aware of.

4.4 Computers Go Personal

The invention of computers with stored programs quickly transformed the entire planet. Until teleprocessing was invented, computers were a space-rocket class of technology. Users had to come into air-conditioned computer centres and monopolise the whole system for a certain time to do jobs by running their applications one by one in sequence, called batch processing. Eventually, it became possible to run multiple programs on one machine concurrently, by sharing the processor, the file storage, and other resources. Engineers started to attach terminals via telegraph lines, allowing users to kick off their applications remotely. They could also receive results back to these terminals. The first teleprocessing systems emerged, and engineers started to connect not only terminals to computers but also computers to computers. The first computer networks were born, with completely new services emerging as well: email, banking, flight reservations, teleconferencing, and many more.

At the same time, the scale of integrated computer circuitry was advancing with an ever-increasing speed, which made it possible to build powerful machines with considerably smaller size. They were called minicomputers. Versatile and more affordable, they were continuing the computer revolution by conquering areas like manufacturing control, scientific instrumentation, and office automation.

The next real shake-up, however was the personal (individual) computer. It came after Intel managed to implement a CPU on just a few microchips. At first, it was mainly used for text processing, which quickly killed the typewriter. But more application areas came very soon when fast computer networks began to be built locally in offices, buildings, and campuses, where many personal workstations could share storage, data, and printers. The Ethernet became a new low-cost way of connecting computers locally. These local networks began to connect to each other with long-haul links, and so the internet was born. People were able to connect from home, cafés, on the street, everywhere.

In the early 1980s, our institute was indeed a centre of computer technology in the country, both in computer science as well as in engineering. All modern commercial areas of computing (teleprocessing, minicomputers, and even supercomputers for processing satellite data) were represented, with groups of engineers, hardware as well as software. Yet the country still did not allow email, for purely political reasons. The free exchange of information through the internet was still prohibited.

The success stories of the 1970s showed the advantage of a totalitarian system putting a significant resource in one spot and delivering cutting-edge technology. But where could we go from there? Other branches of the economy began to suffocate without resources to modernise. The economies in all the Eastern Bloc countries were in crisis and did not seem to have a vision for the future.

It was already the era of Gorbachev's Glasnost in the public space, and a new policy was put forward for running the economy. The Central Planning Commission was now to be augmented with competition, leading to a free-market economy. But how do you restructure when there was no free labour market and no social security system in place? Capital was not available, and the West was still suspicious about the reforms. The uncertainty in the political sphere prevented foreign businesses from investing in our computer industry, even on a small scale.

Gorbachev's changes for the Bulgarian computing industry simply meant that it lost its sponsors at the Politburo level; all the rivalries merely moved down to the ministerial and corporate level without rules or coordination from the top. There was no opposition to this in parliament. Even before that, carefully crafted changes in the political elite always prevented anyone from the top claiming the credit and becoming the next icon in an otherwise cultic-prone society. Having lost sponsors on the top, the computing industry was no longer in vogue. This was the beginning of its downfall, until it was finally killed with the fall of the regime. But for the time being, yet another period of delusion was taking place. An entirely separate corporation was decreed, which surprised everybody with a new strategy: building computers based on Western components. Justification: we buy with hard currency, and we sell in hard currency. So why not just assemble the units? Besides, it was cheaper with the currency rate on the black market.

What would that mean? A peaceful transition of the political system and a brotherly hug with the West? Or was it just a way to prick the pride of highly educated and smart people. We, the mainframe architects, were very proud at the time and often looked down on others. This did prick our pride. However, it was not only about pride. The rules of the game had suddenly changed, but the basis was devious and deceitful. There was no other option but rise to the challenge and play that game. The management in our corporation decided to build on our own microchip technology.

It was the age of large-scale integration. One chip could now encapsulate a whole processor unit, with its instructions built into it. The technology used a photolithographic process in the nanometre range. The design of the electronic circuits to be built was performed in whatever size was convenient for the designers and then photographed. The photograph then was used to produce a mask. The mask was used to lay the circuitry on a semiconductor crystal, using laser technology and a very fine chemical diffusion process. It worked at the ion level by etching out or depositing material on masked areas. Many layers of circuits with connections between them could be created on one base, thus forming a large logical circuit or processor. If one had equipment, for manufacturing chips, then to manufacture a microchip with a desired functionality, was simply a question of having the masks for layering the circuits. One could either spend years of design to produce them or one could buy them on the market, but there was no established market for that yet. Not for customers from the Block anyway.

Well, the Russians were able to get the masks by slicing chips manufactured in the United States. They would get samples of chips available on the components market in almost any country in the West and remove layer after layer from the chip, creating masks from them by using a similar physic-chemical process in reverse to expose the layouts and photograph them under a microscope. Then they could start testing and manufacturing them without much effort.

Using this technique, the Soviets produced an analogue of the Intel microprocessor used in the first IBM PC. The goal was to manufacture our own PC fully compatible with IBM and pirate all their software. We quickly embarked on designing a PC, coming up with a quite competitive design. But this was just a swansong for our plight in Bulgaria. The Americans found what happened and quickly introduced measures in their microchip manufacturing which made slicing impossible. It led to a crisis in our civil electronics manufacturing.

With the crisis in Russian IC technology, cloning became almost impossible. Yet for the time being, Bulgaria was able to manufacture advanced products based on Russian and Bulgarian chips that could be sold in the Third World. But here was the catch: In order to make money, our government embarked on converting these products to military applications. This was intended to go to countries like Iraq and North Korea. I remember a whole delegation of engineers from North Korea coming to see our designs and documentation. These chaps looked poor and gloomy, possibly terrified with the time ahead when they will be back home reporting what they learned. We were told to give them any assistance possible.

Not everyone felt comfortable with these projects. Many of the old guys felt betrayed by the government. We gave the best years of our life and now started to feel marginalised and unsecure. There was still nothing like a free and fair labour market. One could change jobs, switching between one mafia to another, without making much difference in one's life. Looking for a job in the West was still forbidden, and no one there wanted to hear about us, anyway.

The whole culture in the institute was changing. Many of us used to voluntarily stay after five o'clock to do the work we loved, but now, we began to hate it. From an academic-style design bureau, where one often bumped into a university scientist or a technology wizard, it gradually turned into a military-style lab with strict access control, barriers, and passes, a computerised system designed in-house. Our own products were now depriving us of our freedom.

At this time, my boss was offered a job as director of a new R&D institute. Still counted as one of his entourage, I was invited to join as the head of multiprocessing. It all looked great at the time. I hoped a time was coming when we could start something completely new by trusting each other and doing things differently. Looking at the barriers on the entrance of our workplace, it did not take me too long to accept it.

It was a mistake. It was naive to think that anything would change in the way business was done throughout the country, without fundamentally changing the whole environment in which the companies operated, the principles on which the society was founded, the working culture, the trade partners.

4.5 Cracks in the Concrete

After the war, nuclear physics and engineering were the first to bring technological advancement in the country when a very small nuclear reactor for scientific research was built in Sofia, with help from the Russians. The first commercial nuclear power stations were later built on the Danube river, also based on Russian technology. No doubt the computerisation programme in Bulgaria, together with the advancements in other sectors of the industry, changed the workforce, the technological discipline, and the working culture of the country as a whole. Some factories, for example, those producing memory devices and media, were built with some form of assistance and licensing from Western countries; they adhered to high safety standards, comparable to those in the space programme. We respected the Russian technology too, precisely because of their achievements in space and nuclear science.

The advancements of the Eastern Bloc in technology were heavily dependent on the cheap labour of the scientists and engineers of our generation. We were called scientific and engineering workers and were trained to show discipline, act responsibly, and work hard without expecting to be paid more than anybody else in society.

However, in the 1980s, the economy started to make hiccups, firstly for technical reasons, because of the embargo, but also because of the degradation of the morale of the white-collar workforce. New developments and growth were in recess, but technology and qualified people were still needed to maintain what was already built. Technological discipline was still needed and in high demand. Whatever the political system, one would not expect the industrial safety standards and procedures for dealing with civil disasters to be ignored.

After all, we were the countries claiming to be governed by the people and for the people.

May 1 was Labour Day in Communist Bulgaria. It was regularly celebrated with a parade, a half-day-long march with flowers, portraits, and slogans on the streets, until marchers finally arrived in front of the party and state leaders, demonstrating allegiance to them and praising the Communist system. Participation was mandatory, with selected organisations requested centrally to send a certain number of participants from their employees. People from our institute represented the technological workforce in these parades; we were proud of our achievements as a nation of science and technology. The representatives of the government would be standing on the tribune of George Dimitrov's mausoleum. Across the street was the building of the former tsar's palace, converted to a National Arts Gallery. Among the leaders would always be the first secretary.

But in 1986, something unusual happened. On May 1, when we were called to the parade again, I took a film camcorder and shot all the way that morning, taking clips of my colleagues and the scenery around. There was a light rain. Traditionally, the flow of the parade would come from Boulevard Dondukov going west and then would turn round the corner of the ministerial offices to go east down the Largo towards the National Assembly. Approaching the mausoleum on the right, we were bemused by the fact that the first secretary was absent from the tribune. In fact, the group there was quite skimmed down to several unfamiliar faces.

When I later developed the film from my shots, it was completely blank. I played a lot with this device before and had made quite a number of nice family reels. So I knew it worked well. What was this? The thought of a radiation exposure did not even come near my mind. The answer came in the following few days. A major accident with the reactor of the nuclear power station in Chernobyl, Ukraine, which was just across the Black Sea from Bulgaria, took place a few days before. After trying to keep the disaster and the radiation reports secret, the government finally gave up when the radiation reached countries in the West, and they were alarmed by their radiation warning systems. What proportion of the population was affected and what dose we received from the radioactive rain was never revealed. Parades usually took place at the same time in all major towns.

After they could no longer keep it secret, the country declared a state of high alert, with advice for self-protection. Yet we knew that the iodine isotope radiation from sources like the one used in the Chernobyl plant had a very short half-life. So it was the first hours that were important for protection from direct radiation. Obviously, just a few chosen from the elite were warned about it promptly. Well, I do not blame them because that might have well been the procedure for civil disasters. It is a principle for all societies to save the leaders first. However, the intention apparently was to keep it entirely secret from the world. But that did not prove possible due to the atmospheric conditions over the region, which spread the cloud over a very large territory. The following measures were important for preventing contamination of food. But they were inadequate compared to what could have been achieved if they had warned people to stay home at the beginning. They could also have called off the parades which took place elsewhere in the country.

Investigations into the Chernobyl disaster never came to a clear and satisfactory conclusion; all documentation at the time was classified and kept secret by the Soviet KGB. Even after the papers were declassified, there was no consistency in the new reports. We learned the disaster happened during a regular safety drill at night. Apparently, the personnel were not properly trained, and procedures were not strictly followed. Some information even suggested that standards were violated long before the disaster, during the building of the plant. Concrete structures were found cracked, but this was disregarded at the time.

Unlike in Ukraine, the effect of the Chernobyl disaster on the population in Bulgaria, as far as I know, was never investigated, analysed, or reported openly. There was an increase in neurodegenerative diseases and cancer in the following years, which might have been a result of that, but it cannot be supported without reliable statistical data. At least a lesson could have been learned in regard to the way our own nuclear plants were run on the Danube River. We felt like guinea pigs for Soviet nuclear experiments.

4.6 Postdoctoral

In the late 1980s, an agreement on academic collaboration was reached with Britain at a very high level. Several of my closest colleagues had already visited there. I had been quietly wiping my tears over parallel computing research like a child who never gets the toy he wanted, but then I received an invitation from Professor John Gurd to work with his group in the University of Manchester in the UK. Instead of risking having an inconvenient, noisy dissident and troublemaker by stopping me, our governors decided to let me go.

When I arrived at the Department of Computer Science, I realised the academic world in the field of parallel processing had moved on. The Data Flow Machine hardware project, which inspired me in the past, was over. The data flow concept could not be adopted straight away on a large scale as a general-purpose architecture, which it was originally intended for. The idea was far too ahead of its time. It required a radical change in the art of programming. The main obstacle was its asynchronous way of working. The firing of parallel operations would have a potentially different order on each run of the program. This is because the goal was to achieve maximum loading of the available resources on the spot. However, the system load could change dynamically because of other users and other events taking place in the larger environment. Yet the asynchronous mode would produce the same final result if the program was correct. This unusual way of operation would make it very difficult for programmers to debug their programs. It would be impossible to reproduce the same sequence of events on each run in order to localise a bug. Finding a new approach to debugging was going to take a long time and a lot of hard work.

In the meantime, its adoption stood in the way of the large US chip makers and all the industry behind, who invested heavily in another direction: making fast components. The new architecture was immature, and no one would embark on it on a large scale unless it was a top government or industrial policy. The West had other priorities, dictated by the need of the military and politicians engaged in the cold war. IBM and the chip makers did try cautiously to introduce the idea on a miniature level. A small window of several instructions in the sequential program order was subjected to checking for data interdependence. Those, which could be executed without conflicting with the rest, would proceed with execution. This so called 'out-of-order execution' is now adopted by high performance chip makers.

The data flow concept turned into a niche technology later for so-called grid computing when IBM put forward its 'tuple-space' technology. Grid computing was seen as creating a pool of loosely associated, remotely connected computers, which could act as a giant supercomputer, offering high computer power for a short time before disconnecting and associating with others for another job. This idea would be able to deliver computing power on demand, like the power stations for electricity, hence the term *grid*.

For the time being, universities in developed countries (the United States, Canada, Australia, Japan, and France) were no longer focusing only on high-performance numerical calculation but also on elaborating and clarifying the concept of information processing in general. Modernising the interface between human and computer was also important. In Japan, the focus was on so-called fifth-generation computers and knowledge bases. These were seen as advanced information systems able to communicate with users through a language close to human; they were preparing the way for artificial intelligence.

On the other hand, a new exploration of parallel processing had given rise to architectures that no longer required to work with shared memory but were passing data between them in the form of messages. They used the locality of the data at the place it was generated; they were not expected to exchange data between them remotely very often. Many algorithms had such commonality, and it was believed that passing messages between processors would give them the flexibility to work on common tasks by forming an association for a short time and then break it after the task was done. This was called distributed processing. A similar technique could also be used for remote computers on the network that would act as application servers and sell its services on the network like a utility. A new standard was emerging, later called Message Passing Interface (MPI) for loosely coupled computers working as a grid.

In Manchester, a small group was working with transputers. They built the so-called "T-Rack," a machine of hundreds of transputers, used as a test bed for multiprocessing with message passing. The transputer was a British invention, a microprocessor and a programming language called OCCAM (named after the philosopher William of Ockham), who promoted the idea of solving problems with the simplest solution). The chips were equipped with dedicated data links to connect to each other, making large, multidimensional, localised networks of processors. In the application area, the architecture was more suitable for imbedded devices working in the field and controlled in real time (for example, collecting data during geophysical explorations).

The main problem of this hardware architecture for more general use was that one could only send data and messages from one processor to its neighbour. To send to any other processor in the network would require some form of mediator code to run in any of the transputers. The idea was not new. The internet, which was a giant network of machines, already did that on a macro level; the solution was a multilayered network architecture. This is what I proposed at the machine level for the Manchester T-Rack: virtual channels built on top of the hardware ones to provide connections from one processor to any other processor.

The virtual channel solution was accepted by the T-Rack group. With good experience in data protocols, I built the design quickly, tested it on the T-Rack, and prepared a paper to submit. My pride was pricked when I bumped into the classical deadlock problem due to congestion on the network. I resolved it theoretically by proving it will not deadlock if the network had a certain ring structure, which the T-Rack had.

This was the first time I practiced real parallel programming; I really enjoyed it. For the first time, I had a terminal connected to a UNIX server machine, shared by all participants of the project. I also had an email address on the internet and discussed ideas freely with everyone I liked.

There was a wonderful spirit of freedom on the T-Rack team. Everyone was free to define the scope and goals of their work as well as the methods to get there, as far as their work fitted in the broader context of research in this particular field. Every individual result on that level was seen as a result for the whole university. So the PhD students were basically left on their own, with minimum supervision and intrusion in their goals. But if someone happened to get stuck, help and encouragement were always unobtrusively on offer from a close colleague or a supervisor. They all were full-time students, and there was no conflict of interest between them and the supervisors. Relations with the external postdoctoral visitors like me were very courteous, informal, and friendly. We had meetings with the PhD students every week, where everyone reported on the progress of their work. The administration was minimised down to one or two pages of minutes in telegraphic style.

The focus on managing the team was on individual work and achievements, as in most academic institutions, but there was a sense of togetherness and collaboration in the thematic set for the project and the department. The scope was also indirectly set by the whole computer science community working in the same area. There was no ideological or commercial pressure, apart from the anxieties in regard to the funding. Naturally, groups had to compete for funding on merits, internally as well as externally. In our organisation at home, all these mechanisms worked through the squabbles at the ministerial level or the Politburo, either politically dictated or personally and subjectively motivated.

From time to time, we socialised at parties. Though I was not very good at jokes, I was not afraid to tell political jokes when I could. Neither they were afraid. There were lots of jokes and laughter. It was Thatcher's era, when the TV program *Spitting Image* was at its best. One of the leaders also took me to his church. It was my first experience with a live service in an Anglican church. The most striking impression was the kindness and welcoming faces of the people there, especially the children. Smiles were on people's faces on the street too, relaxed and joyful, compared to our grim faces on the streets in Sofia.

I saw people sleeping rough on the street of Manchester. My colleagues explained that there were shelters for them, but they did not like it there; some found it difficult to cohabit with others. So they preferred the light, the noise, and the bustling freedom on the street. I thought if those people found it difficult to cohabit in a hostel, what about me finding it difficult to live in a whole country like ours? It was a cynical thought, which would not have occurred had I known I would be looking for a shelter myself in this country very soon.

One day, my English colleagues took me to a play in one of the lecture theatres of the university. It was about the life of Alan Turing, who they knew was a favourite computer scientist of mine. For the first time, I heard about his relationship with Arnold Murray. I was shocked to know that his death at the age of forty-two was actually a suicide, committed after he was subjected to hormonal treatment. Homosexual behaviour was strongly condemned in our country and still prosecuted, while in England, it was decriminalised some twenty years ago. The drama of Turing's life had awakened me to the personal liberties the country was then enjoying after hundreds of years of wandering in the realms of ethics, civil order, prejudice, and justice, staying in the forefront of Western democracy.

I read a short history of Britain and learned that the nation formed from various people: the Celts, the Anglo-Saxons, the Vikings, the Danes, the Normans, and others. It was the case with many other nations on the Continent, but this isolated corner of Europe perhaps allowed the mixture to brew differently and give rise to radically different styles of running and sustaining a country. A country is governed from one place, but it's not possible without a team of people entrusted with a degree of autonomy. Otherwise, the governor ends up with running the affairs with slaves in tyranny, not a team. But how do you make sure loyalty and certain standards in that relationship are always met? The answer was a written code, an agreement. That was how the Magna Carta came to be in the thirteenth century. The charter between a king and his nobles made the first breakthrough in English law to the way of more tolerant and democratic principles of life and a more compassionate coexistence. But to live in this relative freedom and sustain it was only possible with another written code: the Bible, which had already been multiplied in thousands by handwriting since the fourth century, until the first printed versions in English appeared in the sixteenth century.

As my project in England was drawing to a close, the most burning question was what to do. Go back or defect? Defect, but how? The going-back option had cried out loud as soon as I pondered it. What? Are you the most stupid person, not able to make a simple serious step forward in your life? But I knew I was going to do just that. I said to myself I was finally acknowledged; I was supported and let go, so I had to return with the knowledge. I was convinced that I did well, that I carried valuable experience, and this could be the start of something really good for my country. I was naively dreaming starting new projects with cooperation with UK academic labs and companies.

But when I tried to make a plan of exactly how I would do it, I could not figure it out. I already had a group of people, yet I was not really in charge. There was no market, either. Anything we could do as a team would have to be endorsed by our administration and include central planning up the ladder. I had no sponsor in the high ranks and did not believe I could woo one with my impractical nonconformist acumen.

I had been sending my CV around the UK, looking for jobs, for quite some time, but none of the applications led to an interview. The employers were apparently not comfortable with my official status of an academic visitor. It could potentially damage the relationships between both countries. Frustrated, stressed, and depressed, I felt unwell. It was at that time when BBC news programmes announced that the regime in Bulgaria had fallen. Soon after that, I was on my way back, after picking up a copy of the Magna Carta from the souvenir shop.

5

A Time to Tear

A time to tear and a time to mend. (Ecclesiastes 3:7)

5.1 Seismic Waves

Back home, the report on my work abroad was met with cold response by the board. The whole attitude was to have secrets on the back of their minds and use the cooperation with the West just to gain know-how and technology. The country was still in cooperation with totalitarian regimes like North Korea and Iraq under Saddam Hussein. This was happening despite all proclamations of Gorbachev to dismantle the evils of Communism. How do you dismantle it without having the right partners and customers? Finding the right customers required real political reorientation, without hypocrisy. I wanted to decline working on these projects and go back to Manchester. But that would jeopardise the projects still going on there with other people. I was forced to resign from my post.

At the same time, senior managers associated with the old regime were trying to get rid of people who did not show allegiance or the necessary level of commitment to them, so they could keep their positions. No one cared about the skills, knowledge, and experience of so many educated people being laid off. The tragedy of the nation was that these skills were indeed no longer useful in the crumbling centrally planned economy, which was unable to restructure and function anymore. High-ranking officials quickly changed from communists to 'socialists' and democrats, embracing Gorbachev's perestroika slogan. However, managing the change through restructuring and providing proper social security for the people being made redundant was a low priority. Managers of state companies and institutions were busy privatising businesses or surviving in their positions in the cloud of turmoil. Now in charge of the Soviets, Gorbachev was planning to change an evil empire through a Prague Spring vision from the 1960s: Communism with a human face. It looked far too late; the East needed transformation, not fixing.

Gone were the years of exaltation when nuclear power, space exploration, and computer technology were proving that the liberated power of human reason alone was able to conquer the forces of nature and subdue evil in society. The socialist/communist state, which was once meant to guarantee jobs and satisfy all our basic needs of existence, was giving up. The Marxist prophecy that the abolition of private property will lead to an abundance of material wealth, equality, and fraternity, a society of perfect harmony, proved to be a delusion. Private enterprise was now called back, self-interest reinstalled. Long live greediness.

I knew there were just a few places in our industry sector where I could work, and they were all making people redundant. I knew I had to be flexible and prepare to change professional orientation, but where were the jobs? With the help of friends, I managed to find a foreign consulting company which was helping Americans outsource electronics manufacturing in the Soviet Union. They asked me to set up an office in Sofia.

It was a risky business. The only communication means from Bulgaria to the vast empire on the other side of the Black Sea, a country completely closed to the world until recently, were telephone and telex. Fax was just being introduced, but only a few enterprises in Russia used it yet. The only reliably connecting device in my office in Sofia was the telex, an old German electromechanical post war piece with a punch paper tape. Cute.

When the lines could make it through, I was lucky to speak to someone on the telephone, but my accent could not be disguised, foreign or Georgian at best. I was often faced with iron voices, not very helpful or even threatening for bringing foreigners to "exploit Russians and help stealing their resources." The most one could achieve was to arrange unreliable meetings, and that was all. The rest had to be done after travelling on thousands of kilometres into the unknown. What made life easier was the fact that Russian technology was crumbling, and they badly needed advanced seismic exploration equipment. The Americans were offering a joint venture for producing cutting-edge telemetry electronics with solar panels. But we had to convert to Russian electronics.

At this time, Boris Yeltsin was in opposition to Gorbachev, and economic policies were unstable and changed every day. After a scary period of unemployment, the first in my life, having a job looked too good to believe. My experience was all in digital computer circuitry, and the job also required some knowledge in advanced analogue electronics. Fortunately, all I was asked at the beginning was to use the office I assembled in Sofia for a base to organise meetings and interpret for them in Russian. Their existing Russian customers helped with contacts at other sites, which in their opinion were suitable for possible implementation of the system.

On one of the places the young lads were smiling at me, winking, and whispering that they had already done the job. They found replacements for almost all the components on the manufacturing list, using locally made ones. I said to myself, "Ah, okay, reverse engineering. We are good at that, aren't we?" and smiled back at them. They looked trustworthy and so there was nothing technical to do there. I could not do a better technical job anyway after years of work as line manager and administrator in digital technology. I just had to make sure the dialogue flowed and both sides understood each other in detail, making checkpoints here and there.

With all my life experience, I realised this technical project was not going to happen because the Russians would not need technical assistance or even documentation. They already had the blueprint by reverse engineering the hardware they bought from the United States. They would only be interested in selling their system in America for hard currency. Nevertheless, my American bosses were keen on using any possible chance to continue the relationship and to explore even more opportunities in the vast empire, so I shut up.

A delegation of Russians was sent to visit Houston and see how the product was manufactured and used in the field. In the swamps of Texas and Louisiana and in the Gulf of Mexico, we had great fun going on airboats and buggies among crocodiles and exotic wildlife, laying down thousands of microphones and explosives for seismic explorations. Echo signals from the detonations from each individual microphone got amplified and transmitted to a central system on a ship nearby. Signals from all channels from one explosion had to be pre-processed in real time by a powerful field computer in parallel before they got recorded on tape for further processing in the computing centre in Houston.

In the R&D department, I was shown the diagrams of the multichannel electronics. It was based on an American microprocessor with far superior characteristics, compared to the transputer we used in Manchester. This was a familiar technical area. My heart started to throb. How could I get a job here? When I was invited to dinner by the R&D boss I was very excited, but not sure. I knew he would not extend a job offer if he was not sure I would accept it. I did not believe I would be head hunted. It could indeed be just a show of gratitude for accompanying and taking a good care for him in Russia. During the meal, I only needed to say, "Can I get a job here?" There was a good chance that it would have happened. But I did not. Why? What was it that inhibited me to such an extent? Looking back on it today, it's easy to see that all unrealised dreams were due to disbelief, pride and lack of confidence because of not seeing God's hand in creating the opportunity; a hand that was able to divide the waters of the sea and make a path for the Israelites to go free. (Exodus 14:21-22) "Okay, they would give me a job, but what kind of? Would I be able to do it? What if they say no?" At the end of the meal, he gave me a Bible: the first Bible I'd ever owned.

As the visit was drawing to a close, I learned I was to be given a treat: a day to spend in Houston on my own. This didn't sound very good to me. I sensed these were my last days on the job. But I decided not to despair and make the most of what was left ahead. I asked my companion, a young lad from the company, to take me to the Johnson Space Center. There I spent the day among the rockets and spacecraft and the history of NASA. Among the most spectacular were the Apollo mission exhibits and Saturn V, the rocket that took man to the moon. It was not just a dummy but almost a complete version, including the Service and Command modules, all assembled with surplus from the Apollo missions. Laying majestically on the ground, it looked like a retired gentle giant which was once filled with power and glory, the glory of the thousands of people involved, some of whom sacrificed their lives in the effort to fulfil humankind's dream to reach the moon. I looked on the enormous, over a hundred million horsepower, jet engines on the bottom, which failed at the beginning of the space exploration programme but eventually gave that historic push to Apollo 11, allowing the spacecraft to escape the gravitational grip of the Earth on a successful journey to the surface of the moon.

Back in Sofia, as expected, I was made redundant. A sense of defeat perched heavily on my shoulders, making me bitter and angry. I opened the Bible I was given and read the first page: "In the beginning God created the heavens and the earth. Now the earth was formless and empty, darkness was over the surface of the deep, and the Spirit of God was hovering over the waters. And God said, 'Let there be light,' and there was light."

I was immediately struck by the thought that these were the verses read by the Apollo 8 crew on its way to the moon: the first manned spacecraft that reached to the moon and returned, without landing on it. I recalled the words of Kennedy's speech: "As we sail we ask for God's blessing on the most dangerous and hazardous travel man ever made."

In Blenheim Palace, England, I recently read from Winston Churchill: "Courage is the first of human qualities because it is the quality that guarantees all the others".

5.2 The Fall of a System

Do not say, "Why were the old days better than these?"
For it is not wise to ask such questions. (Ecclesiastes 7:10)

The centre of Sofia sits on the remains of an ancient settlement. The streets today apparently follow the plan of an ancient Roman city, with the road coming from Macedonia on the west forking in two: one going southeast in Thrace towards Plovdiv and Constantinople; the other one heading northeast across the Old Mountain, into Moesia towards Ruse and Varna in northern Bulgaria. In the early 1950s, the space behind the fork was chosen for a monumental building, Партиен Дом (the Communist Party Convention Centre).

In 1990, the country was in turmoil. The Convention Centre, now situated between the State Council (formerly Todor Jivkov's office, which was being prepared for the new office of the president, according to a new Bulgarian constitution) and the Ministerial Council, was set on fire by protesters. Its mast used to be crowned with a five-point red ruby star, regarded as a symbol of Soviet Kremlin. Someone also tried to burn himself alive in front of the building. The star was quickly taken down. The next day, people were hired to chisel flat all the ornaments with the symbol of hammer and sickle from the frieze of the State Council in preparation to accommodate the new president. This was not an easy job, as they were apparently carved in hard granite. It was the hearts of all the nation, cast in stone, that needed to turn soft, but this was just a little Bulgarian reformation, later called 'Velvet Revolution;. Soon after that, Dimitrov's mausoleum was dismantled, and his remains were removed and buried in a cemetery. All these changes brought some glimmer of hope, but they did not make people feel better, as there was a rough time ahead for sure.

Despite the hype of political changes and the good intentions coming from the high ranks in Russia, people like me were actually faced with resolving an immediate practical problem: making a living. In Bulgaria, with no job market and virtually no social security system in place, I felt like a gypsy. We used to look with contempt at gypsies, but with their infrastructure, which worked well even in the most vicious totalitarian age, they looked more prepared for the coming time than the white-collar class of engineers. We seemed to have resorted to complaints and grumbling like recently orphaned children. Grumbling was a typical reaction from the recent past, when the only thing one could do, if trying to change even a little of the world around, was to burn out without even a trace. But now, it all changed; we could hardly believe it, but we were set free. Hungry but free.

We were brought up with an iron rod in a social system which believed that free trade was wrong. In our generation's .culture, trade was reduced to the transport of goods that were sold at a fixed price. In the early days of the Communist rule, trade was even considered immoral, and making a profit was equal to profiteering or cheating. There was no encouragement of entrepreneurship; private enterprise was illegal and prosecuted. Networking with people for business or any material gain in the public space was despised and denigrated to the level of nepotism.

However, this was a hypocrisy. People in higher ranks promoting this morality did not practice what they preached; they were, in fact, part of an invisible, informal network of mafias, built on secrecy and nepotism. Publically, the state was supposed to care for our personal material needs: job, house, food, clothes. To be without a job meant you were either a criminal or severely handicapped. Salaries were very flat and promoted that attitude. Factory workers, engineers, and governors were supposed to be equal and prosperous, led by the party and the state. But there were privileges for people on the top ranks and severe housing problems for young people. Just like in Orwell's *Animal Farm*, we were "equal, but some were more equal than other"

It was a time of social and political unrest. People were either made redundant or not paid for months. Hundreds were made redundant every day, mostly mature engineers, economists, and white-collar staff with over twenty years of career behind, like me. Some people had incredible skills and knowledge, yet they were useless for the country now, as they had to learn to become entrepreneurs. But enterprises for what? There was no guidance or support from the government for that. The computer industry was disintegrating, without much hope to ever be restored. People were leaving the country with any possible means. Emigration reached a peak not seen for centuries.

For some time, I tried to carry on with my own consultancy business. I bought a fax machine and started advertising my skills in outsourcing IT, consulting, interpreting, building computer network systems, and so on. This was quite naive. because foreign entrepreneurs were not interested in investing in a country with a collapsing infrastructure and unstable political system. Internally, a great mafia-type privatisation had just begun, but I was not part of any gang.

I joined the so-called National Trade Union, campaigning for the growing number of people who were laid off for political reasons. On one occasion, a medium rank officer, a relative of mine, had been dismissed from the army on political grounds. I went up to the attorney to resubmit his papers for appeal, which had been 'lost'. The general reassured me that "he will be restored." I never had an inclination to be involved in politics or public affairs. Although the current situation was portrayed as a democratic process, it was in fact a process of mafia wars, conspiracies, and intimidations. There were shootings on the street.

North of Bulgaria, the fall of the regime in Romania was violent and scary, and the top leader, Nicolae Ceausescu, was executed. Earlier in Bulgaria, the top leader had been deposed with a coup, followed by the Velvet Revolution, but a year later, the political and economic systems were still in chaos, although politicians were busy with crafting a new constitution. They wanted to go down in history. People constantly marched in the street for one political cause or another.

There was a petition to restore the monarchy. Tsar Simeon II, who was in exile in Spain, was well and fit. His sister, Princess Maria, who lived in America, visited the country for the first time since World War II. There was lots of excitement. However, the majority of people involved in politics in Bulgaria were not in favour of the monarchy. If it were to happen, it would be a very long process.

5.3 And Marriage Follows

Husbands, love your wives. (Ephesians 5:25)

I lost many friends at that time; bitterly disappointed, I realised they were no more than just rival co-workers. But what a tragedy it was to see that the relation with my best friend in life, my wife, was fading away.

She was a very independent girl but easily followed authority. However, my authority in the marriage had never been truly acknowledged. She lost confidence in me as a man who could provide what she wanted in life, especially financially. We used to love doing things together, but they were no longer there. Going to the fashion shops after work did not interest me. I only went to the shops when I needed something and was always irritated as I could not find what I needed. I disliked smelly, noisy bistros and coffee shops. Good concerts, plays, and films were rare, often showing even more bored people than we were. There was nothing interesting to discuss, except our dismal present and little hope for the future, filled with emptiness and meaningless.

I realised she needed a hug, some empathy for the way we felt, at least from time to time. It might have dried up in seeking a reciprocal response. When love becomes reciprocal, it is no longer love. It starts eroding in lust and quick bodily satisfaction. One day, I noticed with horror how much the intimacy of our relationship had eroded over years of neglect.

We were colleagues by profession, but computers had never been a passion for her, so we did not share much in that. She was more interested in people than in machines, as most women do. They find their identity through attachment, rather than in asserting their self, but she was independent as well, however never felt confident in anything she was doing alone. She needed constant encouragement, which I failed to provide. Later in my life, I realised I was wrong to give my work higher priority than my family. It led to wasting even more time later for fixing things that were already unfixable. A short burst of activity in supporting orphanages with abandoned children, kept her focused for some time, but then it stopped. I noticed how much our attitude towards fidelity in marriage changed. We started to talk about an open marriage, but it pained me the moment I allowed it in my mind as a possibility. Perhaps I was not modern enough. I thought I had to do something about it, but I did not know what.

I was a man of strong opinion but thoughtless action in family matters. There can be many sources of friction in a marriage. We did not have many in the beginning, but later on, they started to pile up. My strategy in family conflicts then was to withdraw, to hide away from them by finding peace in my work. Another bad side to my character was that I expected her to read my mind; I did not say what I needed in time of pressure. Pressure appeared to be a permanent feature of my life anyway. While my sister needed support during her divorce, I tried to visit her more often, but my wife was not happy that I had more time for my relatives than for her. It was true I did not spend enough time with her to keep the romance going. But I did not know how an open marriage was supposed to work. Perhaps I was too much of an individualist? Perhaps I had the wrong attitude, thinking I owned her, like a possession.

Perhaps it was better for me not to marry. The highest call for a man, according to the Bible, actually is *not* to marry (1 Corinthians 7:1). But my nature was not fit for celibacy. I am not in favour of it now, either. Its sanctity is very difficult to uphold.

When my sister died, I turned my anger towards my closest friend: my wife. I blamed her for being selfish and not giving me enough support. But I did not say much vocally; it was all burning inside me in destruction, and there was no one close enough to share with or advise me. I was missing a soul mate. It was indeed right to make my family first priority and then my siblings and relatives. I could have won her support in helping my sister earlier and my ailing mother later, had I set the priorities in my life right and been more positive about it. These things needed time and discussion, but I was not the sort of person to spend time in 'useless talk', sitting on the opposite sides of the table and trying to affirm our own positions.

Crucially, I did not believe our relationship could be repaired. Things had gone too far to believe that sitting on one side of the table and finding a way to defend our common values could help. But divorce would be too high a price to pay, for both of us. I had seen it in the marriages of my sister and my brother. So what could I do? She could divorce me, but she was practical. She would not win anything. I was still her last resort. But she did not want to follow me in leaving the country.

Eventually, I called my daughter aside and said I was going to leave the country again. This time, I made it plain that I would not return, even if I were to die. I wanted her to come with me, but she had a boyfriend and said that they were going to marry soon. They had different plans for their future. There was nothing more to do than give her my blessings and take care of myself.

5.4 A Time to Give Up

A time to search and a time to give up. (Ecclesiastes 3:6)

During all these years, I believe an unknown force kept me from stagnation, as I was on the move all the time. And now again, as if someone was saying to me, "Come out," I said, "But where do I go? What do I do? What do I live on? What do I live for?" Life stopped having meaning and stopped being possible. I used to think that loyalty to the country, if nothing else, was a virtue. I did love our country: the mountains, the sea, nature, parts of its culture. But the people no longer needed me. In fact, I was like a burden to everyone, even to my family, useless indeed. I realised I was stupid not to take the opportunities to flee abroad which emerged in the past. Now they were gone. Would another one ever come?

My plight in those days was not the only one; many were in my shoes. We liked our profession and would like to see a continuation of it: jobs and prosperity in a country which had some vision for information technology. This vision was quickly disappearing. As it happened, we used to be like privileged children with expensive toys. The country needed computers, and we made them. But in the end, the rules of the game changed, and they took our toys away. We were told that we had grown up. We were given freedom and let go in the wilderness, made redundant. We had to learn to fly like birds which had grown up in a cage. I blamed myself over and over again that I did not manage to leave the country earlier.

Many were like me, people from my generation who were supposed to live the most fruitful days of their life in a system that promised equality, brotherhood, friendship, if not love, prosperity, and opportunity for all. Yet now, it looked like many were in a rush to become rich, stampeding others. The spirit of the time could be best understood by a pop song, the lyrics of which came from the poet Damian Damianov. Written with a degree of prophecy in the last years of the totalitarian decline and decadency, it heralded the coming total crash:

Къде изчезна добротата	Where has the goodness vanished?
Измислица ли беше тя	Was it a fiction or a tale
Или пък приказка, която	the world has never known?
Не съществува на света.	It was yesterday somewhere here,
Край мене тя до вчера беше	a smile, a look, a warming touch of hand.
Усмивка, поглед, топла длан.	By the dread of this day has it disappeared
Стопи ли я кошмарът днешен	in a world engulfed by evil? My life.

В света от злото завладян.
Животе мой …
©Дамян Дамянов,

The song, covered by the national pop icon Lilli Ivanova, was heard on the radio over and over again and was some sort of consolation. It showed there were other people feeling like me.

My independent consultancy did not win a single customer. My family lived on the proceeds from selling our car. In the past, I was reluctant to leave the country because my family didn't want to. Now, it was obvious that our family was broken; my authority as husband and father was nil, in fact never acknowledged. I once again suggested that we should all leave together and try to restart our life elsewhere. News from emigrants who successfully found jobs in Western countries were heard more and more. It all sounded adventurous, but I was sure that was the way to go. Perhaps I was not very convincing, and they did not want to follow. My wife still had her job. She also had her father's family to rely on. I realised my failure as a head of family, and that was very painful. She had always relied on her parents more than on me.

For the first time, I felt not only disillusioned and useless but also scared. There was nothing to hold on to. I was ashamed to go to my father, who still lived in our old family home. The last time I visited him, he was tried to find me a job in the area, which made my soul cry. For the first time, I felt a strong affection for him. But I could not see my future life developing there. My brother was working abroad lecturing engineering in the Third World countries and I lost contact with him. I heard it was hard for him but I could not help. Old friendships based on work relations dissolved since I became a black sheep. They were looking for new alliances, building new networks, and making friendships according to their fortune. I knew I was worth for something much more important than all these petty hassles here, but I was a shattered, lonely soul. After years of distress and hardship, I fell ill with constant headaches and a lack of energy.

Life lost its meaning. I looked back to the years that had passed and realised that perhaps half of my life had gone. It was as if I heard a voice asking me, "What have you achieved? What are you trying to do? What is the meaning of all this?" I began to realise that I had always been hurrying from one activity to another, chasing my tail like a dog and kidding myself that real life would begin just a little while later.

I had turned forty, so you could call this a middle-age crisis. However, despite my depression, I had a tremendous urge for survival. It was an age when I believed I deserved to enjoy the fruits of my life. I firmly believed that I had done well professionally. I just had to carry on fighting. I felt a strong sense of injustice, but there was no one to blame. These days, while hundreds of people queued for bread, I killed time by making yet another attempt to read the Bible by randomly browsing through it.

I came across Matthew 4:4: "Man shall not live on bread alone, but on every word that comes from the mouth of God." This verse immediately struck the whole of my inner being and made me shudder. I suddenly felt the presence of the author, inviting me to talk, but I did not know how. I suppose my thoughts silently said something like this: "God, people are queuing for bread outside. If you do exist out there, you know what is on my heart because you are God. Your world here has broken apart and fallen. Deep down, I know these failures do not mean your failure, but it is hard not to feel that way. Help me understand and see your purpose, then I may surrender to it."

After I blamed God for all of it, I felt a bit better.

5.5 Exodus

> Better one handful with tranquillity than two handfuls
> with toil and chasing the wind. (Ecclesiastes 4:6)

One of the things my mother did was to never rush to lift up a child who stumbled and fell on the ground. She was often entrusted with looking after several grandchildren, and I always loved to watch her reaction when something like that happened. She would calmly approach the child without rush and start talking softly, trying to persuade them that it was not a tragedy, that it could happen to anybody, and encouraging them to get up on their own strength. If the kid was already crying and distressed, it was usually because it had seen panic in the face of the others, not because it felt pain. But if my mother managed to stay calm, the kid never cried, despite its pain. Of course, in serious distress, my mother would hug them and kiss them and try to comfort them. Perhaps this was one reason that her three children had that Spartan attitude on failure: get up, dust yourself off, and try again.

In fact, my current situation was one that I knew would not be helped by crying. I had to analyse it objectively without emotion, make a decision, and move on. I decided to try leave the country, alone.

I did not need an exit visa anymore; at least something good had come from the changes. But I no longer had an entry visa for the UK, so I applied for one. This looked like a hopeless exercise, but eventually, after staying on a queue all day, I managed to submit an application to go to a scientific conference. All the staff there were local people, employed by some foreign office's mutual agreement, and most of them were very rude and unhelpful. I could understand to some extent their difficult job; thousands of people were on siege of the embassy, trying to get a visa. I thought they were bribed and usually put through applications out of order, if there was any order at all. No one expected to receive a response by post, so everyone had to check for their result in person, queuing and waiting and waiting.

Then, the coup against Gorbachev in the Soviet Union came out of the blue. Rumours about restoration of the old regime spread. There were unfair trials for alleged corruption going on, with different sides prevailing according to political or mafia-like battles behind the scenes. I felt unsecure having done that job for the Americans in Russia, where many people were hostile to doing business with the 'imperialists'; to them, people like me were only spies. There were often killings on the streets in Sofia.

I decided to go to the embassy again and ask to see the British ambassador personally, something I knew the staff were not allowed to refuse. When I sat in front of him, I must have looked quite upset. He asked me why I wanted to travel to the UK. I looked straight into his eyes, paused, and then said, "For a conference." He smiled and said, "No problem. Just wait in the hall to receive your passport."

That was it. When I got it, I realised I didn't even say thank you. Now I did not know who to thank. But it was not a time for emotions. I had to pack and run away, alone. I was somehow sure it would work this time, without any snags.

We grew up in a culture that praised rational thinking and a Stoic way of living, where only the fittest survived. In this culture, those who achieved and produced, who kept busy, were naturally more valued than others. In the Greek culture, the majority dictated the value system through the new political invention of democracy, as opposed to the dictates of a ruler. This was a great achievement in the ancient world, but the decisions of the majority were not ideal. It emphasised the material and overlooked the spiritual needs of humankind. This gradually led to a boorish, vulgar society, especially in the East, where little distinction was made between idleness and stillness, and where the spiritual life later degraded into idolatry, cults, and the occult.

So I was bracing my Eastern European self again for survival, to make my living in a foreign country. I had no faith in God then but some hope still left inside to keep me going. It was my last chance in the fight for survival. A friend of mine kindly offered me hospitality for a short time while I looked for a job. I had to be quick, so I employed a different strategy. I hid my PhD in my 'back pocket' and went for a job advertised in the newspaper. Those jobs did not need a permanent work permit. They were the kind of temporary jobs that would not make the business suffer if someone were to be unexpectedly deported.

There were many marketing businesses at the time, looking for people fluent in Russian. A magazine publisher hired me to sell advertising space to Russian companies seeking to expand in London. It was a talking job, measured and paid by the time you spend on the telephone trying to sell ads. I did not believe I could talk so much in my life. They were impressed by the time I was able to spend in conversation and by the huge number of contacts I had in Russia. This was my capital from my previous job with the Americans. However, months passed without being able to sell a single advert. They were only paying a basis, and I considered leaving, with the feeling that selling was not a job for me. I had to learn first how to sell myself with the gifts and skills I already had, but at least I had this job for now to keep me going.

Lonely and depressed, I would drop in on Sundays to churches in central London. I knew nothing about the Anglican doctrines or rituals, and it was fun to see the clerics sweetly pointing me to the Greek Orthodox church nearby. No one tried to explain what the gathering was all about. Eventually, I ended up in a small church in central London. Here, young lads with smiling and beaming faces were advertising an evening course on Christianity called Alpha. I joined, and new friends I met helped me with some leads for finding a better job. Eventually, I found a company designing devices for biomedical research in proteomics, the science of how different proteins behave. This was effectively a technician job to work on their product- a robot for dispensing protein for research. I was not allowed to do any research or design or development, just production work. This humiliated and angered me as a proud academic hiding his PhD. But I knew I had to swallow it and carry on if I were to survive.

I had a job to keep me going, so what more did I need? I was still not well, under stress, and worried about the past and the future. I knew no one was going to give me a permanent job until I had a permanent work permit, and vice versa; it was a vicious circle with no solution at the time. In the church newspaper, I saw an advert for an affordable flat just down the road from the church. A Christian missionary living abroad was looking for tenants. They needed recommendations, of course, and I had luck with that. I might have looked trustful with my greying hair.

5.6 Believing without Seeing

Blessed are those who have not seen and
yet have believed. (John 20:29)

Bread and roof provided, I felt some sort of relief and security. The job was not demanding, and this let my mind free to engage with what I was hungry for lately. Even though I only had enough money to just survive, I was in London and decided to make the most out of it. Many of the museums and galleries were free entry, and I devoured books from the library about British history and culture. I bought the *1662 Book of Common Prayer* in a bookshop; the chap at the counter smiled when he recognised my Eastern European foreign accent and shabby jacket. Nevertheless, I looked inside it with zeal, trying to know more about the roots of this culture: what it was all about and what made it tick. At last, I had the time and embarked on reading the Bible diligently, like a study book, from front to end, trying to grasp the consistency of the message in there, just like I would have done with any science research project.

Then I read *Mere Christianity* by C. S. Lewis and started understanding the logic of the Christian ethics and faith, literally like a scholar with a serious dose of reason. This book shifted my world view and helped me begin to understand the culture in the country. It exerted a strong influence on my value system, but that was still just another philosophy. "Okay, then," I said to myself. "I understand." And that was it.

I kept going to Alpha. It was a very small gathering at the beginning, which took place once a week. Each session began with a simple meal, and then we had a talk on specific subject of the Christian faith. A discussion in small groups followed where we could ask questions. Someway along the course, we first sang a song. The lyrics were based on the Psalms from the Bible, but in a modern, pop music arrangement. For the first time after many years, I sang. The only other time I sang as an adult was in the army. As children, we sometimes sang patriotic songs at school. These were modern worship songs from the Vineyard Church in America, and there were some written locally as well.

It was lovely to chat with people who came to the course; they were genuinely interested in each other's life and openly shared a lot from theirs. I eagerly looked forward to the next meeting and always asked myself what made these people running the seminar shine with a radiating smile. I remained suspicious for some time. After all, I was a scientist and an intellectual, I thought proudly. I did not trust emotions shown openly, considering them an indicator of a mental problem. But there was no compulsion or pressure.

For the first time in my life, I saw people showing empathy and compassion to wounded souls like me, strangers to them. Why were they doing it? The staff were volunteers; no one was paying them to do a job, and they expected nothing in return. There was nothing pretentious, pompous, or patronising in these people, nothing to suggest they knew it all. They looked so natural with faces filled with love and a genuine need to care. I realised I never had that in my life experience, except for the early years of my childhood, when plenty of love was extended from Granny and my mother. The rest was putting a mask on my face to hide my true self and making my way through with elbows and fists in a hostile world. I wanted to have more of this here, relax and be nice to others too.

We were well through the course program when I started to feel the urgency to decide. No one was pressing me with anything to do or say. I could leave anytime, without giving any reason. I could also stay till the end and say goodbye, without an explanation. Some actually did. But it was all coming from within me. Did I believe it or not? Was it true? If it was not, then I did not need it. I was fed up with brainwashing all my life, with all sorts of philosophies, political doctrines, manipulation, and hypocrisies. "I have to check it is true and genuine," I kept saying to myself. Some questions were answered, but some were not; some I did not ask but still needed to reconcile myself with them.

I agreed long ago on the need for a common moral standard in society. But where should the moral standard come from? According to C. S. Lewis in *Mere Christianity*, everyone had that in themselves, more or less from nature, but although having similar standards, people still had big differences in behaviour. Extrapolating from there, everyone agreed that no one should do to others what they would not like being done to them by others. However, people always try twisting this principle to work for them, even if it could be against the interest of others.

People's attitudes were not the same on all aspects of life. And then there were ethics of all sorts, including Nietzsche and Hitler. All preached whatever was a predominant force in their lives. World views and religions were not compatible with each other. Few of them had a moral teaching, anyway. So where was the truth?

It did make sense to me that all should agree to accept the moral standard of the Bible, a book that has been the standard for human relations for thousands of years, so long that it could be considered unbiased and genuinely independent. If it survived the time, it might be true.

But then, it was not scientific at all; some of the texts were very naive scientifically. It took me some time to understand. A sort of scientific truth was there, but compressed and mystified. Very little scientific knowledge was there, if at all. If that was the Word of God, he certainly did not intend to provide scientific knowledge in there. Modern science was not given to those who wrote the texts, anyway. Although it was sensible to consider the book superior in all aspects of human life, I came to the conclusion that scientific explanation about the laws of nature and how nature works was not the focus of it. It was all about human behaviour and relationships and human purpose in life, something invariant of time, culture, and technological knowledge. If other knowledge and facts were there, including primitive ancient science, it was only to facilitate that central message about relationships. Once I adopted that attitude, I felt more at home with the Bible.

I had to interpret the texts with the help of the Alpha team. I used my reasoning to find out what it meant to the people in the context in which they wrote and then extract from them the relevance it made to life today. I also had to distil and differentiate history and facts from poetry. There is a lot of poetry in the scripture, alongside other texts, but poetry often does not speak the truth word for word. Rather, it expresses it metaphorically, allegorically. When the psalmist writes, "Let the rivers clap their hands, let the mountains sing together for joy" (Psalm 98:8), we do not believe the rivers have hands. Rather we stand before the Lord and feel how the whole Creation resonates with our joy.

That aspect sorted, I decided I could believe the Bible was the Word of God, even though it needed to be interpreted. But crucially, did God and the supernatural really exist? Once I accept that God exists, I had no problem believing in the supernatural, because if God created nature with its laws, he certainly would be at liberty to intervene at any point in time to override these laws. I realised it was not possible to prove or disprove the existence of God with mathematical logic. But surely there should be some evidence, at least. How much evidence should there be? I accepted that God would not want us to believe by coercion. He created people who had free will. He would never force himself into our lives. Several texts in the Bible suggested that.

Keeping it all rational, I could see God did provide evidence in the spiritual realm of morality, ethics, and divinity, as well as in the material realm of physics, science, and history. This evidence was enough to put our trust in him. Some were amazed by how finely tuned the universe is. Yes, indeed I said, but it is close to mind that otherwise, we would not have been here in existence. Then I suddenly realised that the most amazing thing about it was how vulnerable we actually were here on the planet precisely because of the fine-tuning. It suggested that someone, a mind, a person, indeed, must be sustaining it every moment.

For me as a computer scientist, the mere fact that the laws of physics are rational and can be expressed in beautiful mathematical equations became a clue for an intelligent creator. The crucial moment of believing was when I saw that the genetic code, which controlled my development from a single cell when I was conceived, was digital and beautifully designed, just like the computer programs I was writing. This code is involved in controlling essential functions of my body. Who wrote that code?

Some would say mother nature, but where did nature come from? Where did all that come from? What are we? Where are we? It was indeed far more reasonable to believe that nature was created by someone uncreated than to think that the 'nothing' created itself. I found it difficult to see it as if it has always been there. I mean, even with reasoning, we could hardly grasp the concept of infinity in mathematics, or the "finite but closed" universe. Even though the question is beyond reasoning, I see that to ask where the universe came from is not the same as asking where God came from because he is God. In other words greater than the universe. I was content that nothing contradicted my reasoning as a scientist in order to make a leap of faith in what I was investigating.

Eventually, it dawned on me that the texts of the Scripture had an amazing power to explain the way people related to one another, fought each other, suffered, or prospered, just as the science of physics explained how matter behaved. As C. S. Lewis wrote, "I believe in Christianity as I believe that the sun has risen: not only because I see it, but because by it I see everything else."

Yet a significant amount of scepticism still remained in me. I shared it with my friends in our discussion group, many of whom were already believers. They said not to worry because the Holy Spirit would sort it out. He, they said, is the only one that converts; neither your reasoning nor anybody else is able to.

"The Holy Spirit?" I said. "I just managed to grasp who Jesus was, and now this. Or God, am I going to miss you?"

I heard a smiling voice whisper in my ear, "Good! You are already speaking to Me."

5.7 Amazing Grace

> And everyone who calls on the name of
> the Lord will be saved. (Joel 2:32)

The final snag to faith was to believe that God is personally interested in me.

I cannot remember when and how we started praying, but it became a routine in the middle of the course. However, when I was alone at home, I found it difficult and odd. Had I turned mad, speaking to the walls? Then my brain started to heat up again. Immaculate conception? Mmm, okay, supernatural. But did the person Jesus Christ really exist historically? Yes, no problem. Was he the Son of God? That was more difficult. The things he said do support that claim. C. S. Lewis's rationale with the list of options made sense: 1. Lunatic/Mad? 2. Con? 3. God? You have to make your choice.

Oh, my choice? Not the Holy Spirit's choice? Sounds good.

But it was still just an intellectual exercise, until one weekend, we went down to Ashburnham, an old English place for spiritual retreat and reflection. We were going to learn about and call upon the Holy Spirit.

A lot of people who fled from the war in Yugoslavia turned up in the evening worship and prayer. Many of them were visibly shaken by their recent experience. Some lost their loved ones. Images from TV programmes showing atrocities in the Balkans came into my mind, mixed with my memories. I imagined the battle on the bend of River Cherna in Macedonia, where my grandfather was killed almost a century ago in another Balkan war. The misery of the Balkan people, always in conflicts, broke my heart. Then more and more pictures came, like from a movie: my sister's body in the mortuary, my brother with a pack of punched cards asking me for help with his computer program, while I was pushing Mum in a wheelchair for a check-up in the hospital. And then there was blood everywhere in a mist or smoke, as if coming from some of my Granny's animals being slain before Christmas. I did not know. I could not bear those memories anymore. I wanted to be forgiven and let them go, but those who could forgive me were already gone.

I had an enormous desire to drop this burden and forgive others too, but I could not forgive the world turning its back on me. I felt tons of rejection, rejection from work, country, and home.

We sang a song:

> Father God, I wonder how I managed to exist
> without the knowledge of your parenthood
> and Your loving care.
> Now I am Your child, I am adopted in Your
> family,
> and I can never be alone.
> 'Cause Father God, You're there beside me.
> I will sing your praises.

Tears began pouring down my face. I had not cried since the funerals of my sister and mother long, long ago. I wept and wept and wept. My tears turned into crying, and then friends put their hands on my shoulders and started praying in tongues I could not understand. Then I heard someone translating, "You are forgiven. You are going to have a new beginning."

At some point, I realised the evening session was about to close. I noticed I was not the only one weeping. My old self was dying. That evening, I surrendered. I gave my life to Christ. We only have one life in the flesh, but our spirit with God's spirit can morph into a beautiful butterfly and take us to new heights, our new life in spirit going forever.

In the days that followed, the Lord took me on a journey through all my past and explained so vividly what actually happened in my life. He knew in advance what I was going to do, according to my destiny, but the experience had been a preparation for what was coming later. This journey back in time was a lesson in discerning his perfect will for me in the future. I was so thankful that he made even my past life meaningful. He had always been there for me, even before I knew him. Before I honoured him, he was there loving me and taking care of me. He did not fight my battles, but carried me right through them. He did not make them easy so that I could take delight in my achievements. I often made a mess out of my life by trying to do things my way. This was against my interest and well-being, and it did not help anybody else either. I ran on my own strength, ignoring so many good opportunities, often proudly chasing false images. I threw out what God had given so graciously, things that were nurtured with so much care and effort.

But apart from being so foolishly stubborn, I did keep to certain ethics in life. Now that I knew he was the master of my life, I wanted to thank him that he made me this way by nature, striving to be good. Now, it all had meaning. What would have been the ultimate meaning in life if the Lord had not been? For what other reason was I to be ethical when trying to fight to succeed in life? People died, good or bad, but the reason our natural goodness gets blocked is because we doubt and stop believing good is stronger than evil. As a result, we surrender every now and then to the wrong master.

In the following months, I realised the Lord was not so much interested in what I did than in who I was, my character. What we do stems from what we are. Looking back, I was not pleased with what I was: selfishly ambitious, and proud, with lots of resentment and anger accumulated over the past years, which I was now able to let go. I used to think of myself a martyr, while in fact, I was one of the privileged. Peace rested on me, and I stopped being so self-involved.

Whether we have an affluent upbringing or not, we always remember our youth with a sentiment of appreciation, with a feeling of something good that was gone. Looking back to those years, I had to acknowledge that not everything was bad. Like many others I had a good profession, with challenges and a passion for technological advancement, despite my humble upbringing in a small country which was not well known to the world. I thanked God I was part of that computer revolution on the world stage and for my family where I was loved and respected. But I was a sinner, just like the members of my family and the people I worked with, who rejected me. Inevitably I caused hurt to many too. I realised I had to drop the bitterness and aim for reconciliation. To my surprise, I found now that whatever I intended to do, I began doing with prayer, before, during, and after. My first prayer was for a new job. I still had my ambitions, but they were looking outward, to do something for others. I recalled my daughter, my wife, and my father, the three living kin I had responsibility for.

6

A Time to Mend

And a time to mend. (Ecclesiastes 3:7)

6.1 Baptism in Medicine

After two years in England, I realised that there was no going back. Letters from Bulgaria were all full of desperation and indignation about the turn of life there; the economy was shattered and broken, many lived in poverty, below the means of subsistence, and there was high unemployment, especially for the white-collar class like me. Many former colleagues had emigrated, which made me think a chance was given to everyone. My daughter had married, and I had become a grandpa. The news made me happy and sad at the same time. I had to do something about my family. However, I was still not able to support them.

My prayers were for a new job, and I became so much more focused. Computer science was not in my heart anymore. The engineering itch had come back to put in practice all that I researched and studied for years and see a tangible result. An enormous desire came to bear fruit, to see things happening in real life now. I had passed the age limit for purely academic work, anyway. When I had the passion, it was the right time, but I was not in the right place. Now that I was in the right place, it was not the right time. I had to find a quick way to make a living, not only for me but for my family as well. Academic work was not going to provide that.

I had the feeling I wasted so much time, yet life was going on, and I had to make an urgent resolution. "What am I to do with the rest of it?" I did not have the answer yet, but I did not want to postpone my living any more for later. Life was here and now. My experience as a manager under the Communist rule was not a credential in this country. And in the end, was not sure if I would like a management job or not. There was no time for experiments. I needed a secure job. My track record was not helping me. Employers were suspicious with someone holding high qualifications and at the same time doing simple jobs, though they were useful. These guys could not possibly understand the audacity of emigrating to Britain from nowhere. There were many educated people in their fifties from Eastern Europe, like me. Why would they risk employing me?

Healthcare IT professionals were in high demand in the UK at the time, as they worked in the interdisciplinary area between medicine and technology. Biology was changing fast by employing lots of informatics turning into bioengineering, and good IT skills were in demand. Also, the physics of medical image analysis in radiology and other hospital departments required high-performance data processing, where my experience could be useful. Film-based radiology was soon going to be replaced by image interpretation made on computer screens. However, images, unlike text documents, created huge volumes of digital data. Each pixel on the screen, one single tiny spot, needed tens of bits of data to encode the colour and the brightness. One X-ray picture could contain millions of pixels. So these methods were not quite feasible for off-the-shelf machinery, but recent advances in networking speeds were making this possible.

Pictures from body scans needed to be stored and transmitted in digital form. Multimedia machines were emerging with larger disk space, faster internal memory, and faster network cards. The challenge was to allow scanning devices to store and exchange digital data over the network in a standardised format, understandable by all applications.

A short study in medical physics put me on the right track. Soon after I sent my CV out, an offer came for my first medical engineering job in a small private company. They were designing new systems for storing, archiving, and distributing digital images in hospitals. A new standard, called DICOM, had just been agreed by the industry, and I was tasked with implementing it. They desperately needed someone like me.

DICOM was not just another file format for storing information. Apart from the pixel data of the medical scan from a patient, it employed a rich metadata set including the method of the data acquisition, scanning device parameters, timings, safety and demographics and much more. Above all, the way this information was transmitted and stored was essential for reliable communication and safe keeping. It needed new networking protocol, specific for patient data management and examination control. Another standard, called HL7 (Health Level 7) was in development for medical data other than X-rays.

This was the first serious commercial software engineering work I did hands-on. In the beginning, it was just a one-man project, and I was delighted. The network speed of 100 megabits per second was on the edge of making medical image management practical. Any possibility for performance boost had to be investigated. There was a new paradigm called multithreading which allowed the computer program to be split in two instruction streams, called threads, running in parallel. Multithreading could increase the speed of the program significantly if run on a powerful machine having multiple processors available on demand.

Writing a multithreading program was quite a challenge; all threads exchanged data via shared memory, and it was easy to make a mess by writing in one memory location while reading from the same location in another thread at the same time, before the relevant data was actually there. Critical sections of the program accessing common resources (memory, networking controllers, and so on) had to be protected by semaphores, signalling when someone else was already there. These semaphores were not yet available in the programming language; I had to create them from scratch with subroutines. My past experience with Dijkstra's discipline of programming paid off. The design aimed at receiving the images from the scanner in parallel with compressing them, to save storage space before they were archived. As a result, the server I designed and implemented for receiving and archiving compressed images was the fastest available on the market at the time. The next step was to compress multiple rows of one image in parallel. When I said to my boss that I would like to present my work on the Radiology Congress in Birmingham I noticed a sparkle of jealousy and worry in his eyes, but in the end it all went well. I said to myself "...nothing new under the sun" (Eccl 1:9). No matter where you go: east or west, human nature is the same since the time of old.

The company expanded, and a group in the United States, which was initially only involved in marketing, also extended its development wing. We got clinical certifications for our product in the US and the EU, and installations on a global scale were picking up.

This was my first real-life encounter with the UK working culture in engineering. I got along well with the lads when involved with the other parts of our product: the image display and image management. Most of them had graduated recently in purely programming disciplines, and the most they knew about data communication was a simple file transfer protocol. They did not know much about networking protocols and asked why the medical standard needed to be so complicated. Being very pragmatic in everything they were doing, they had an eye on making money, keeping things as simple as possible, and were very open about it, not ashamed. "We are here to make money by serving others." Mmm, this was something new for me, and I liked it.

Yet my life was still in a mess. My daughter came to Britain with her child; her marriage apparently had broken down. So we had two broken marriages, and I prayed for wisdom on how to restart our lives. What could I do? There are many instructions about marriage in the Bible; some are binding, but some are just guidance. I prayed and listened, and prayed and listened. In the prevailing thoughts that were coming, I decided not to be too dogmatic but accept the reality of separation, with the understanding that there was freedom in Christ there for us to decide. In my view, she could give her marriage a second chance, so her husband came and joined her. The enthusiasm of a new beginning worked well at first. They supported each other. But it was difficult for them in a foreign country. He was an actor, and performing and expressing himself without a full command of English was not easy. He tried directing as an independent artist and cast a rock version of *Macbeth*; with a few friends and fellow actors, they spoke a few words from the script and sang rock songs. But there were other opportunities possible; perseverance was the key. Yet after the initial excitement had gone, I realised they continued to run on their own strength and lean on their own understanding. Divisions that made them separate kept coming back. It did not work. Eventually, they got a divorce.

6.2 A Time to Dance

Everything I did, I tried to do in accordance with what I now believed, and I knew if I did not take it seriously, it would be a disaster. When I read 1 Corinthians 7:15, I thought I should start my life anew. Then I felt my daughter would need the support of her mother for her child and started praying for a reunion. Soon after that, we were all reunited, after more than five years of separation. Yet there was a bumpy time ahead. My wife and I had changed so much over the years. Our attitudes on family relationships were now even more different than before, and we had to start building trust again from scratch. Settling in a new country was not easy, either. We had to move to a rural area, where my new job was. There I began to see that cosmopolitan London was not England.

The media at the time was not very amicable to the Eastern Bloc countries, especially Russia. Bulgaria was seldom mentioned. I noticed few British knew where that mysterious country was on the map. When it did turn up in the news, it was always about something bad: corruption, killing, poverty, welfare of animals, and so on. Some people at work were xenophobic, patronising. The British apparently confused the Balkans with Greece. They heard about the culture from their childhood because Homer's *Odysseus* and *Iliad* were on the curriculum. But few had the vaguest idea where Bulgaria was. The poisonous stories of drinking wine from the skulls of the enemy and the mythical figures like Medusa might have not been seen as a myth. I realised these chaps were just trying to make a point about where I came from and to affirm their superiority. Some, however, looked depressed, without self-esteem, and I took pity of them. I prayed in my heart for all of them, a lovely bunch of lads lost in their own ways. Nevertheless, the majority were easy to get along with, friendly, and a pleasure to work with. One can come across difficult people anywhere and at any time. But I was much more prepared now to face the challenges of communication at my workplace, even without much experience in the working culture here.

Outside work, the Lord gave us lovely Christian friends, British and foreign alike. They accepted us in a very unreserved and loving way, genuinely and kindly interested in hearing about our past experience and about our attitudes, not just out of courtesy. They helped us a lot in any way: inviting us for meals, going to social events, sharing their family Christmas dinner with us. It was only after Bulgaria joined the EU in 2005 that the British got a better idea of where our country was. Yet I later realised the Balkans never had a favourable reputation among the people of our new country of residence.

After years of separation, I felt like I had married my wife again. In marriage, husbands have the ultimate responsibility for failure, and I accepted it the first time. I was able to see those parts of my personality that were difficult for others to tolerate or appreciate and learned how to be more tolerant myself without compromising too much. I realised we should not fall back in the past tracks of existence. We had gone through and shared together so much. It was useless to try to repair things we both did in the past, stupidly and selfishly. It was better to value what we had and do things right, here and now. After all, I still loved her. Over the years, I managed to live like a celibate; I did not start any new relationship because I feared it would complicate my life, just when it started to sort out and heal. Our old relationship was fractured, but we had almost forty years together behind us. In general, she had been honest with me and was still my best friend. I would not let my problems now spoil all that. I would not let them bring feelings of sadness, bitterness or jealousy and anxiety once again.

I had been baptised as a baby and had a high regard for that act, since it happened at a time of religious oppression. When I came to Christ I knew there were lots of disagreements about the terminology and the rituals of infant baptisms in the Church because it is a basic sacrament in all denominations. But there is a clear message in the Bible about baptism, which comes down to the following three: the dedication of Jesus (Luke 2:22); the baptism with water for the forgiveness of sins by John the Baptiser (Mathew 3:11); and the baptism with the Holy Spirit Jesus ordained himself (Mathew 28:19; John 3:5-7). Whatever word we use: baptism, christening, dedication or else, it is important what we mean by that word. I believe my baby baptism was a dedication to the Lord from my Granny. It did not make me a Christian at that point of time but it did make a difference in my life, though I did not know the Lord at the start of my life. When I married, we were pagans. In terms of doctrines, denominations, and religions, I now considered myself nondenominational. After receiving Jesus in my heart, I was confirmed in an Anglican church. I recognised the importance of the Reformation for restoring the supremacy of scripture and faith over human-made rules, doctrines, and rituals. That was how the Lord revealed himself to me. As I changed jobs and homes, I joined a variety of Evangelical Alliance and Anglican churches.

I did the Christian course again with my wife. It did make a huge difference to her life, but her transformation was more gradual, over a long time. We did another course on marriage. Later, we confirmed our relationship in a service where other couples were also present. We did not have a wedding ceremony in church, but I had awakened to rituals and realised the importance of the act of marriage and the words we speak, not just on occasions but in everyday life too. The words every believer speaks with conviction have power, especially in public. When both, husband and wife are believers, marriage can indeed be a holy matrimony, a beautiful, harmonious relationship between a man and a woman and their children.

We decided to take our grandchild to live with us, allowing my daughter space for her marriage to heal. Our granddaughter became like our second child, and I felt God had called me to sit again the exam for parent on which I failed the first time. He gave back graciously all that was stolen in the past, the sweetest moments I missed with my own child, her mother, when she was little.

I did not have Dad and Mum, who were believers to bring me up in a world surrounded by faith in God. I did not listen to stories from the Bible. I did not hear prayers and lullabies. But I was very blessed with my grandmother, who showed love, shared compassion, and persevered in openly going to church, even during the hardest time of political oppression. I made a firm commitment that my grandchildren would be given this opportunity in life. Hoping that for my daughter, personal faith would be won in maturity, I realised that for her child, it would be such a blessing. To fill the world of an infant with the love and hope that comes from Jesus was the greatest gift grandparents can give. We sent her to a Church of England preschool.

The kid took great interest in England's kings and queens, and so did we. Visiting castles and stately homes on weekends was our main entertainment. My wife's favourite period was the Tudors. She learned the names of all the wives of Henry VIII, their personalities, and their fates. We appreciated the architecture of every town or little quaint village, with its old town hall, church buildings, and pubs.

Almost every little village in England had at least one church from times of old, with people still worshiping every Sunday. They reminded me of Granny. They shared the same spirit as the poor Balkan villagers, who gathered to worship Christ every Sunday. They were well off compared to my compatriots, but they were not rich people, either. And yet they gave money to restore and maintain their cherished little organ. It enabled them to continue singing their beloved traditional hymns. With the same generous spirit, they also kept their purses open to support one or two missionaries in the poor countries of Africa.

The British are adventurous and they like the bliss of the equatorial sun too. Suspicious about their motives in Africa I once talked to a missionary. He said that it was only when you get there surrounded by black people, the only one white being you, that you truly make yourself humble and vulnerable. Only when you realise that you are the 'different' one among many, only then the love of God, that is in you, is revealed to them. Yes, he said, we do have lots of people in this country who need that love too, but Africa is a unique training ground.

The church was in decline, they said, but I would not believe them, having met with many people involved in the Alpha movement in London and all over the world. Decline or revival, a mere immigrant could not tell, but I could see the difference with where I came from. These fellows here loved their laws, history, and traditions and would like to preserve their continuity in the future. They also had the necessary spiritual influence on their society to do it, regardless of what majority they represented in the country. When Prince Charles and Diana became estranged, there was some sort of disenchantment with the monarchy. Outspoken republicans saw an opportunity in it, but the majority of the British people were deeply concerned and saddened. I realised that the Royal Family and their past imperial glory were not just a tourist attraction and pageantry but were strongly interwoven into the fabric of the society. It is accepted not so much because it rules over them but because of its continuity and longitudinal presence in the public space people identify with them and like them just as they accept and love a family of their own relatives with their good as well as their bad. The Royal Family is seen by Christians as a model for every other family in the country and a symbol of nationhood. When it is hurt, the whole country feels hurt.

When Diana was lost in that tragic car accident, the moods swung in all directions, dangerously threatening the stability of the country. The whole Christian community was praying against the spirit of infidelity, disunity, and resentment, hoping for love and peace. A Christian monarchy depends not so much on the prudence of the monarch as on the prayers said by its people. However, quite a few people, mostly immigrants, predicted the fall of the monarchy and sneered at how come modern Britain, a country on the forefront of democracy in the world, was still a monarchy.

The answer to that question can only be grasped through the prism of Christian ethics, which is still governing this country. A person who is not willing to kneel down or bow to any authority, even though just ceremonially, for the sake of tradition, is simply a crude pagan, who hates superiority over them but loves trampling others. Democracy in such understanding, unlike in the ancient Greek culture, is not so much about equality and a dictatorship of the majority over the minority as about grace and opportunity for all. Although the aristocracy is disappearing, the culture that it represented remains. Millions of Britons who are not hereditary aristocrats enjoy their lives, wherever they turn to be in the social strata, without looking into other people's cups too much. People respect the lifestyles and views of others and try to be ladies and gentlemen, a status now built not so much on inheritance or material possessions but on a quality of character, on willingness to serve others.

We lived in the heart of England and delighted in getting to know the culture as much as we could. We were regular churchgoers, where we made friends of all ethnic backgrounds. The country has been receiving vast numbers of immigrants every year. Churches in rural England usually have at least a small nucleus of sturdy, elderly British pillars of the faith, but the rest of the younger congregation are usually very mixed, as they change places of living quite often with their jobs. We realised it was a very dynamic, non stagnant society.

We gradually became completely immersed in the social life and culture in the area. Theatre performances outside in the summer were great delight, when it did not rain. A time comes when you stop bothering what the weather does. Just take your umbrella, raincoat, and wellingtons, and go in the mud. That is the point I guessed when the Britons recognised you as one of them. We enjoyed walks, a great way of socialising too. Having lunch and a glass of beer in the pub or a cup of coffee afterwards was delightful. Most walks on the south of England are level ground, but there are some hills, which the locals called "downs." I was puzzled for quite some time why they called them downs, when it dawned to me that it came from the British way of seeing a hill, when you are on the top of it. They all laughed, and I was proud of the joke I invented, usually not that good at jokes at all. Britons like others pulling their legs and laughing at themselves too.

In Albert Hall in London, they had the last night of the Proms concerts every year. Once we joined in the patriotic songs. The British look humorously to their patriotism, yet they take their national identity to heart. We applied for British passports and were waiting, holding our breaths. Just when my worried wife started teasing me that she was going to get me a T-shirt and trunks with the Union Jack for consolation, the passports arrived. We were very happy. The following year at our office Christmas party, for the first time in many years, my wife and I danced together, rocking like youngsters.

Approaching the millennium, life looked too good to be true. My wife was looking after our granddaughter, making friends, and sinking in the English country life. We took turns with friends picking the children up from school. There was a lovely family atmosphere and a lot to absorb for her from TV, theatre, castles, museums, and her social circle. On our fiftieth birthdays, we celebrated like teenagers. We felt young again.

6.3 A Time to Build

And a time to build. (Ecclesiastes 3:3)

In the meantime, I was taking delight in my job; with a bunch of other enthusiasts, mostly young lads, we got busy making the first commercial digital imaging data systems in the country. My work was giving me great satisfaction because our product was successful, and the bit I designed provided a key strategic capability. I was stuck again in work. Relationship with my wife had improved, but I didn't spend much time in building and keeping it going. I was happy as it was, not making a big effort to change the way we used to communicate. Instead of letting my new self grow and lead in this new phase of our marriage, I was gradually drowning in my old pattern of workaholic. I remembered the time I wrote parallel software in OCCAM for the Manchester T-Rack. Ironically we now lived very near Ockham, the place of that medieval philosopher who preached simplicity. I noticed our company tried to make money by every bit of knowledge the team had and still keeping it simple. Yes, as simple as possible but we must not make it even a bit simpler than that, I thought.

In the summer, just before the millennium, a total solar eclipse occurred in England. We watched it from the street in front of our office. For some of the young chaps on the team, this was the first time to observe such a phenomenon, and they were excited. The astronomers also expected another rare event: the transit of Venus in front of the sun. That was to come in five years, but the scientific community was quite agitated. Usually excited by such events, this time I felt nothing until the point of the totality, when the road where we were standing plunged into an almost complete darkness. For a moment, I felt weak, lonely, and abandoned, and I went back to my office.

One foggy night, on my return home from work, walking along the same street, which I loved a lot, a car travelling at high speed ran into me and knocked me down, unconscious. It might have lasted just a few moments, though, because when I came back to consciousness, I was lying on the road in the darkness, in severe pain in my right leg and arm. I could see the red stop lights of a car far ahead of me, so I might have flown above and behind it after the impact and fell to the ground. It saved me because otherwise I would have been run over. While the driver was probably thinking to drive away, all I remember was desperately trying to overcome the pain and crawling to the bank, so that another car would not run me over in the darkness. I was groaning in anger all the time. "Why should have this happened?"

Then a woman came from the nearby house; having heard the noise from the impact, she apparently already had called 999. The ambulance did not come right away, but she stayed there and calmed me down. While I was laying on the ground, moaning, I saw a young girl in white trousers approaching cautiously in the darkness. She looked like an angel, and I realised it was the driver. One thought immediately struck me that it could have been my daughter. Poor girl; it could have happened to anybody behind the wheel while coming back home late, tired from work. My anger disappeared immediately, and I felt I had forgiven her. Without saying anything, I wept. I heard the woman who first came to rescue me tell her to go. And the girl disappeared from my view.

In the hospital, I realised it was not just a bad dream but reality. In the A&E, they found my right elbow was smashed into pieces, and my right leg was damaged below the knee. Fortunately, after a quick X-ray, no life-threatening injuries to the head were found, which proved once again that my brother was right. He always said when we ever bumped our heads on something hard, "Don't worry! We carry tough Balkan heads on our shoulders."

I felt some pain in my neck, but the focus of the doctors' attention was on my leg, which was put in traction and quickly became like a black balloon. I later knew they were quietly discussing amputation. There, in the patient ward later with five other patients, all elderly people, the Lord gave me a poem in English. Until then, all my thoughts and dreams were in my native Bulgarian:

> All fibres of my heart
> have already been scanned
> with invisible rays,
> all atoms measured
> with piercing waves.
>
> They found it normal,
> and that was the end.
> I am still feeling that burning pain.
>
> Every end makes a beginning,
> the poet once said;
> now they are mounting
> a hadron scanner over my bed.
>
> Not much time
> in this rigid dimension,
> and we do things
> with incredible tension.
>
> I believe another one is left open
> to reach infinity,
> but we still look in the vicinity.

Why was it about my heart? I did not know.

Friends from the church and others came and prayed for me on the bedside. The greatest cheer I received, though, was when the young lads from work came to see me. I wanted to help them with any advice, but they were managing well in my absence so far, without anything critical happening.

The bones of my elbow joint were fixed with eleven two-inch screws, and I was encouraged to exercise it straight away. I felt like a robot now, but my right leg was in traction, so I felt I was human in pain. They drilled a hole all the way through my Achilles bone and put a metal bit in. It helped attach over a kilo of weights to it, pulling my leg all the time. For forty days, I could not turn in bed or move away from it all that time. The worst embarrassment in my life came when I had to ask the nurse for a bedpan to serve my bowel movement. Well, Lord, if that is how you build a new character, let it be. The Lord said, "What about those astronauts you admire? In their squashy capsule, they were not served any better for a week on their way to the moon, were they? What you get compared to them is luxury."

The first steps on the way to recovery brought the inevitable question: Why did it happen? Where was God? I noticed the enemy tried to butt in. I realised God created the laws of nature, and he would not intervene to suspend them just because I was inattentive and doing my own thing again. One of those laws was that if two material bodies collide with great speed, they break, unless, well, I did not pray for protection, did I? But did I have another sin?

There is a direct link between illness and sin, according to the scripture. That certainly made sense to me, for the simple fact that if we follow an unhealthy lifestyle (whatever it is: bad diet, obesity, stress, or smoking), it makes us more prone to disease. Also, psychological impact from hatred, rejection, jealousy, anger, frustration, or fear can cause short- and even long-term illness to the body. That is the law of human physiology. There is also so-called generational sin, when predisposition to certain illness gets passed to generations through the genes. It comes down to the original sin of Adam.

But it would be untrue, unbiblical, to always link disease to sin, as it was in the case of the man born blind (John 9:1). Jesus clearly declared that no one sinned in that case, neither the man himself nor his ancestors. My case was trauma, as a result of an accident, and I continued to ask why God allowed that happen to me. I started asking that question in anger, just after the concussion. That anger gradually subsided, and I had peace about it when I read that famous verse from Isaiah 54:7: "For a brief moment I abandoned you but with a deep compassion I will bring you back." Perhaps because my profession now was in the health industry, he wanted to put me in the position of a patient so I knew who I worked for now. I realised that I would have a full recovery, and I stopped asking questions. I just somehow trusted God was going to give me back everything I had lost and damaged. Just as He did with many other things.

The ward in the hospital was full; all six beds were occupied, and on the opposite side, a man came later with a stroke, partially paralysed. However, he was chatting all the time. His speech was not slurred, and he was very entertaining, touching on physics and science. He found a good listener in me, someone who could ask sensible questions here and there to make him feel connected. A friend of his came to visit him, and when he heard I was a software engineer, he was very interested and came over to my bed. I heard from him for the first time about the Enigma project in Bletchley Park, engaged in deciphering secret Nazi communications during World War II. This top-secret information had been declassified just a few months ago; nobody could read about it from the public domain before that. The man also told me about Colossus, the electronic device used in the decrypting process, a precursor of the modern computer. We argued with him whether the American ENIAC could be "dethroned" as first computer or not. With visitors like him, I felt relieved, and time in the hospital bed, to which I was 'chained' passed much quicker.

After forty days, following my grievous pleas, doctors let me off the traction and put my leg in plaster from the toes up to and above my knee; then allowed me to go home. It was an immense relief to be able to stand again on my other foot and look outside through the window down in the park, where daffodils and crocuses had blossomed in the early spring. I was able to walk on crutches. My broken elbow joint was implanted long ago with metal within hours after the accident and was not very painful. It was an extraordinary surgical and orthopaedic job and aftercare. I have never seen in my life such nice and caring people before. I felt like a child in the hands of my mother again. My heart will always remain grateful to them all- doctors and nurses of various ranks, not just knowing well their professional stuff but truly loving human beings, working intensively hard all days and nights.

The experience, which interrupted my life and took at least a year away from my productive career, changed me permanently. It taught me to always be obedient and humble because my life was not mine, anyway. God gave me life; therefore, I lived for him, and he was entitled to have it back at any moment, even if it required suffering in the process. He was sovereign. He was still building my character. I was glad I was still a work in progress and I learned I will remain such all my life on earth.

Christmas was coming, the millennium Christmas. It was two thousand years since God's coming on planet Earth in the appearance of a man.

6.4 A Time to Scatter Stones

A time to scatter stones. (Ecclesiastes 3:5)

Months later back to work after my miraculous recovery, I found myself in a professional quagmire. The team dynamics had changed, with new recruits eager to assert themselves in what used to be a very flat and friendly working culture. Now, there were squabbles for hierarchy emerging with increasing force. Some of the new recruits ambitiously embarked on converting the code I wrote to object-oriented design, without knowing what they were doing. It only needed a wrapper to make the code object-oriented, but they would not listen to me, a mere émigré, who did not know how to cross the road, a nuisance to drivers. Instead, I had to fix errors they made when they broke the code while meddling unnecessarily with old low-level routines. After the code was fixed I offered training on the existing multilayered design and DICOM, the medical data protocol on which it was all based, something they were missing, but they were not cooperative. Showing contempt, they were mainly interested in quick career progress. I liked their passion for being trained and certified in object-oriented design. It was the right time but after long absence, I felt I lost touch with the newcomers in the team and needed time to come back to it. The old team that used to perform well was now driven by pride in stormy conditions, but the management was inexperienced in handling it. Some found internal competition would work well for them even if it would mean breaking the company.

It was the right time to be more involved in corporate management. On a visit to our HQ in the United States, there were opportunities to get more involved in strategy and decision making on a different level. However, I did not quite feel I was up to it, still recovering from injuries and expecting another operation. Besides, I knew I was not very good at company politics, though I would have loved to take the challenge this time, had I been fit enough. But it would require stressful engagements of different kinds.

On that trip, I took my wife with me. This was her first visit to America, but I could only accompany her on the weekends. Limping, I took her to the Empire State Building, where the panoramic view of the city was breathtaking. We both were in awe of the great achievements of the American civil engineering and the heroic work of the builders of the 1930s. In the following week, she went alone to visit Liberty Island and took the tour with the ship round the harbour that simulated the view emigrants from Europe would see on their arrival: the Statue of Liberty welcoming them to the New World of freedom. She paid tribute to her grandfather, who came here from Bulgaria in the 1920s; his ship was not accepted because of epidemics in the city, and they returned.

She was very excited and happy, and that made me happy too, never mind the exhaustion from limping, jet lag, work, and driving in New York. There were still no satnavs at the time, and one had to drive by map. I was pleased to see that American cities, having been built anew from a plan, were laid out neatly, very easy to drive. Streets crossed on a grid, and you could count them by number or name. The plaster had just been taken off my right leg a few weeks earlier. In the comfortable seats of the Metropolitan Opera, where we went to see Placido Domingo, I fell asleep. I was not very thrilled by cultural icons and opera anyway, but I enjoyed the jazz in the Lincoln Center the following weekend. I loved the spacious concert halls and their cosy, clean, neoclassical interior, the illustrious marble plazas, and the shops, nothing comparable to the squashy, polluted old Europe.

While passing by the World Trade Center and the Twin Towers on our way to the airport, I was told she managed to pop in there, too, and was fascinated by what was inside. I said with a slightly envious voice that she always saw more than I did, but I would catch up the next time I came to New York. We did not have a clue that in a year's time, there would be no more Twin Towers. It was exactly one year before 9/11.

Back in England, I heard the news that our little company was in negotiations for a takeover. That did not sound good to me. There were opportunities there in the skirmish, but I knew I would not play them well. I thought I'd better look for another job elsewhere.

Next year, out of the blue, came the September 11 attack. Soon after that, we felt the new economic climate had caused problems for our business too. We were a US company, after all. But the majority of our customers in the beginning were hospitals who used to receive UK government funding for modernisation of the radiology departments. The clinical staff naturally was also a stakeholder in these projects, and some high-standing medical academics usually sponsored the whole project. They had a high interest in realising the benefits. So the first systems were installed and ran with few problems.

We got more customers after 9/11, and as the technology matured, we about to break even to profit. Instead, we had more and more cases where clinical staff was no longer supportive. The radiologists really had a tough time switching from film-based diagnostics to images displayed on the screen. It was a very big change, which involved training of staff on new technology, and there was friction between staff who were used to the old things and new recruits, who were enthusiastic about change. The working culture was changing at times, very steeply, and few hospital management teams were able to handle it successfully. The situation needed support on a national level in order to make modernisation happen. That came later in some six years' time with the so-called National Program for IT, but for now, small businesses were left to struggle on their own, with limited resources. From supporters, the IT departments in some NHS hospitals turned into competitors for the modernisation, bidding for funding themselves.

As a result, clinical radiology departments were trying to get away from storing and archiving images on computers by holding every possible technical restriction against it. They just did not like diagnosing on screens. They loved hanging their X-ray films on light boxes. Also, it was too much data on their networks; they had to store huge amounts, and they had no experience with that. The profession of a PACS (picture archiving and communications system) administrator had not been born yet; it had to be either radiographers, who had no experience with computers, or system administrators, who did not have the medical imaging experience. Such people with multidisciplinary skills were not yet available. The imaging department was hanging exclusively on the continuous support from the vendor.

The existing infrastructure in the NHS hospitals was not ready to implement electronic imaging storage and management. Apart from the images, other medical records were still on paper. Hospital or radiology information systems managed billing and scheduling, and they had to be integrated with the image management, a process which took almost a decade because of the disparate workflows each hospital had in the radiology departments. The environment allowed vendors to quick-fix problems by employing obscure proprietary protocols that were not standard and charging the customer a lot. This approach left customers with closed systems, which evolved over time without further integration. They did not realise they would one day be locked with only one vendor, which would be too costly, too late. I was firmly part of the alliance that promoted standards in order to bring the costs to the hospitals down, but that did not seem to be in line with the new business strategy following the takeover.

I had to look for another job, but first I wanted to see my father. My first visit back to Bulgaria after many years away and tribulations in my personal life would have been a pleasurable experience, had it not been for the fact that Dad was dying with cancer. The little town where I finished my first school looked shaken down in misery. The hospital looked in terrible state; there was no heating.

In Sofia, the country's political elite was again in a bitter squabble, this time between socialists and democrats. They put so much energy in blaming each other for the past instead of looking into the now. Both sides in effect originated from the same former Communist circles, anyway. What the country needed was a national reconciliation.

King Simeon II had returned from exile, and contrary to all royal traditions, got involved in politics. Not accepted as a king, he put forward his candidacy as prime minister and won. His time in office brought moderation, calmness, and more civilised relations in the politics of the country. Corruption and abuse of power diminished, and the country was on the way to joining NATO and the EU. However, people expected quick improvements in eliminating poverty and restructuring the ruined economy, which needed time. He continued after his term in office as a chairman of a coalition but lost the following elections. He never pushed ahead firmly with restoring the monarchy because Bulgaria still had very strong republican sentiments, and that would have created tribulations affecting the democratic process in the country.

It looked like the Third Bulgarian Kingdom was coming to an end. The majority of people did not like the idea of restoring the monarchy. There is nothing wrong being non-monarchist. However, people cannot benefit from earthly kings before they acknowledge their king in heaven. (1 Samuel 8:7). The functions of the state, to care and protect its citizens, to provide historical identity and continuity, to promote common values and faith, were gravely eroded during the sixty years of Communist rule. Yet there was a chance for revival and restoration. The nation and its leaders, the intellectual elite, and the church did not seem to grasp the importance of the moment. Yes, analysing the past, the country with its institutions was guilty for not standing up fully to the Nazis, for choosing to submit to an overwhelming force, like the French did, in a moment of weakness. But violent resistance and self-sacrifice was too high a price to pay and would not make much difference in practice. When Simeon II returned from exile, he could have publicly repented on behalf of the ancestors for any form of collaboration with the Nazis through the institutions of the time, which inevitably took place when the monarchy was in power. This would have brought national healing and reconciliation on a much deeper level. It could have brought the spirit of remorse and removed the sense of guilt for the past. After all, the monarchy was forcibly deposed while the country was still under foreign occupation.

Instead, the 'democratic' politicians, while denouncing the Communist state, in fact silently approved its methods of terror and dictatorship, the forceful deposition of the monarchy, when that state was established. That was grotesque. To agree to take the crown off the head of a king who already had it, was to reject ourselves as members of a nation, already recognised as sovereign throughout history, good or bad. Apart from anything else, the monarch represented the state. Even his personal qualities were less important than the office he represented, but few had that understanding after more than half a century Communist rule.

Few people cared anyway because many hoped to get away with the traumatic divisions of the past by adopting a new national identity: citizens of the EU or otherwise. Some of the media, like Radio Voice of Truth (VOT) called for a national prayer, repentance, and reconciliation generally, without involving a monarchist agenda or guilt from the distant past. But few others joined. Simeon did not reach for the crown of his father, a crown the writer Stephane Grueff called "a Crown of Thorns." Yet the country gained peace, and Simeon, thank God, became one of the main instruments of it.

Of Ecclesiastes and More

I noticed the younger generation in the country was not like ours. A new value system was forming, also based on discontent but now with the degraded morals of the materialism and pornography. In the past, we served a moral purpose of the larger community, the welfare of the state or whatever, despite our resentment of a system which restricted our freedom and the morality it preached. However, this generation did not believe in anybody or anything: no idea, allegiance, or cause. They were growing rebellious, arrogant, and cynical, seeking meaning and purpose where it could not be found. In the public transport, one could often hear heated discussions which would always finish in blaming the fellow next to them or the government, or cursing themselves: "What people are we? What a country. Rubbish." I took pity upon them. It made me sad, and I thought I may have a mission here, but not with technology; with the Bible instead. Maybe I was wrong, generalising for all. Anyhow, I found it difficult to strike a positive note.

The misery around had managed to take over my spirit too. My elbow was in pain. I feared I could become disabled with my right hand if I did not act promptly. I had to go back to England for an operation. However, Dad needed an operation on his cancer too, which could extend his life. I felt hopeless not knowing what to do. As I was sitting next to his bed, he saw the anguish on my face and tapped on my shoulder. "Do not worry," he said. I felt ashamed that I had let him see me down and concerned as always, instead of demonstrating strength encourage him for what was coming. He changed a lot after seeing the end of the regime. He talked a lot about his mother, my granny, showing respect for her Christian attitudes during the totalitarian time. Then after a pause, he said, "Look, I am over ninety. I would not go for an operation anyway. I have lived long enough. I think I have lived it all. Don't worry about me. Go back and take care for your family."

I left the room, hiding my weeping. My Dad did not like men weeping. He used to be stone-hearted to others, including members of his family, but he was stone-hearted to himself too. I felt guilty I could not do much for him, a man of integrity. I prayed and felt he was right. I arranged for people to care for him and went back to my family in England.

He died in June 2001 having served his country to the best he could, always giving his time and work higher priority than his family. He departed at just the right time; he would have felt extremely traumatised and betrayed by all that happened following the collapse of the regime and the bankruptcy of the whole country: the rush to become rich, the abrupt discontinuity with past and present, the total rejection of the past values, good and bad. Whatever happened and whatever he believed, those were the best years of his life in which he was decorated "People's Order of Labour" and the "Order of the 9th of September." Who would wear these today with pride? They would rather shoot you. Whatever the past was, good or bad, this was his life, and these awards were the recognition for his hard work and loyalty to the country. Sad.

Before I left, I called in his patch of land, a vineyard, now a desolate place. Verses from the Bible came to my tongue:

> Why have you broken down its walls
> so that all who pass by pick its grapes?
> Boars from the forest ravage it,
> and insects from the fields feed on it.
> Return to us, God Almighty!
> Look down from heaven and see!
> Watch over this vine,
> the root your right hand has planted,
> the son you have raised up for yourself.
> Your vine is cut down, it is burned with fire;
> at your rebuke your people perish.

Let your hand rest on the man at your right
hand,
the son of man you have raised up for yourself.
Then we will not turn away from you;
revive us, and we will call on your name.
Restore us, Lord God Almighty;
make your face shine on us,
that we may be saved.
(Psalm 80:12–19)

6.5 A Time to Gather Them

And a time to gather them. (Ecclesiastes 3:5)

The first time they were putting me asleep for an operation,
I was not afraid. I was sure I would come back. I awoke with
an uplifted spirit and joked that God brought me in the hands
of the doctors as part of my training. Being a patient in the
capacity of a medical engineer who knew about medicine
and healthcare was a funny experience indeed. However, the
second op a year later, to remove the metal, also required
general anaesthetic, and that was very scary. I thought "What
if I do not wake up?"

So what? If I did not wake up here, I would wake up in
heaven, without any pain. Simple. This was our belief. It would
be like the twinkling of an eye between our moment of death
and our awakening in heaven, because we would be out of
time. But we do not know exactly when Jesus will return. It
might be billions of years. It is a lot of time for the living human
mind, like eternity itself. The thought suddenly threw me into
doubt. Would Jesus come again at all? I knew I was under a
strong attack and called a friend to pray for me. Peace rested
in my mind again. When they wheeled me down to the op
theatre, I stretched my hand to the anaesthetist like the first
time and fell asleep.

When I awoke, although there was not much pain in my arm, I felt sick for a long time. The op however was successful. They took half a kilo of metal out of my elbow. Back home, I gave thanks to God for the successful operation and went to focus on hunting for a new job. What my inner being needed, though, was a long, long rest, just sleeping and doing work in the garden. But my retirement age was still way ahead. Maybe I should ask the Lord for a simple job like gardening?

No; my proud self jumped again. So I got up and sent out the next lot of CVs.

Initially, the advancement in medical informatics was mainly in new technologies for body scanning and data acquisition. At the same time, advances in general computing were mainly in increasing core computer performance and developing software applications in specific domains of knowledge. There were fewer changes in systems architecture. It was mainly implementation of new application systems and software support, which at the time meant fixing bugs. Professional development for IT workers was quite steady; it was not so difficult to catch up with new advancements. There were some waves of innovation, like wireless data communication and mobile devices, but it was not too difficult for an IT professional to surf through them and secure a job.

The next change came with the quest for crossing the boundaries that were created by rival companies with a variety of incompatible computing platforms. An application created to run on Apple could not run directly on a Microsoft Windows machine. Though the applications were written on a high-level programming language and were meant to be portable to different brands of operating systems, the process wasn't straightforward because there were different data formats and different ways of connecting and managing events. It was an issue for hospitals, especially because they normally ran a multitude of platforms from various manufacturers. The new approach was called virtualisation, which used the age-old idea of simulation. Pieces of code called virtual machines could run on one processor and simulate the interface of different operating systems, so that the applications running on top of them did not see the difference.

The arrival of the smart phone, however was another stepping stone for humanity- a computer in the pocket! In the beginning it was just a simple organiser: diary, calendar, music and a phone call a button away. But then, as the gadget quickly became smarter and smarter, we slowly became so dependent on it: mailing, texting, banking, searching information, shopping, travel information, maps, camera, news, radio, TV, learning, meetings, weather, health monitoring, book reading...All that in a single chocolate bar size gadget, in my pocket! Teenagers today do not have an idea about the life we had without all that. They do feel however restricted, vulnerable, marginalised when they are deprived of their smart phone, as if their whole world disappears.

For some time, I had a desire for more customer-facing experience, and after a short period of job hunting, I joined a global provider of integration services for healthcare devices. They built their success on developing toolkits for standard connectivity. My new job was to consult on issues they had with customers when connecting to other manufacturers in the field and to troubleshoot any problems they experienced. It involved capturing network communication data and checking whether the information exchange was compliant. This job raised my profile globally, as I had to engage with many specialists in major companies involved in medical imaging.

Travelling the globe for work is a blessing. Meeting with different people and seeing the history and culture of Western Europe and America was quite enriching for an Eastern European who had spent most of his life behind the Iron Curtain. It was a bit over the top, too, for a man in his fifties. Flying every other week and writing reports while jet-lagged was taking a toll on my health. The job also had a lot of pressure. It required me to work on my own budget, market my service, and find customers. Very stressful.

Working in the United Sates gave me the opportunity to think again about immigrating to America, as finding a permanent job is so much easier when one is already at work there, and contacts with other professionals are easier for networking. I liked the country, with its vast territories of still unspoiled mountains, rivers, valleys, and plains; the climate was similar to the one I grew up in. One weekend in Seattle, I drove up near Mount St. Helen, which in the early summer stood like a heavenly place topped with snow. Next time, I headed south to Tacoma, driving round the canals and the inlets of the bay to the Olympic Peninsula. The views from the heights were magnificent. Going north from Seattle, I found the beaches on the Pacific coast beautiful, but the water in the sea was freezing cold in midsummer due to currents coming from the north. Going east through the Snoqualmie Pass was very invigorating; I could see people still skiing on the slopes.

On another occasion, I was called by a company in Andover, near Boston, to troubleshoot their new ultrasound machine, which was unable to connect to the image archiver because of a very subtle error in the connectivity subroutines. From there, during the weekend, I went to Cape Cod, a peninsula extending like a giant elbow into the Atlantic. It was a beautiful conservation area of many species, crossed with hiking and cycling trails. There I sat on Marconi Beach, deafened by the roar of three-meter-high waves coming from the vast expansion of the sea; the coast curved along the peninsula to the east to calm the rough waters. This roar perhaps never stopped for millions of years since this side separated from the coast of Europe and North Africa. The tectonic plates floating on the molten core of the Earth had kept moving until the American continent was completely separated from the rest of the land by the Bering Strait, a relatively recent event in the geological history; it's even recorded in the Bible (Genesis 10:25).

It was late afternoon, but the moon was clearly visible rising from the ocean. It reminded me of who was responsible for all the tidal waves above and beneath the Earth. Were all these movements of matter ultimately self-sustained on their own merit since God wound the clock and left the scene? I don't think so. An angel of the Lord came and sat next to me, joining in meditation. I came here in the spirit of technology, but my mood suddenly turned quite philosophical, as if I was visiting this primordial chamber of life creation, the ocean, precisely here in the New World for some important reason. But what the reason was remained a mystery to me.

I remembered Lime Regis in England on the other side of the vast expanse, where a similar view to the sea can be experienced from the hills. As we were walking down to the Jurassic Coast, a lady from Canada came up the stairs to the car park, clutching a precious rock with ammonite fossils. She had come here with a special mission of hunting fossils, and there was her reward. Nothing is more exhilarating than the face of a person running with their passion to learn, to investigate, to touch something from the primordial times.

On this site of the ocean, the spirit was on me with technology. Marconi Beach was the site of the first transatlantic radio telegraphic transmission, performed in 1903 between America and England on the other side. Almost nothing remained from the original equipment and the towers, but just to be here in the mood of communications history was quite a moving experience.

On that trip to Massachusetts, I also went to visit the iconic MIT. The old building looked quite insignificant and even shabby inside, a bit like my alma mater, the Technical University in Sofia after the crisis. I sat on the green in front of the great dome and did not even try to visit the iconic targets I meant to.

The urban culture of the United States was not for me. I found the townscape of skyscrapers megalomaniac, spooky, and depressing. The sight from inside a skyscraper was attractive and uplifting, but only in those which looked to an open space, to blue sky and sunshine, like the ones in Chicago near the lake. I also felt the society was driven by an excess of consumerism. I learned my lessons that I should take responsibility for making money because there was no other way we make our living. However, to start a friendship with the question, "How much do you earn per year?" breaks the spirit of having it.

The majority of Americans were not that materialistic. I found my colleagues- engineers and scientists, open-hearted and hard-working people, very pragmatic but friendly at the same time. But my soul was after the small towns of Europe, where one did not need to get into a car to go to a shop round the corner; it was a much more settled lifestyle. One could enjoy the weekend in peace and comfort, walking around a little town and into the countryside. Relocating to America would mean I may not have my own home for some time. I was tired, and my mind was looking more to retirement than to a buoyant career fight.

I was still thinking in the context of my enlarged family. My daughter had just remarried, and I worried about how that was going, as I rarely spent quality time with them due to all my travel. Then one day, she and her husband stunned us with a decision to return to Bulgaria. They believed it would soon be part of an enlarged Europe and had seen opportunities for them there.

As we were coming to terms with their leaving, they announced they were planning to take her child, our granddaughter, with them as well. It was a huge disappointment for me. She was already a British girl. She didn't even speak

Bulgarian. Though my wife and I spoke mother tongue at home, we always communicated with her in English. When I told my daughter that my granddaughter should stay with us, I was faced with such a fierce response that a bitter conflict would have been inevitable had I decided to push further.

In the years past, I learned that we should always praise and value our family and children, whatever the circumstances. We have to do what we can to make our family even better, but it is important to value what we have at the moment. My hasty response to situations that emerged in the past was almost always wrong. As it happened, my daughter's family did well after returning to Bulgaria. For some time, I felt abandoned, left alone, but then I was glad I had time to do my own things again.

For us with my wife, England was where our home was now. We had become emotionally linked to the problems of this country and the way people were resolving them. We had lots of friends now and felt at home here, grafted on their culture. We had sold our flat in Sofia long ago. It was painful when I had to get rid of hundreds of books (including a luxury edition of the full collection of Einstein's works), furniture, crystals, and many other possessions. I made so many moves in my life which in the long term looked all good, though they were painful at the time. But they all affirmed my conviction that I was a stranger, a foreigner in this world, and that heaven was my true home.

I realised that moving to America could have made a difference, but it was too late. Opportunities do not stay long. When we are called to move, we should do it promptly, for apart from the things we are involved in, God does many other things. We do not have the whole picture, though our faith allows us to view more than we would see otherwise.

Thinking about the past again, I realised I had never actually enjoyed life to the full. Even when I felt on top of making a living, I still could not relax fully and enjoy it. My mentality of a "prisoner behind bars" spoiled it all, as if it was forbidden. This was the moment, I decided to go skiing in the Alps with a Christian travel company. It was the trip of a lifetime, with fun on the slopes and socialising during the evenings with other Christians.

On the last day I went on as many tracks as I could on my own. It was early in the morning. After a couple of runs across the area, I saw a lift without anybody on it; it was just a man clearing snow and supervising it, and I jumped on there, hoping for a private descent this time without crowds. It turned to be quite a long ride, which ended up at the base of a giant rock extending up in the sky.

No one was there. I saw a signpost saying "Danger: ungroomed piste! End of skiing area!" Then, after I disembarked, the lift suddenly stopped, and the silence that followed was so immense that it made a loud cry. I realised I had to ski alone down on an almost virgin snow; about three inches of new snow fell during the night, hiding any hazards. It was a very steep slope; scary. I looked down to the snowy valleys and up the surrounding peaks. It was white heaven all through the past few days with beautiful sunshine. However, that morning, the peaks were half-surrounded with clouds and mist. Total silence. I looked up again and literally heard the silent presence of the enormous nuclear reactor beneath which raised up these mountains. All of a sudden, I sensed that the Creator of all this was near too. My legs trembled. I lay down on the snow with my skis still on.

"What do you want from the life I have given you? Why does every man want to know everything, understand everything, and try all hard jobs?"

"It is such fun, Lord."

"Enjoy, but you don't have time to grasp all of it. I put limits on you. All you get is information, and the little knowledge you manage to filter out is at my discretion too. Why do you ask for more? The more you get to know, the more you will not know; it is infinite. You will never get the full picture while on earth. All you do is obstruct my best plans for you. Enjoy life. Stay still, and accept life as it comes to you. Know that I reign."

I came down safe, after over an hour descent through a virgin snow.

Back to the warmth of my cosy little chalet room, I took a shower and plunged into the bed, exhausted. Through the window, I could see the snowy hills in the dusk, illuminated by projector lights. The tractors were already working to groom the tracks for the morning. Half-asleep, I could hear my fellow holiday makers who returned earlier singing "How Great Thou Art." Why did I need to go back to my office next week? The Lord was changing me. My zeal for ambitious IT work was turning sour yet again. There must be something more than just that. Was I not a prince in my Father's Kingdom?

6.6 The Science of Life

In the first years of the new millennium, I joined a small company working in biomedical image analysis, an offshoot from the University of Oxford. They were using image processing techniques to quantify specific bio molecular activity in the human body. The way to do this was called "molecular imaging." A particular substance used by the body for food or other physiological activity can be labelled by removing an atom from its molecule and replacing it with an isotope of that atom. Thus, without changing its basic biochemical properties, the substance becomes 'marked' by becoming slightly radioactive and could be traced wherever it goes. A small concentration of this material can be injected into the body. The concentrations are not meant to be harmful. The body then can be scanned with a device that is able to detect the radioactivity and its location in the body at the organ or even cell level. Based on the data received by the detectors, a software application can reconstruct an image in three dimensions, showing the distribution in the body and its concentrations.

The applications we were creating could help, for example, evaluate the rate of metabolism of sugar in different organs. Applied to the brain, it could help diagnose Alzheimer's or check for tumours or cancerous tissues. In pharmacology, this method could also trace the distribution in the human body of a new drug for treatment and the dynamics of its activity and concentration. These applications were helping doctors see considerably more than in other scanning methods, which showed anatomical features of tissue but not functional ones and their dynamics. Methods like these were soon to replace the art of traditional diagnostic interpretation on two-dimensional images in radiology departments.

My colleagues were very smart software developers as well as scientists, real wizards of image processing techniques. They needed someone to help them structure and format their data for export and import. This was essential since, unlike researchers who used whatever tools they could grab for free, hospital clinicians had to use certified applications from different manufacturers and had to adhere to healthcare safety standards. Applications from other manufacturers needed to further analyse and process the data; for example, to control the beams of a radiotherapy machine to treat cancer. The whole project, entailing many years of expensive research, was in jeopardy just because the software was not interoperable with other manufacturers. I had to help them build a new communication platform which would integrate their product in the standard data management environment of the hospitals across the world.

The area was still in academic research; transferring the results into the industry involved creating strict, formal and clear definitions of new concepts and creating appropriate information containers. New data formats had to be created and agreed to by international standardisation organisations. It was quite enjoyable to organise and conduct testing and certification with our partners and to present results on conferences. It was lovely to see the team inspired by their achievements and the fact that they were not excluded but recognised as part of the global industry, able to collaborate and exchange data with other applications.

It was also a time of breathtaking advancements in genetics. A new technology, able to sequence DNA and read out the genetic code with computerised machinery, allowed scientists to map all the information from the human genetic code, the genome. They began to understand for the first time in great detail how biochemistry inside the human body actually worked. Shortly after that, machines sequencing genes became less expensive, and that opened a possibility to completely transform the way disease was diagnosed and treated. Based on our genetic make-up, doctors would soon be able to predict our predisposition to certain types of disease. This personalised medicine would soon leave the research labs and be implemented in routine healthcare practices. However, the transition needed new data formats and smart applications able to understand it without requiring doctors to make low level decisions. It also needed new types of databases to store and keep medical data about individuals from the cradle to the grave. That on its own was scary and raised serious issues about data privacy and security.

Oxford was just what my wife and I dreamed of: a simple life without much fuss. I walked or cycled to work. Lots of cheer on the streets coming from students carrying books in their rucksacks and rushing to the lecture rooms. My wife's favourite places were the bookshops where one could pick a book and a coffee and read like in a library. There were nice cafes and restaurants. You cannot get bored in Oxford. We had a great time going to museums and concerts in the churches. In the iconic Sheldonian Theatre, where the graduations took place, we saw wonderful musical performances. The town was small enough to feel cosy and big enough for fine shops but not too many to take over the academic spirit on the streets. We often went to parties and loved mingling with the dons and chatting with intellectuals.

One weekend, our children came to visit us, and we went out punting on the canals near St Catherine's College, something we always wanted to try. I found it quite easy rowing from the back of that funny rectangular boat and steering. It was going so well, with my wife and my granddaughter in the front, that it puffed up my pride, and I did not notice when we came near a willow, gently bending its branches over the river. There was no time to react, and when my head hit the branches, I toppled down into the shallow water. My ladies laughed and had a great time. I was so happy they had such fun. In the evening, we all enjoyed Shakespeare's *Midsummer Night's Dream* in the park.

Just as we were planning to settle there more permanently and buy a house, we began to notice the first symptoms of illness in my wife; her mobility suddenly started to deteriorate. I had to spend more time taking her to the university hospital.

No one likes being made redundant, especially just when you think you have got a career for life. Medical imaging was a very competitive area of business, and our company was facing the prospect of being taken over. The team dynamics started to change with different opinions over which way to go: academic research or clinical industry. My job was relocated to Germany. After many years in England, I did not want to leave. I was too tired to make a big move.

It was not possible to hide everything from my wife, and I knew she was a worrier. I shouldn't have made a fuss about my redundancy because she was always feeling guilty for the whole world. We decided to leave Oxford and move back to where we used to live; we had more friends there, and it was closer to the major clinics in London as well.

Stricken with sadness and anxiety about my job and the crumbling health of my wife, I suddenly looked at my profession in healthcare IT with bitterness and anger: a billion-pound industry to care for sick people, bringing health through pills, pills for everything: for painkilling, calming, erections- a diabolic 'sick care', not healthcare industry. Lots of politics, less love and compassion, only greed and pride. Lots of information; little knowledge. Managers learned how to rush but not how to wait. Not much care for the healthy to stay that way. Why didn't God create a new job in Oxford? Why was I made redundant? Why was my wife getting ill? I was almost yelling in my room behind closed doors, with cynicism, angry at God, when the telephone rang, and I was called for another job in London.

I was hired to prepare radiology departments for the digital age; it was a great privilege. People began to realise that major fundamental breakthroughs in life sciences achieved in the past decades could not be introduced in clinical practice without first modernising electronic patient records on a national and even international level. At that point, digital medical image management became one of the most important elements.

The first commercial systems based on the integration standard we promoted years ago proved the technology was working and viable, but significant investment was needed to implement it across the country. To counter this problem in the UK, the government launched the National Program for IT (NPfIT). They developed and published quite elaborate technical specifications, defining in detail specific data formats and protocols to achieve interoperability between systems of different manufacturers, precisely what was heralded in the pioneering stages years ago. The goal was to improve patient safety and bring down the cost of integration. The concept of interoperability was no longer seen as just communicating data between systems from different manufacturers, but also interpreting that data correctly when computer-aided diagnosis was introduced. This was why high-level network standards had to be combined with artificial intelligence machines (AI).

The strategy was to keep vast amounts of data for a longer time and to increase the role of computers in helping doctors analyse the data and make decisions about the right diagnosis and treatment. The major NHS trusts in the country were divided in several regions, and vendors were allowed to bid to service them. Naturally, only a few blue-chip companies were able to respond to requirements for 24/7, zero downtime service and strict adherence to medical and safety standards. Even they found it challenging. There were risks, but standards ensured high quality and safety in an area where people's health and life were at stake.

The NPfIT attracted a great deal of criticism in terms of the huge cost involved and blocking the free market. The issue was highly politicised. It was true that the costs were high, but all areas of innovation have high costs for the initial implementation. The NPfIT created islands of NHS trusts dispersed across the country to serve as models to follow and standards to adhere to, something very difficult to achieve quickly with a free market. It also created hubs with clinical and IT staff, trained for the new digital technology, who could serve as centres of knowledge and expertise later when these systems were replicated across the country.

Project management is thrilling and exhilarating but stressful. I used to be fully committed to a job, going to sleep with my projects and waking up with them. But my enthusiasm for such demanding work was running out. I had to drive from home to central London an hour every day and another hour back after work. Approaching sixty inevitably brings the unease of life fulfilment, when you feel you have to slow down because of age and health. At a certain time, you realise that our bodies are just not fit to go forever. At the same time, you become aware of so many missed opportunities in early life.

Mark Twain was so right when he said, "You will be haunted not by the things you have done but by the things you haven't done." But then I remembered that meeting with the Lord in the snow in the Alps. I recalled what he said: "I reign." And peace filled my heart again. I was able to pause for a while, listen to the wisdom, and see that there were still many opportunities in later life. We just need to change our attitude to be able to spot them. My wife's health was still failing. When was I going to spend time with those I loved, hugging her and saying, "I love you"? Perhaps I never said it with its true meaning. This is a treasure, and it did not need any effort. I was suddenly filled with sorrow for the missed moments we could be truly together.

I looked through the window of my flat to the beautiful garden outside, listened to the songs of the birds, and realised what a treasure I had. My Christian friends called and prayed for me. Although tired and not very productive because of the worries, my health was still okay, my mind was still working, and I had gained tons of life experience and professional knowledge. These were all my good things in life which I could use in a different way now, perhaps working at home.

6.7 A Time to Mourn

And a time to mourn. (Ecclesiastes 3:4)

In 2005, Bulgaria celebrated joining the European Union. My children were hyped up, but they realised there was hard work ahead. Young people thrive on being challenged. They are up to it. In good old England, we were looking towards peace and quiet. There is that moment when you realise you are entering a different season of your life, perhaps the last one before you depart. I was suddenly overwhelmed by the desire to shower kindness on my wife; she might die soon, as her health was rapidly deteriorating.

It all started when she found it difficult to rise up from her chair and then later on to turn in bed at night. It got even worse when I had to get up several times at night to help her to the loo. Detailed and lengthy examinations with neurologists in London and in Sofia did not lead to any definite conclusion. They wanted some very invasive and painful tests, which she did not agree to.

Symptomatically, they decided it was multiple system atrophy, the worst form of Parkinson's. The cells producing neurotransmitters in the brain die. Without them, important neural signals cannot reach their destinations in the organs they control. As a result, vital body functions start to deteriorate. Medical science did not know why the cells producing the neurotransmitters die. But only after more than 50 percent of the cells died, symptoms would appear. Doctors in this case prescribed medication that added the missing neurotransmitter in the body. This treatment supported the neural system, slowing the progress of the disease, but did not deal with the root causes.

Knowing prayer was what mattered most in this situation, we gave it a go. She and I went on several healing ministry sessions. Yet there was a barrier no one could remove. She firmly believed she had a hereditary illness; her father had died from a neurodegenerative disease. If the clinicians did not know what to do, she did not believe God could repair it, any other way. I tried to encourage her by pointing out that even with a genetic predisposition, gene expression depends on many external events: the environment; what we eat and drink; how we exercise, rest, and relax; what we watched and listened to; our mindset. But she remained firmly convinced in her mind.

All DNA tests showed that she did not have any of the known Parkinson-related genes. The Human Genome Project finished recently, and research for mapping all genomic information related to neurodegenerative diseases was underway. But this was just filling a database. Research for treatment was in its infancy.

I read some books on generational sin which could help on the approach to prayer, but I was guilty of becoming increasingly sceptical. She kept saying that she wanted to die; it was very frustrating to go against that in prayer, as I was not sure what God's will for her was. Each one of us has an appointed time to surrender, but we do not know it in advance. One day, she said that Jesus is Lord and that she was saved, confident in her wholeness. She just wanted to see certain places before she passed away.

While she could still make a step or two by holding on to me, we tried to fulfil her wishes to visit as many places as we could in a wheelchair. We had great fun in Gibraltar, where we were allowed to drive up to the very top and spent lovely time with the monkeys. We enjoyed the stunning views from above to the bay; in that gorgeous weather, we saw Africa across the strait. We had sweet moments in the galleries and museums of Europe. In the Sistine Chapel in Rome, a dream from teenage years, exhausted we managed to sit on the bench and stay as long as we wanted. Our eyes were circling round without being able to stop on anything because there was so much there on the walls and on the ceiling, all the Bible stories in frescoes. The colours were so vivid after a recent restoration. Having rested for a while, we noticed the scene of the Creation of Adam on the ceiling just opposite, which immediately took dominance over all the spectacle. It was so realistic, down to earth. Adam, sitting on the ground as if just awakened to life by the breath of the Creator. The heavens were also unmistakably there, represented by a white backdrop of sky with the angels surrounding God under a veil. But he was very human, sweet old Daddy, stretching his hand to touch Adam's finger and charge him with the stewardship of the planet Earth before retiring 'to rest' from his work on the seventh day. She later bought from the art shops a picture, cropping up the hands from the Creation scene. In her family they had many little statuettes. Among them were David and Moses. The hands from the Creation scene in Vatican were to extend the collection.

The hands, I suspect, must have been a strict order from the Pope. They resonate with the moments of electing a new Pope when traditionally the hymn 'Veni Creator Spiritus' (Come Holy Spirit) is sung. In it the Holy Spirit is called 'Finger of the Hand Devine'. Beautiful hymn. Michelangelo's relation with his powerful sponsors from the church who always wanted to interfere with his artistic revelations was very bumpy. His passion was always to make sculptures while the church always wanted him to paint. The original iconic sculpture to David with the sling, on display in the art gallery in Florence, we could not visit but my wife was well satisfied with the replica on the town square. These were all dreams come true from her childhood family lessons on Renaissance.

Airline staff were very kind to us these years and provided a special platform for her wheelchair. She was lifted up to the aircraft door, and then I could walk behind her, down the aisle to the seat. However, I found it increasingly difficult to drive and attend to her needs at the same time, and I nearly had an accident in London; we had to stop driving this way.

Very soon package tours with their fixed schedules stopped being an option anymore, and we did not have money for private arrangements. We bought a special disability car that allowed me to place her wheelchair in the car, so need to transfer her to the car seat anymore. She was almost completely immobilised; could still stand on her feet for a minute if there was someone to lift her up and hold her. But that was all.

We hoped to travel abroad in the car to see more places. However, her condition was deteriorating rapidly; not able to stay relaxed in the chair for more than half an hour, although we got a very modern one, with adjustments, pressure relief cushions, and head support. There were moments when she felt very uncomfortable with cramps and tremors in the limbs, and there was nothing I could do to make her feel comfortable. She did not know what was causing her discomfort. Nevertheless, we had very sweet moments in the National Trust and royal gardens in England. Her disability card allowed us to park on spectacular places. We loved the flower show in Winchester Cathedral and going on the seafront on the southern beaches and the cliffs.

After a couple of years, she began struggling with eating, and swallowing sometimes went wrong. She needed someone to feed her on a regular basis; her hands turned woody. With all the rest of her basic needs, she had to be hoisted into her bed or chair for going around. The only pleasure that remained was watching TV or showering in the wheelchair. Rubbing her body and feet with a towel after a shower gave her an immense relief. During these special moments, she would look me in the eyes with a thankful heart and a barely noticeable smile, which made my heart melt. She was turning into a head attached to a body that she could no longer control. Her mind was not affected much, though, and was aware of everything going on.

After lots of prayers over the years, she got much better spiritually and went on a kind of plateau physically. However, her speech increasingly slurred, which became a big problem; she found it frustrating to communicate with anyone helping her. We acquired a talking tablet, similar to the one Stephen Hawking was using, but she did not like it still able to communicate through facial expressions and simple gestures.

Visits from friends gradually decreased. People just did not know what to say or how to cheer us up, knowing our situation, so they disappeared, except for some faithful Christian friends. As she felt embarrassed with her dignity affected, she no longer wanted to see people, anyway.

The situation we were in was changing me as well. For the first time, I found purpose and meaning in the little things around. I learned to accept the day as it came, without making plans and getting anxious for not achieving them. It was lovely to care for her, except for periods when her anxiety and agony increased; I just disintegrated without knowing what to do. At such moments, I prayed in tongues or in my mind. I kept to the promise that we will not be tested more than we can bear. It helped me when I looked to the cross where Jesus was once hanging, and I compared with what he had to endure for us to have life. We were going to spend eternity with him. Life had meaning: to glorify him in our life as in our death.

My Christian brothers were a great support throughout this period; we often met for breakfast, bible study and prayer. I remember once reading from the prophet Habakkuk in tears:

> Though the fig tree does not bud and there
> are no grapes on the vines,
> though the olive crop fails and the fields
> produce no food,
> though there are no sheep in the pen and no
> cattle in the stalls,
> yet I will rejoice in the Lord. I will be joyful in
> God my Saviour. (Habakkuk 3:17–18)

One Christmas, I helped her stand up for a moment and pretended to dance her favourite waltz from Shostakovich. Two years later, in the early spring, she passed away after getting an infection in the hospital.

When I lost my sister, my mum, my brother, and my father, I had a horrible time, but this was different. For the first time, death had become a reality for me personally, something that was awaiting for me too. It is true: we get connected in marriage, and when our better half dies, bits of our own flesh rip off and go in the grave too. We had been married for over forty years.

We had a thanksgiving service in the church, where our children, a few friends, and neighbours came to say goodbye. Her best friend took me to the crematorium afterwards, as I was not able to drive. The only other person there was the priest from my church. Her friend sang as the coffin disappeared slowly behind the curtain.

She was a sweet girl, honest and loving. She wanted to enjoy life: music, theatre, parties, food, seeing places, architecture, history. I felt sorry I did not provide enough. I did not protect her enough. After she was gone, it was a relief for her and for me, but I suddenly felt the emptiness. I felt really, really lonely in this world. When we were separated for years, I was lonely, but that was different. I knew she was there, far away, and I hoped that one day, she would rejoin me. I wished she was still here and that I could rub her feet and look her in the eyes with gratitude and love.

We buried her ashes in the churchyard, where we sat on the grass among the graves when we first arrived, looking to buy a home in the area. It was so peaceful with the birds singing in the woods and the sun shining. She said, "How beautiful! I could wish to die and be buried here," words now come true. She also said she had never thought, even in her wildest dreams, that she would be able to come and live in England, and she was extremely happy we were buying our home there.

> No one but You, O Lord…
> You are altogether lovely

and You're all I want to see
and when my life is through
I'm coming home to You.
That's all I want to do
just come home to You.

7

Epilogue

For everyone who calls on the name of the
Lord will be saved. (Romans 10:13)

I heard this question many times since I became a widow "If
you were to live your life again, which parts you would live
differently?" It was probably because I was behaving as if all
my life had finished. My wife passed away, my children had
gone back to my country of origin and it looked like they had
no intention of coming back again. I had health issues. But
lamentations were not a permanent feature of my character,
neither was running after the security that children could
provide for their old father. Yes, so much happened that we
shared together, but everyone has their own life and I was
thankful we did not have to be a burden to each other nor to
have to share all our problems intensely again. Past experience
is a strong bond for every family but it does not have to be a
bondage.

What would I do differently? We do not have a dress
rehearsal for our earthly life. Rather the earthly life is a dress
rehearsal for heaven. Better think of making the most of what is
left of it. I believe I am still 'work in progress' for the Lord. The

real question for me is "Where is the Lord calling me now?" Here in England or somewhere else?

After the political changes, poverty in some areas of Bulgaria reached unprecedented levels. In the Roma communities, the situation was really critical because of hostilities; crime was out of control. The Roma were still at the bottom of the society, despised and abused, and that provoked violent behaviour. There were strong sentiments of segregation in the rest of the population, because of the Roma's unusual culture and the crime that sprang out of poverty. That led to conflicts and isolation.

While still a carer for my late wife, one week I took a respite and joined a small group of evangelical Christians from Britain for a visit to the Roma community in Sofia. The streets were poor, with garbage scattered around and no proper sanitation. Yet they had a small Christian community and their own pastor. They needed help in organising activities with the children, Bible teaching, and ministry. My fellow evangelists, elderly people from Britain, were a remarkable group of sweethearts, who had the strange belief the Roma were one of the lost tribe of Israel. That was quite controversial, and I was about to ask them what they meant, what was their evidence? However, my heart melted seeing the love for these kids on their faces before they uttered any explanation. What better evidence did I need? I realised their belief was just a test for proud, educated scholars.

We humbly sang with them to the Lord, clapping our hands, and then made a tunnel with our arms, through which the kids passed, one by one. As each one emerged from the other side of the tunnel, we stopped, and the child was prayed for and blessed, called by name personally. As I was very privileged interpreting from English to Bulgarian, I could see the moment when their name was called. The face of the child changed from depressed and gloomy into a big smile, eyes beaming with radiance. I think a tear or two dropped from my eyes that day. At the same time, there was gypsy music and dances in the little square, where the leader of our group preached to hundreds through an interpreter provided by another church in Sofia. There I met an old friend and colleague of mine, a Christian, who was providing literature for the event. He suggested that I could far better serve the Lord with my profession.

I came back to England refreshed. Then thoughts about starting to write something appeared to dominate the days ahead and I did give it a go but later I went to Bulgaria again, this time to teach Medical Informatics in the University. It did not fill me with joy. I saw many people of my age competing for jobs there. For me it was not a good pay but it was probably essential to them, so I felt like robbing the country of their resources at a time of crisis. The students and some of the staff liked the new subject I was opening, but others did not. The attitude towards ex nationals, returning from the West, was that they should come back with millions to give away, preferably with a 'famous name' attached that they could use as a teaser in their bids for governmental support. However I did not have a famous name, neither was I bubbling with money. In the end I felt like useless intruder, so I came back home to my book writing.

Reading back what had been written I was not pleased very much. Too much anger, too much 'I..,I...' less about the Lord. Some friends found that the story was very sad, too pessimistic, with little hope even compared to the Book of Ecclesiastes in the Bible. I concluded that I need Part II to show my firm determination in making a new beginning and lift up the spirits. But which bits of my life so far I would like to live again differently?

For many years since I was born in the flesh, the Lord has been keeping me on the move for his own purpose. In the beginning of my life, I did not know him; I was blind to his presence and so often acted blindly. Later in life, he reached down and saved me. I became more aware of his good plans for me but still often failed to stay in his blessings by doing my own things. Sometimes, he wanted me to move, to come out of things I was doing, to "make the most of every opportunity" (Ephesians 5:16). But I settled quite often too low on the mediocre. He kept saying, "Up, up, up," yet I still did not follow and headed down. An opportunity often required to speak just one sentence in a conversation that the Lord brought about and to fully commit myself to the change of my life that would follow. Yet I did not speak that word, either showing pride or fearing failure. No opportunity remains unchallenged after you take it but that should not be a reason for not taking it.

Having sought God's wisdom for your future work as a leader, a moment will come when He will open a door and put you in a place where you will feel unmistakeably on top of everything needed for you to succeed: your knowledge above the knowledge of any rivals, your experience- the best of all; people will be there needing you desperately to tell them what to do and you will know it! Everything you may still be missing will be provided with the capabilities of people on your team or they will come on board just in time you need them. You just need to perceive it and trust the Lord. The main temptation at that moment will be to puff up yourself with self importance and plunge into narcissism. Instead, all you are going to do is to go straight for the goal set up before you, building up and trusting your team.

Other times in my life, he wanted me to stay still and wait for him to open another door, but I rushed in like a headless chicken. I often did not realise how many good things I already had and allowed myself to be tempted with chasing false treasures. I realise that far too often, I let go of the good things I had in life, especially professional knowledge and skills, with unreasonable quests for change, for something new, hungry for yet more knowledge, new experiences or fame. I drowned myself in information but failed to distil the wisdom. I abandoned good health and family, chasing highly demanding jobs, which were no longer dictated by the need to provide but to satisfy my selfish desires and proud ego. The Lord's purpose was not in them. Science, as any other profession, may demand sacrifice of family life and other things, but it would not produce good fruits if the Lord's purpose is not in it.

To be in the world means to be in the wild, where the laws of nature rule. Yet we have a foretaste of God's Kingdom here on earth when we come to faith and start following him. If we do not follow him, we find ourselves in the company of those who are "controlled by bit and bridle" (Psalm 32:9). Yes, it is difficult to know when to wait and when to act, to know God's plans for us. We struggle to understand God's sovereignty and our free will. Philosophers and theologians over the centuries pondered upon this question, and they still do. I am content to accept it as a paradox, since there are so many paradoxes in science too. How does that work? I do not know, but I believe it. And it is not 50-50. It is 100 percent destiny and 100 percent free will, in which we actually make our destiny. But we need to discern God's plan, his agenda in the broader world, so that we can become part of that plan by our own free will. The Lord will always give us the desires to do it, and will seldom force us into it. However, we need to seek wisdom in humility and prayer, and make him the source of all our important decisions in life (Romans 12:1–2).

I looked at the misery of the person I used to be and was glad that person died when I first encountered grace, which made it possible to forgive others, forgive myself, and let it go. Only then was I able to enter the Lord's rest (Hebrews 4). Before that, I was robbed by the most precious moments in life.

When I first visited the country of my birth after the political storms subsided, I felt I was without roots. Thankfully, my only roots were already in the vine (John 15:5). I was a branch, a living one, not the one destined for burning.

The world praises achievement in its own way. I was not a high achiever by its standards, but I have become a great achiever in the Lord's eyes. He took me from the middle of nowhere, showed me the whole world, and made me succeed in jobs I would never have been able to do on my own strength, facing challenges and having great fun. He always acknowledged my decision of what to do next and never got angry when I tried to do my own thing. He was pleased, letting me entertain all my obsessions, until I realised that my passion for him was the only one that satisfied. All our talents and achievements come from God, and to him belongs the honour, the praise, and the glory.

The most important decision for each one of us is the response we give to the calling of our Creator. I would like to see this book as an inspiration for the coming generations, to see them not be afraid or ashamed to put love in the cornerstone of their career and their life, to see their potential unleashed to the full, to see them saved for eternity.

May the Lord give me the wisdom to know when my timing comes so that I have the strength to finish well, to surrender my life to him in peace and not being a burden for anybody. He is my Lord. He has given me life, and he is entitled to take it back. When the time is right I would take delight handing it back and coming home, where he reserved a place for me to rest until he returns. We may fear going into that rest. How long will it take? It depends on the means and speed of travel. Time is a mystery. It might run faster for you than for someone else who boarded the fast train of the universe. One thing we know with certainty: there will be a new earth and a new heaven when we awake. It will be a magnificent journey with God throughout eternity.

I hope I will not die but pass beyond like Elijah. If I die, there should be laughter and no sorrow. Think of me as someone who just went out of sight. You better make sure you get there too, so I will not miss you. While you exist in this restrictive, material world, you are free to act and receive freedom and the gift of eternal life given to you by the one and true living God. He will come in the material world again, to judge the living and the dead. There may be millions or billions of earthly years until I am awaken, but for me, they will be like a blink of an eye because I went out of time. My life surpasses death. It does not break the continuity which started with my physical birth. Then I boarded a body, bound in space and time for a journey, just to be born again in spirit to partake in the Creator's mission on earth. There is no end of the life which started with that birth. We shall laugh together when we meet again, and there will be no remembrance of death, only life everlasting.

PART II
The Wonder of Life

1

THE WONDROUS YOU

Most certainly, your life started as a tiny microscopic cell in your mother's womb. All cells in plants and animals are similar. They are constructed with long molecules which exist because of the property of carbon atoms to bind to each other and make chains. Those chains form a backbone to which other essential elements like hydrogen, oxygen, nitrogen, phosphorus, sulphur, calcium may attach to make more complex structures: carbohydrates, proteins, and fats- the building material of life on Earth.

There is not much difference in principle between these organic macromolecules and the ordinary ones like water. But scientists have not yet found a plausible explanation of how they could come into existence spontaneously. It is the sheer size of the structures that makes them so special. The longer they are, the more strangely they start to behave, folding themselves or binding to others persistently in a very specific way and even replicating themselves under certain conditions. Their properties are so amusing and intriguing that one may think they came from another world. Take for example the so called fatty acids. They are fifteen or seventeen long chains (tails) of hydrocarbons: carbon atoms bonded with each other and with two hydrogen atoms as well. On one end a smaller composition of other hydrocarbons, including oxygen, phosphorus and nitrogen atoms as well, attaches to the 'tail' like a head. The head however is polarised because of the specific structure of the bonds connecting the atoms. The resulting molecule is called phospholipid, a building block of the cell membrane. Take a volume of phospholipids, shake them and all the heads will align and bond to each other to form a surface that can potentially close its ends and create an enclosure. The cell enclosure is made of two such surfaces in which the phospholipids are back to back with their tails. What a miracle! Yes, my book of cell biology explains how the natural process works and I still wonder. Where have all these forces of attraction came from?

The cell membrane encloses a fluid compartment that consists of a nucleus and numerous microorganisms: organelles. One type of organelle, mitochondria, acts like a booster of energy for the cell. All cells in the world look alike, but what makes each one unique in behaviour is its master control, encoded in the genes. Genes are in the nucleus, an inner compartment protected by yet another membrane. A small piece of control is encoded not in the nucleus but in the mitochondria. Primitive organisms, including microbes, are either single cells or a conglomeration of cells.

It was so fascinating for me, a computer scientist, to learn that this controlling information in humans is encoded in a linear fashion in twenty three long organic molecules, called chromosomes, folded and packed in the nucleus. Fully unfolded from just one cell, they could stretch as far as the moon. They are all made of DNA (Deoxyribonucleic acid), a chain which spontaneously curls in the form of a helix under the forces of the molecular bonds between its constituents. Two strands of the molecule, precisely complementing each other's constituents, are bound together so that they are securely protected against forces trying to change them.

The picture of that super long double helix structure immediately made me associate it with a Turing machine and its tape. What is even more striking is that this information is encoded digitally by using four types of simpler and shorter molecules called amino acids. Strangely, there are only twenty amino acids in all terrestrial living organisms, plants and animals alike. Four of them serve as an alphabet and are used in the DNA of the genes to encode important information, not only about reproduction but also about growth and functioning of the organs of an adult; for example, how to synthesise particular proteins needed for energy release, repair damage, and other physiological functions, including how to engage with our environment. The process of control involves *transcription*, during which the double helix is unzipped in a particular location, the information from there is copied, and transferred into another molecule with slightly different encoding. Then the 'tape' of the DNA is zipped back. Astonishing. Every computer scientist can see there is an alphabet and a language here in this design. It suggests there is a mind behind it, a Creator.

Yes, each member of the human race starts as a single cell, an egg of the mother. When fertilised by the father's sperm, it starts to replicate. First it divides into two, and then those two split into another two to become four all together. And then each of those continues to replicate, on and on. At each stage of division, the total number of cells is doubled, and so after many stages, the number of the cells increases exponentially. Looking like a bubbling sphere in the beginning, the group slowly begins to take the shape of a new living organism. Each of the cells, same in the beginning, develops and differentiates in the process to perform its specific role in the body, but it always stays in harmony with the others. The differentiation is controlled by the instructions programmed inside the cell and by the environment. The DNA chain unzips in different areas and exposes (expresses) just the genes needed for the particular cell differentiation. Gene expression is important part of the development of a human body, a process covered with mysteries scientists are working hard to uncover. At some point, nine months after conception, these replications slow down, and you are ready to be born. Cells continue to replicate after birth, especially in the developing brain, but not at the same rate. It is amazing what our bodies represent as a biological structure. Trillions of microscopic cells, working in sync. Is this a natural process or a miracle?

For me, it is both.

Taken in isolation, cells are not that smart in behaviour or complex in structure, yet they are more complex than a factory with hundreds of wonderful machines, performing complex biochemical processes. Bound together, trillions of them, they form a human being: you. A trillion is a ten with twelve zeroes behind it; that is more than the visible stars in our galaxy. In each one of them, you have a tape with information that is long enough to stretch to the moon. The human body is a galaxy of its own.

It is fact that the cells comprising most animals and humans come about after a single cell, from the mother, combines with a sperm cell from the father, and starts replicating over and over again to form the body organs and ultimately a new individual. Think of it. All the cells of the body of the mother were some time ago created this way too, including that originator cell of her child, an egg from her body. The body of the mother started from a single cell too- an egg from her own mother. It means tracing back over generations, in simple terms, one cell has been replicating over and over again and kept alive for a very, very long time even though many generations of individuals from the family chain had died. But for how long? When did this process actually start? When did the first human being of my 'clan' come into existence?

According to some scientific theories, human organisms developed as a result of the reproduction of ever simpler and simpler organisms back in time. On the lowest level of the construction, organic macromolecules are thought to have come into being from simpler ones under certain conditions. Science is now engaged in trying to pinpoint and recreate a plausible scenario for that. However, it's hard to determine whether a certain long chain of events took place over billions of years.

According to an existing hypothesis, the beginning of life in primitive organisms started in primordial times, billions of years ago. It happened in deep ocean vents, where magma coming from beneath the ocean floor interacted with water. If we take the picture of volcanic magma turning into dust when it cools down, then we could appreciate the story of Creation in the Bible as a metaphor of the same process. That primitive organism divided and lived until it became someone living today. During that time, it has been changing, modifying, and adapting. That affected the genes themselves. The blueprint carried in our genes, according to modern science, imprints a unique exposure to events that have been happening over millions of years up until now, the evolution process suggested by Darwin, who did not know anything about DNA. His theory was that during this process, the organisms of multiple generations changed and adapted to the environment. It is now found that some of the changes were firmly fixed in the genes because most changes occurred through random mutations of the genes. As the environment changed during geological history, so did the organisms as some mutations were beneficial for survival, but others not. Those who's random mutations were not beneficial for the new environment died and became extinct. Only the 'fittest' survived, a process called natural selection. It is not a fantasy. Farmers throughout history used artificial selection to improve their crops and stock. The Bible talks about it too. (Genesis 30:31-43)

The advancements of science in areas like genetics, anthropology, archaeology, geological dating, and others strengthened and further enriched Darwin's theory of evolution, helping put together more bits of the jigsaw of life, although it opened even more blanks and arguments in other areas. It became evident that the process of natural selection was not only driven by competition to survive, but also by some forms of cooperation between members of one or multiple populations.

Evidence for evolution is abundant but not conclusive. There are gaps in the evolutionary chain observed in fossils, that need to be filled with evidence if all hypothetical claims are to be accepted beyond doubt. For example, science has evidence that members of one group of species evolve, but there is no abundant evidence for evolving from one species to a completely new one. It might be that other mechanisms are involved beyond natural selection. Take as an example the strange extinction of the dinosaurs. It might have been a result of a catastrophic cataclysm, a collision of the Earth with another massive body, which selectively made life for entire group of species on Earth impossible. That could be called natural selection too but of a different kind. What happened and is still happening cannot be isolated from external events taking place anywhere in the solar system and indeed in the whole universe.

At the same time, studies of our origin as a species discovered striking new evidence supporting the biblical references of the origin of humankind. Research in the ancestral lines of the existing human population, based on genetic analysis of the mitochondria, which is passed by female ancestors through their eggs, found that all the people existing in the world today must have originated from a single woman: the so-called Mitochondrial Eve. Similarly, studies of the Y chromosome in the nucleus of our cells, which is only passed by male ancestors, found that all the population today must have originated from a single man who existed at the same time in human history as

Mitochondrial Eve. This does not mean that both individuals were the only ones existing at the time. It only suggests that the other lines of descent, if any, became extinct.

The discovery of the DNA structure in 1953 was a fundamental breakthrough in life sciences. By 2003, the Human Genome Project was able to read out all the information recorded in the human DNA. This information led to an explosion of new discoveries about the way the human body develops and works. However, scientists still do not understand all of it in full. One day, we might. It is an exciting area to work in, which opens a new era for the treatment of disease.

2

MATTER AND SPIRIT

The ancient philosophers like Aristotle viewed the material world as infinite in space with no beginning or end. However modern science accepts the big-bang theory and experimentally supports it. Whether the universe had a beginning or not it does obey the second law of thermodynamics, which in simple terms states that all material structures, whether inanimate or live, on a universal scale, are spontaneously changing from order to disorder. The entropy (the measure of disorder) in the universe is increasing all the time. It means ultimately matter is irreversibly in decay. According to the first law of thermodynamics energy in a closed system is constant. It cannot be destroyed or created but just converted from one form to another. The spontaneous flow of energy will stop when matter in the universe comes to a thermodynamic equilibrium. It means no life as we know it would be possible. The universe will then be dead.

Energy is a mystery. We can measure it but we cannot explain what it is and why it is here, in the universe, in the first place. Where has it come from? One direction of conversion: from mass to heat and waves is well proven in the nuclear reactors we build, but the other direction, energy to mass, has not been clearly seen yet in reality beyond doubt. That might be happening in the black holes of the universe and in the first moments of the Big Bang, when all the matter of the universe was created, according to our theories. However the black holes are 'singularities'- places where physicists admit the laws of nature break down. At the moment we do not have a theory explaining what happens there.

Science used to define matter through its structural properties: anything composed of atoms and taking space or has mass. But we know modern science now considers matter as being space itself. Physicists are also trying to distinguish 'ordinary matter' from 'dark matter' or something else. Ever since the famous equation $E=m^*c^2$ turned up in the game, they have been bemused of the fact that ordinary matter could actually 'dissipate' into its so called 'energy at rest' in the form of heat and waves. The energy at rest is different from the kinetic energy, which moving matter has and which turns into heat or else when the material object comes to rest by hitting something big. It is also different from the potential energy every material object has when placed in a gravitational or other kind of field that exerts forces on it. The energy at rest is only connected with the actual mass of the material object.

To make the matter even more confused now physicists are trying to define vacuum as composed of matter and antimatter. Hence matter could actually turn to be 'nothingness' as well. Science of the 21st century is increasingly exploring incoherent models that are very difficult to test. It allows itself to go beyond the rational in a fantasy world, similar to the one described by Lewis Carroll in *Alice's Adventures in Wonderland*. We do not call that world irrational, because it isn't! It is just that our ability to investigate and understand the material world has many limitations, which we will discuss later.

At the same time we are unique among the species on Earth in having the ability to engage with a world beyond matter. This engagement transcends reason without contradicting it. Even some materialists, atheists, feel their scientific work sometimes points to something beyond empirical knowledge, a reality that cannot be rationalised. They would accept as plausible, and even put forward a hypothesis that we might be 'Sims': simulated beings in a giant computer run by super powerful aliens, like in the science fiction film *The Matrix*. Some meta-physicists and theologians elaborated on this hypothesis but there is no way we can prove it or even find out about it. It might be a plausible meta-physical proposition, but to me it sounds more like worshiping aliens which, while living in the same material world as us, chose not to leave any clues in their creation. The Hellenistic culture has already been there in the fantasy world of invented gods- the idols humanity does not need to worship again. I do not believe the existence of super powerful aliens, which created us that way, but even if they did, they would themselves have been created by the one truly immaterial living Spirit of God. Not only is the Spirit real but also primal. In the rest of this book we will consider the rationale for this assertion.

3

SMARTEST ANIMAL OR TEMPLE OF GOD

Man's fate is like that of the animals; the same fate awaits
them both: As one dies, so dies the other. All have the same
breath; man has no advantage over the animal. Everything
is meaningless. All go to the same place; all come from
dust, and to dust all return. (Ecclesiastes 3:19–20)

Natural science considers humans a biological organism, just
like any other kind of animal: member of the continuum of
species on Earth. Without the Spirit of God in us, "we come
from dust and to dust we return," and that is the end of it.
Indeed, without faith, just as part of nature, we are not a great
deal different from the animals. There is no meaning in nature;
it contains live matter, controlled by "selfish genes", lifeless
stars, radiation, black holes: a universe with a birth and death,
though some may suggest it is eternal on its own merit. The
only way we could make sense of nature is to accept the reality
of what is beyond nature- the spiritual. One cannot prove the
existence or the nonexistence of Creator God with infinity and
eternity of higher cardinality than nature. But if God does not

exist, then life has no meaning. We are like lonely animals in the wilderness, where the only other friendly creatures are the animals from our herd, and our only purpose is to reproduce ourselves. Is that what life is all about?

The drive to replicate, to reproduce ourselves, may be coming from the self-behaving nature of the macromolecules we are built of. They gave some scientists reasons to believe they also made themselves by chance, from simpler ones. Richard Dawkins, the anti-theist, explains the wonder of life with 'simple rules' governing individual components of a living system: macromolecules, cells, individual members of a colony like termites, birds in murmuration or else. He explains how living structures are grown 'bottom-up' by self-assembly, and makes a bizarre non-scientific conclusion: there is no design plan for all this. He even claims to 'prove' his statement, to his audience of pupils at school, with an experiment he had performed using a computer program model for murmurations. In fact that model is in computer science terms called a 'distributed system'. The gigantic computer network, the Internet, actually works on similar principles, built into the lower level protocols of each node of the network. And there is a design plan for that, actually not a very simple one! Even though that design still belongs to the ultimate Creator who created man.

We may say there is no human design plan behind the living systems, but does that mean there is no intelligent creator? Where did the forces of attraction in molecules come from? Where did the elementary particles building the atoms and the molecules come from? And ultimately, why is it they have those specific properties? What is the purpose and the meaning?

The universe, though very beautiful and intriguing for a scientist, is a dangerous place for humans to be. To say that life has no purpose is to make it even more dangerous. A human being without the Spirit of God is a ruthless animal. But if we have been given the gift of life, then there must be some meaning in protecting it and sustaining it. We are here. We could try doing something about it. We could make the world a better place before we leave it.

Today, every so often, we need to make ethical decisions we never had before. They bring us back to the stories of the Tree of Knowledge and the Tree of Life in the Bible. Those stories compel us to look to the origin of life, not only from our own perspective but from the perspective of the Creator too. While science may one day be able to explain the self-assembling properties of organic macromolecules, it is not able to explain why so often in its history, humanity gets it so wrong. In the absence of faith, individuals only trust themselves and make enemies of everyone else. But are we really meant to live only for ourselves? Are we really that clever individually or in alliances? Being clever is a blessing. Cleverness may save us in the short run, but not always in the long. Why do the crucifixion and the resurrection of Jesus Christ have no meaning to so many clever people? Does it really contradict rational thinking? Is it really irrelevant to the existence of the human race? We do not even take the time to explore the evidence for it, the events that took place when humanity changed its dating from BC (Before Christ) to AD (Anno Domini).

God, whom we know from the Bible, is a spirit (John 4:24) and does not depend on anything material for his being. However, for a short period of time, he lived in the material world in the appearance of a man. He engaged with the world in the form of His Son to bring about radically new transformation. What was it all about? God created us in his image to be holy and loving like him. However, since our ancestors, Adam and Eve, failed to obey the instructions of the Creator, we were placed in that part of the universe occupied by an evil power. This is not a cinema thriller or just a concept in our mind, but real. There is a battle here between good and evil, but it is not a battle between independent powers. Rather, it is a war between a sovereign and a rebel. This is the scene on which we are called to counteract evil. Our nature endowed with free will may give evil a foothold in our life and corrupt it. But we are justified by always believing that good is stronger than evil and by trying to live by that.

People struggle with the question "Who created evil? Did God create it?" Well, God created us with free will and this already includes evil as a possibility. We are free to disobey Him, which is already an evil act because rejecting God's order has enormous consequences. But there are no simple answers to evil in the world and we struggle with them all our life as Christians. If you think not accepting God's grace will make your life easier then don't accept it, but I am sure it will not make your life easier! Instead of trying to judge God for His Creation why not just accept the Creation as it is and see what we can do to have meaning in it, to keep it out of evil while we live? Instead many individuals try to live by outwitting others for their own selfish advantage, the only principle they think matters.

After all, unlike the animals, whatever our individual experience in life is, we have free will to consciously do whatever we like to others. Because of that, we often do to other people something we would not like them doing to us. Consequently, every now and then, we come to a point of life when we long for justice from a neutral authority. Our human nature seeks security and love from someone and for someone, someone to shield us from the dangers surrounding us or at least to support us in the struggle. We often have goals, passions and aspirations deep down in the core of our heart, which we feel right to fulfil, but they cannot be realised without the support of someone much more powerful than us. In our mutual coexistence, it is not possible to have justice without some principles to define it, a 'standard for universal goodness', acknowledged by all. Without that, any conflict that may arise from our coexistence as individuals or nations could only be resolved like in the wild nature, by the stronger side coercing and subduing the weaker. Sometimes, human conflicts are so dramatic that they lead to violence, suffering, and death. Then we long for an independent, authoritative, just, and holy superpower to vindicate us. We are created with that drive within us. We long for a friendly relationship with that power. Until we find that relationship, there will always be something missing in our lives, and we will feel insecure.

Holiness does not come near evil unless a price is paid. Otherwise, there will be a pollution of sin, and holiness will be gradually diluted into evil. But the fact is that there is a mysterious force here that sustains the gradient towards holiness. The Old Testament tells us that the priests of the ancient Jews were compelled by this situation to sacrifice animals in the act of penitence, to bring forgiveness and reconciliation between the affected parties and restore the ordained order, to keep that gradient going. They were being prepared for the universal spiritual act of redemption with the coming of a Messiah. The New Testament tells us that the Messiah did come to make a breakthrough in human history and effectuate in part, through faith and action, the world as it ought to be. He was conceived in the womb of a woman by the Holy Spirit and born as human- the Son of God, and at the same time the Son of Man, not a superman. His mission was not only to redeem, but to save from the fatal disease we all suffer since birth: death. He sacrificed himself willingly to bring that healing: "For God so loved the world that he gave his one and only Son, that whoever believes in him shall not perish but have eternal life" (John 3:16). This is a free gift, offered by grace, but I do not think it works automatically. The only way we can be sure is to give an answer to him while we live: "Thank you Lord. Yes, I believe. Please forgive my past life of meaningless. I receive this gift".

There is no simpler and better way to define holiness and love than this story summarising the message of the Bible, a message of salvation. Every human being is able to understand it and choose to believe it. This, in short, is the story of the Bible. This is my faith.

If you as a scientist find this story too simplistic or incredibly stupid, don't worry; you are not alone. The ancient Jews rejected the complete story too, even though some of them witnessed it. For a long time, I could not believe it was true either. Apostle Paul could not believe for some time; he persecuted the early Christians. His story of conversion in the book of Acts was indeed remarkable. Many people, including prominent evangelists and preachers, felt the same way before they believed. So welcome to the club.

The good news, however, is that God knew humankind would have a problem accepting this by pure rationalising, and he did something about it. 1 Corinthians 1:21–23 says, "For since in the wisdom of God the world through its wisdom did not know him, God was pleased through the foolishness of what was preached to save those who believe. Jews demand signs and Greeks look for wisdom, but we preach Christ crucified." Here the theologians of today agree that the name 'Jews' stands for the dogmatic, legalistic religion Christ was against. It can also apply to the stagnated legalistic Christian church which made the same mistakes later and still makes today. The name 'Greeks' stands for the pagan philosophers which were content with worshiping idols. It can equally apply to the atheistic, pagan metaphysics. 1 Corinthians 2:14 continues "The person without the Spirit does not accept the things that come from the Spirit of God but considers them foolishness, and cannot understand them because they are discerned only through the Spirit."

It sounds quite elitist, I agree. "You, the believers are God's chosen. Really?" In fact it is quite the opposite. You have to humble yourself, bow down to this 'foolishness' and accept the offer on His terms, not yours. And the offer is open to everyone. The key to accepting the universal truth is the Holy Spirit, on whom we depend in believing and not perishing. He enables us to make a rational decision to choose to trust and believe by means beyond rationality. It is a mystery I chose to believe.

In the years after 2010, I organised a seminar on Christianity for scientists and engineers who exerted a strong influence on society by virtue of their leadership positions. They were meant to be influential to their children as well. Most of the participants said that everyone had their own truth. But where we have two or more incompatible truths, then at least one of them is not the 'true truth'. All of them could be untrue, but to deny the existence of one universal truth is not sensible logically, because that would mean the denial is untrue as well. The debate eventually came down to the belief of the existence of God (theism) or his nonexistence (atheism). Of course, the affirmation that we are unable to definitively know the answer to that question (agnosticism) holds too.

At first it looked like the agnostic view was the most respectful because of the apparent neutrality. If we cannot know the answer to the question about God's existence why do we need to make a choice? Just leave it at that. But humanity can only postpone the answer to this very important question for a very short time until the moment we are faced with a real life question of morality. If we need to make a judgement between right and wrong where is the moral principle going to come from? There are many different incompatible judicial systems in the world, not to mention those hijacked and weaponised by single handed brutal and corrupt dictators. The agnostic world view leaves vacuum in the moral space and a society without a sense of direction.

One of the common objections to theism from those whose world view gravitated to agnosticism was that there was not enough evidence for the existence of God. But how much evidence do you need to have? I agree that having as much evidence as possible is better, because it matters what you believe. It is important to believe what is true. In the science of physics, we have to have 100 percent coverage from the existing facts to declare a theory truthful. It means there should be no single fact that contradicts it. It does not mean such facts cannot be found in the future, which may disprove it. In that sense, any scientific theory is also based on faith. But it is impossible to have 100 percent coverage from facts in the material world about someone who created that world and whose descriptions are infinitely and unimaginably larger, beyond the material world.

However, there is good evidence for the existence of God. God is gentle and does not want to provide so much evidence for his existence as to coerce people to believe in him. He created us with free will. Yet he provided enough evidence to trust him. After we study the evidence, we can take a leap of faith and believe.

The most irrational objection to the existence of God, however, came from atheists. They were convinced there was no evidence for the existence of God at all. Scientists have a strong appetite for rational thinking. But they also are in the business of argument. Most prestigious schools of science have classes to teach students how to argue. Thank God, we cannot do a good job in science and engineering without rational thinking and argument. But the bad side of the scientists, including me, is that they are sometimes unreasonably stubborn. They pride themselves in being intellectuals and often find it difficult to accept that they are wrong. This is because in a scientific discourse, it would imply the other party is more clever. We sometimes pay much more attention to our own personal importance than to the truth.

To assert that God does not exist is just another form of faith, because the statement cannot be proved. It is a choice.

And it is the least rational of all choices because it is the assertion of an universal negative, which is very hard to test. Atheists think of our God as being an entity like the multitude of pagan gods of the Greeks and therefore they would have to probe every single corner of the universe and beyond to check that he is not there. When asked if it was possible that God exists, Richard Dawkins, the most influential anti-theist of our time, said that when he considered all options, he found it was plausible, but he rejected the possibility altogether. It was simply his choice. The fact is that we cannot prove by pure mathematical reasoning either the existence or the nonexistence of God.

It may come as a surprise to some to know that one cannot prove or disprove many things in physics, either. Despite all wonders of nature and its laws, theories in physics which provide the understanding of how everything works always remain just theories. Stephen Hawking, in his book *A Brief History of Time*, wrote, "Any good theory is always provisional, in the sense that it is only a hypothesis: you can never prove it. No matter how many times the result of experiments agree with some theory, you can never be sure that the next time the result will not contradict the theory. On the other hand you can disprove the theory by finding even a single observation that disagrees with the prediction of the theory."

What does that mean? It means engineering operates through faith. And that includes the design of bridges and airplanes. And yet we all fly; we all cross bridges, though sometimes we fear. Science and engineering do well for us. Why are we afraid to take a leap of faith and trust the manual of human relationships, the Bible, given to us by the very Creator of the laws of physics?

Scientists are engaged in uncovering the laws of nature and gathering knowledge about the material world we live in. We are passionate about it. It is often difficult for nonscientists to see the driving force behind it. One may think it is always money or innovations to sell or a war to win. In fact, it is not always that. Most often, it is intellectual curiosity, the strong desire to know what it is and how it works. Einstein as a child was bemused by the compass hand, moved by the earth's magnetic field. Later in life he preferred the quiet of the patent office to earn his living while satisfying the desire of his heart with theoretical physics alongside it, without having to bow down to university professors telling him what to do. He said that the joy of seeing and understanding was the greatest gift he had in life.

There is so much excitement in inventing new scientific models or improving old ones based on existing observations. A new theory in science these days is usually a result of the efforts of many people engaged in theoretical as well as complex and heavy experimental work, depending on modern technology. No one can deny that science, as a collective enterprise, is also driven by the needs of humanity for technological advancement. Our life desperately needs the knowledge that comes from science, but we naturally fail to realise that any knowledge is given to us on discretion from the Creator.

What science uncovers is a hidden knowledge. "The secret things belong to the Lord our God, but the things revealed belong to us and to our children forever, that we may follow all the words of this law" (Deuteronomy 29:29). God deliberately hid this knowledge (Genesis 2:15–17) because it could cause us harm without first mastering wisdom of far greater importance: the moral code and the message of salvation. Loving parents don't give their children knives to play with. They are hidden away, and that protects them. It does not mean that when children become adults, they may not try to exercise their free will by using a knife for the wrong reason. But at least they have been given a lesson about the danger. Within the framework of that message in the Bible, we have been given freedom to experiment, research, and unravel the ways the laws of nature operate as well as make use of them.

Humans, as part of the material world God created, possess a unique feature in that world: to transcend our physical origin by having a spirit in us too, which is able to marry with the spirit of God and engage with him on an equal basis. Together, we embody His temple in the world (1 Corinthians 6:19–20, 12-27, Ephesians 2:21-22,).

4

AMBASSADORS IN THE WORLD

See, I am doing a new thing! Now it springs up; do
you not perceive it? I am making a way in the desert
and streams in the wasteland. (Isaiah 43:19)

Psychologists speculate that we are the only creatures retaining
our identity, our sense of self, over a long period of time (in
fact, for a lifetime). They deny this quality exists in animals.
Yet neuroscientists cannot find any structure in the human
brain that carries our self. The self, they say, does not exist
anatomically in the brain. Even when half of someone's brain
is removed and memories are wiped out as a result of injury,
people still can retain their own identity, with links to the
past. Physiologically, may be large aggregations of neurons in
the brain (potentially all of it) are involved in our sense of self.
Maybe it's just a repeating pattern of oscillations in our neural
network that carries our self. This awaits a scientific discovery.
But although informatics may one day manage to analyse and
model all the processes in our brains in detail, will it find the
ultimate purpose of our lives? Why are we here?

Some philosophers claim that the immaterial soul does not
exist. They assume self-awareness depends only on something

material. Some of them go further, trying to persuade us that there is no such thing as human integrity; that our behaviour exclusively depends on the circumstances and the pressures that come from the environment. We are good, they say, as long as our goodness is not tested too harshly. But history is full of examples confirming that is not always the case. For example, they are not able to explain how it was possible that Maximilian Kolbe, a Christian priest, offered himself to die instead of another prisoner in Auschwitz in 1941. The materialistic view of the soul is not able to explain why some people suddenly change their attitudes and way of life completely; while retaining their sense of self, they become completely different persons. They cannot explain Paul's conversion on the road to Damascus.

The atheists hastily jump into such debates to say that the human brain, having made a 'critical number' of neural connections as a result of the learning process, can suddenly transition into a new state of mind. As if the human brain works on nuclear chain reactions. Such materialistic explanation sounds great but it means nothing in regards to consciousness. It springs from the conviction that human consciousness is purely based on computations of sufficient complexity; in other words, based on information processing as we know it from computer science and AI today. No one managed to map human neuron cells networks to 'brain states' yet, but that is not the point. Can science really ever tell us what human consciousness is? Can we define it? And how has it come to be?

We are, more or less, shaped by the environment. It is the essence of life. We change over time. The longer we live, the less we can identify ourselves with the previous self. Our characters do change over time, for good or for bad. Yet my life experience tells me that there is a dominant pattern in each of us that does not change very easily. Christian theologians call it Natural Law, the law that God set in Creation. It may express itself in the way we are wired at our physical birth, but one way or another, we are also all part of a connected world, where our character expresses itself and our integrity hugely matters. If we lose our integrity, we lose everything. There is a mysterious force in the world which is creating a gradient up towards good in the battles against evil. Where did it come from? That gradient is meant to shape us so that we can become more and more like God and retain our integrity. That is how we are meant to be, but until we receive the spirit of God in us, we might get lost, without direction and purpose in life.

Animals have to adapt and compete to survive in the wild. In contrast, our physical survival as individuals among others is more or less granted, thanks to the knowledge we have been let discover how to use natural resources and the general principles of coexistence we agree to. So far as we keep to them (Matthew 6:31–33). The human race is called to a different model of behaviour, such that could empower us to live in harmony with each other. Yet we often fail. But wherever we are as Christians, we are called to be different, not conforming to "the pattern of this fallen world" (Romans 12.2). We are called to have an impact, to transform the world according to a heavenly pattern, to make a difference by continuing to be in the world but not of it. It suggests we are meant to transcend the physical. We belong to the spiritual.

These days, I ask myself what a difference a retired IT man could make in the world for the better? Technology is advancing with an ever increasing speed by the collective effort of millions of young scientists with razor-sharp brains, and I barely manage to keep pace with the change there; I hope at least to make a humble contribution. I am thankful I can still manage to read and enjoy articles in scientific magazines. Trade and business changed so dramatically in the information age that the dynamics could only be mastered by the youngsters themselves.

Yet youngsters always seem to ignore moral teaching, considering it outdated and restrictive to their ambitions. But regardless of the advancement of knowledge about the material world, the basis for human relationships and ethics remain the same. They do not change. The actions of the characters in the Bible speak a simple truth which is invariant of time, culture, or scientific advancement, and has been accessible to people throughout history, including the uneducated. What young people always need is the wisdom to know their purpose, what they have been created for, and to establish a strategy for their life. They need to get their priorities right; they must know when to wait patiently and when to act. They need to persevere, to be encouraged, and above all, to love whatever they are doing, wherever they are, and to master the skill to be assertive at the same time.

To be confident and assertive in life does not mean to be inflated with self-importance. How can we love and have a purposeful life if we do not know our "why"? Ken Costa, in his book *Know Your Why*, writes, "A question that goes right to the heart of our sense of being and belonging in the world, Why Am I Here? And not just here on earth. Why am I in this city? Why am I here in this job, this church, this club, this group? Why am I here?"

It is not possible to give a reasonable answer to that question without first answering the call of Christ. If it is yes, the priorities are clear. If the answer is no, they remain ambiguous and ill founded. Confidence disappears.

Scientists and engineers, exploring and subduing nature, need to know the Creator as well. Otherwise, they are lost in their own world of self-importance and become subdued by nature instead. Christians need to be able to understand them better, to give them the same grace which they themselves received when they believed. Whatever our world views are and whatever we do, we are not just individuals but relate to each other and depend on one another: in our families, at our workplace, and in church, society, and the nation. Without that connection, whatever we do would be without value.

It is a challenge of even higher proportion when the encounter with those who are lost happens across cultures and nationalities. Regardless of ever-changing alliances, the world today is full of changing nations, as it has always been, since the days of old.

4.1 The World of Nations

> But the line dividing good and evil cuts
> through the heart of every human being.
> —A. Solzhenitsyn

Travelling across the countryside in England on Saturday in the summer, one could see this picture in every village: men dressed in white playing cricket, an almost ritualistic game. There are just a few cricket fans on the village green this weekend; fans and friends of the players, sipping their pints slowly, giving occasional lazy outbursts of acclaim to encourage both teams. Sitting on the other side of the pitch on a lonely bench, I do not follow the game. I do not fully understand it, anyway; I played just once and never spent time to learn the rules. Although I do not know the game, I like the spirit of it. The teamwork does not seem to require a great deal of interpersonal engagement or any close encounters with the opposition, either. It is not so much a tournament as a shared activity, which includes the fans as well. Do not like it? Then play rugby, a violent game for gentle players in close encounter, not like soccer, a gentle game for violent players heading for a collision. Neither of these games are for me now, after my heart started to misfire, so I take the opportunity to enjoy the golden autumn scene behind the pitch and plunge into meditation.

Old jokes aside, it is true that the British like the comfort of their own space and do not want to see it taken over by intruders. Yet they are admirable for their enormous capacity to smile and accept intruders to become like one of them after all, but on their own terms. Something remains from the years of the empire which, despite all its flaws and its failures, sought not to completely annihilate the foreign cultures it met, but to ameliorate and preserve them. I realise I need a lot more time to be able to say, "I am British," yet I am not Bulgarian anymore, either. I feel like an alien wherever I go. If it was not for the Christian friends I had here, life would have been very lonely for me indeed. I like going on a holiday to my country of origin. But I don't feel at home there anymore. I wish I could be a citizen of the world. Instead, I am a mere naturalised citizen. Yet by faith and grace, a friend of God who let me step into His Kingdom.

It was defiance to God which caused the people to build the tower of Babel (Genesis 11:1–9). A new technological invention- bricks, made them think that they became so clever that they did not need God. As a result they were scattered over the face of the earth and were unable to understand each other. From then on, tribes began to turn into nations. Since then, each one of us has happened to be born in a nation. Nations form around language, ethnicity, culture, and state boundaries. With their diversity and, often, incompatibility, in conflict with each other, they exist in the same wilderness as individual human beings in nature. Just as the world of individuals, the world of nations is a fallen world, where selfishness rules. Countries have self-interest and, consequently, borders and defences. How can we cross these borders with the message Christ has for all of us? The language is a barrier, isn't it? I have been blessed with speaking more than just my mother tongue. How can I make the best use of it?

After Bulgaria joined the EU, I went on a trip to Ochrid; it was my first visit to Macedonia. The coach was full of other people from Sofia; the journey was a kind a pilgrimage to our common ancestors and missionaries, the disciples of Cyril. On our return, the border crossing was blocked by long queues, and we had to wait for hours to get through. There are beautiful views in the mountains of Ossogovo. I had time for a short reflection.

What was it that made the ridge of this mountain a border, a divide between people who spoke dialects of the same language? What kind of people were the rulers of this land over the ages: Alexander the Great, the emperors of Rome and Byzantium, Simeon I, Ivan Assen II, Stefan Dušan, the Ottoman sultan, Tito? There have been kingdoms and rulers over the centuries in the Balkans; nations have risen and fallen, but rarely have people of these lands from the Adriatic to the Black Sea been free, and at the same time united, for more than half a century. Now people from Split would find it difficult to understand those in Varna, but the language only gradually changes as you travel eastwards from Split. It was not God's will to have one dominant nation in the Balkans for long. We tried our own Balkan Tower of Babel, Tito's Yugoslavia, and it did not work. Why was that? The great European powers were not in agreement? The East and West meddling all the time, you think?

Why is it, unlike many other countries in Europe, the Balkans experience instability and total social, political, and spiritual shake-up every half a century, with complete obliteration not only of the negative but also of the positive values from the past experience? Why is it that they lose past identity and search for a new identity again and again? Despite many outbursts of revival in Bulgarian history, for example, one cannot identify a long term of peaceful existence. It is difficult to escape this observation, and it is even more painful to accept it. After the collapse of the Communism in Europe, the descendants of the people who translated the Gospel into their own language, before the Germans and the English, found themselves without faith again. Some cynics say, "Have they had it ever?"

The value system of the young generation after the transition to a free market was based on discontent and the degraded morality of the atheist elite. Our generation before them was still underpinned by some Christian values from our grandparents. However, the following generation grew cynical, arrogant, and difficult to talk to. While we and our children were distorted in over-disciplining, their upbringing lacked discipline, immersed in an overdose of unrestrained liberty. Seldom experiencing true love in their family, they became individualists, without a sense of duty. They were also missing their identity. Their identity was no longer given to them by the state, providing jobs and an ideological boost. Frustrated, they had to find an identity of their own.

There was a spiritual vacuum in the hearts of the people, and there was a danger that it might be filled with dangerous explosives. There was a hunger for supernatural experience, and the media was full of occult rubbish. On one occasion, I pleaded to the director of one of the TV channels to stop a programme called *Fortune Tellers* (Ясновидци). We should not underestimate the importance of such events since the occult is not equal to charlatanism. I believe people with supernatural power to dabble in the future do exist. However, individuals with strong Christian faith must always ask themselves who is behind that power and what their motives are. If we do not have a clear understanding of the source of power, it is extremely dangerous to organise or participate in such practices, especially in the media. Christian teachings make a distinction between prophets and fortune tellers. In the history of humankind, according to the Bible, prophets are people with a clear understanding that they were sent by God to protect and guide people or to warn about their wrongdoing. Prophets are people with a lot of responsibility, reaching sacrificial commitment. They are called to do good. As opposed to that, fortune tellers are associated with dark forces and act with unclear, often selfish motives. They are forbidden by God (1 Chronicles 10:13–14).

My country, as all other European countries, had a pagan history of superstition. In Germany, there was a wave of occult after the unification. In Britain, cult and witchcraft have never stopped smouldering. Typical for the Balkans were practicing magic, walking on fire, and others, but even during the Communist regime, people took a great interest in the occult. There were a few mediums who were known to have successfully told the past of individuals and were consulted about the future. Those mediums were protected, supported, and used by the regime for its own purpose, but access to them was monitored and controlled by the authorities. Some people I knew claimed they were helped by them. Their relations improved, illness healed, problems sorted. We cannot deny such claims. In the midst of a spiritual vacuum, created by a godless society, God may provide relief and loving care to those in need in many ways. But if we know the Creator of all things personally, why not make our petitions in prayer directly to him? Each time someone engages in practices forbidden in the Bible, they go into the enemy's territory, where they make themselves deliberately exposed and vulnerable to evil. At the same time, prayer to the one true living God is considered by such people weird religious mental.

The spiritual landscape in Bulgaria was (and still is) badly affected also by cultic teachings, which arbitrarily mix multiple beliefs and make spiritual cocktails far away from the teaching of the Bible. The only prudent way to counteract those, instead of attacking existing practices, is by proclaiming the simple, unadulterated message of the Gospel about the life, death, and resurrection of Christ. Many churches in the country do that, but more is needed to change the narrative of the culture, to transform society.

There was a short period of revival in Bulgaria, after the political changes, which the evangelical churches brought about with hard work. The situation started to improve after the country joined EU. The political and economic integration with the EU did play a positive role not only for rapidly changing laws, trade, and manufacturing standards, but also by the influx of financial help and investment from the richer countries of central and western Europe. The EU integration did help the establishment of a free-market economy.

"But where is the country heading to now?" I was asking myself. With a sincere desire to forget the shameful and traumatic totalitarian past, people are inclined to project a new image by embracing more ancient ethnicity or joining other nations. The emergence of a new amalgamated nation under the EU flag however is not going to happen soon for a variety of reasons. It has never been considered a goal for the immediate future anyway. At the same time trust in local authority has been diminished and has little chance to recover in a new society rid of corruption. The migration we experience in our time confirms that. It puts to the test the very foundations on which the European unification was formed. For these reasons past personal and national identities in the member countries, and not only in the Balkans, seem to be under pressure of being wiped out. As a result we will be left out with a pluralistic world of competing voices without foundations for real representation of people's admirations and hopes. In such a world Christians are less and less heard in the public arena. History tells us that when those voices are silenced completely, nations turn blind, stumble, and fall.

Yet I believe God has good plans for the future of the people of the Balkans. Despite our selfish divisions, he delights in the diversity of cultures. Diversity is part of his plan to unlock each person's potential to do well in a freedom of choice. However, nations fall over and over again in their freedom, when trying to put culture and traditions above God. The Christian faith has no interest in division but unites. Its ultimate goal is to unite all people one day.

The history of the world is a history of wars between and within nations. The roots of the conflicts lie in different values and beliefs, but above all, in selfishness. Anti-theists love to say that all world conflicts are caused by religion and that it is better to stay 'neutral' like they are. But we know that anti-theism is not neutral. It is the most hypocritical, intolerant and aggressive religion of all. There have been many cases in history of abusing Christianity, compromising it from within as it were. The Nazis, for example, including their leader, claimed to be Christians and then went on to commit the world's most terrible atrocities. There is nothing that can stop people, principalities and powers claiming allegiance to Christ without realising the judgement they bring upon themselves. People are able to misuse the name of God while still controlled by their sinful nature. But, "...if anyone does not have the Spirit of Christ, he does not belong to Christ" (Romans 8:9). In most cases, conflicts happen when nations attempt to exert their self-interest at the expense of others. They always find the ideology that is needed to justify their actions. Their ideology is secondary to their desires. Faithful Christians, however, are called to act according to the message of the Bible. Their desires and actions come secondary.

Looking at the conflicts in the world today, we note the same. But it never does much good attacking other beliefs. We are called to try to live in peace and tolerate other views. It would help much more to say what we are standing for, what our own belief is, and how we think it would resolve the problem.

Religion, as a human-made institution in the spiritual realm, is often called to the test in God's refining fire. It was so when Jesus walked the earth in his battle against the religious establishment. The history of the Christian religion that followed was not much different in that respect. The church was often called to the refinery when hypocrisy and misuse of the name of God were punished in various ways; the turbulence during the Reformation period being just one example.

However, we cannot let the cynics reduce to nothing the great achievements of the Christian church over the centuries. The medieval nations which emerged in Europe after the fall of the Roman Empire were predominantly created and shaped by the rule of Christian ethics, much more so than by the pagan culture of the barbarians. This happened despite the painful conflicts which took place in the process. No one can deny the positive role of the community of Christian churches, which crossed boundaries during the development of early Europe and later unified moral standards and values in society. Despite its coercive nature at the time, Christianity amalgamated and consolidated society by accepting the love of Christ as a binding principle in human relationships. The loyalty to these principles resulted in greater freedom and creativity in all aspects of life, including science and engineering.

But we have to learn the lesson from that period of Christianity. We are free to choose our system of government, but we cannot make it a government of God by a mere declaration. Any system of government can fail to provide defence against dishonest individuals, who are free to choose their own morality and ethics. Ultimately, there is no defence against the manipulations of powerful groups in society with different ethics and vested interests in government. Any such declaration can potentially end up with abusing power, unleashing demonic forces, and creating unstable, transient governments.

Today, the theocratic Christian state has been replaced by the liberal state, where economics, business, politics, social justice, and state government have their own pursuits and laws, separate from the disparate moral systems of its citizens. We have to acknowledge the fact of this separation but continue to strive to keep the state laws grafted onto the moral principles of Christian ethics, as a basis to unite our values in all aspects of life. However, in the meantime, our faith can be divisive, as is any other world view. World views and beliefs of people in general are incompatible (Hebrews 4:12). Yet we are called to live in peace with everyone, as far as it depends on us (Romans 12:18). But we cannot expect to be immune from accusations that we are troublemakers. We are for good reason provocative when we admonish that the liberty we enjoy is a gift from the cross of Christ and that by being ignorant of that fact, we can no longer live in his grace.

The hope for the citizens of the liberal state of trade, then, remains in buying the message of Christ. We should 'sell' this message to the leaders of our society in business and politics, teachers at schools and universities just as we reach out with it to all private individuals. This message is free for us, but it was not free for him. The cost was his life as the Son of Man. It is for his purpose that political, economic, and government structures today exist, regardless of what kind they are. Above all, we should continuously pray for all people in government, and there should be no difference between our values in public and private. We should pray for the governments of all countries, even those considered enemies by the politics of the day. Pray for the eyes of their hearts be opened to the love of God and His wisdom, pray against the demonic powers that make leaders do evil. War is the last resort of resolving any conflicts.

The Russian dissident Alexander Solzhenitsyn wrote in his book *The Gulag Archipelago* "If it only were all so simple! If only there were evil people somewhere insidiously committing evil deeds, and were necessary only to separate them from the rest of us and destroy them. But the line dividing good and evil cuts through the heart of every human being. And who is willing to destroy a piece of his own heart?"

The vision for the future of the nations is the one of the prophet Isaiah: "They shall beat their swords into ploughshares, and their spears into pruning hooks; nation shall not lift up a sword against nation, neither they shall learn war anymore" (Isaiah 2.4). This is not a utopia. We have a choice: experience a glimpse of that reality by stepping in the Kingdom of God now, or carry on "beating our ploughs into swords" (Joel 3:10).

4.2 The World of Science

Who has put me here? By whose order and direction
have this place and time been allotted to me?
—Blaise Pascal

Some Christians do not like scientists because they look monstrously clever, with no heart. Similarly, some scientists dislike Christians as uneducated and dangerously fanatic. There is an unspoken, ungrounded opinion that these two categories of people are enemies. But does it have to be like that?

It has not been like that in the past, even after the church no longer exclusively owned the scientific enterprise. There have been many scientists with a Christian world view: Blaise Pascal, James Maxwell, Michael Faraday, and Gregor Mendel, to name just a few. There are still scientists with Christian faith, but for no reason, this profession nowadays is seen by the world as predominantly non-Christian. When a scientist starts talking about Jesus, his colleagues immediately think there's something mental going on. "There might be God out there in the energy of the stars, but Jesus? This is crazy, too simplistic, stupid", they would say. But is it not true that scientists often go 'crazy', in their own way? Einstein's theory of relativity looked crazy at first and was not accepted by the scientific community. To this, the reply was, "It is indeed crazy, but the question is whether it is crazy enough to be true."

It is perhaps true that the majority of scientists today are materialists. They deny the spiritual realm, ignoring so much evidence for its existence. At the same time, they are reluctant to acknowledge that science has limits and cannot provide meaningful answers to all the questions we have. There is something in the human spirit that transcends the material world. From the moment we are physically born until we meet our Creator in the spiritual realm and establish an ongoing relationship with him, we are unsatisfied and search for meaning and purpose. But the Bible provides direction in the otherwise meaningless material world.

The Response to Atheism

First of all, Christians have to acknowledge all the mistakes the church made in the past. The case with Galileo is an example where we should stay humble. We should also keep in mind that scientists and engineers work hard; we should be thankful for their work, by which human society as a whole benefits enormously. Yet they often do not know their why, and because of that, they are often exploited and even cheated by irresponsible administrators and businessmen. They also tend to argue with zeal just because their profession requires them to do so. They like lucid talk and are easily angered by lack of it, sincerely convinced that argument is always required in order to do their job properly. We have to respect their knowledge in the specific areas of their work, where we may only have a vague understanding as amateurs.

Secondly, we have to examine our motivations. We can only have a meaningful debate if we act from the position of love, not of superiority. The Word of God is superior and takes precedence in all conclusions, but we are not superior to other people. We have to be honest and admit that not all the knowledge about the material world is in the Bible. We cannot, for example, build an electric motor or generator by reference to biblical texts. It is a book of a different kind: a book of salvation. Yet it is our duty to present the message of salvation to others with grace, knowing that it is God who ultimately converts people in his timing, not us. We also have to be prepared to admit that we do not know the answer to everything on Bible teaching and interpretation. We should help others see the love of God in it without patronising them. If our encounter leads to acrimonious arguments, we should just shut up and leave.

The majority of secular scientists actually are tolerant agnostics by heart, but the rest, who are anti-theistic zealots, fervently and honestly believe we are hypocrites, belonging to an esoteric club for some personal material gain. To some extend this is due to the cults they have seen, which abuse Christianity with their own obscure ethical platforms. People will always look at what we do, not what we claim and we must always acknowledge that we often fail. But I always tell them that it is different when we tried hard but failed, because of weakness. It is different when you do the wrong things deliberately without restrain, just because you are convinced there is no one above or near to judge you. The difference is in God's judgement. We are safe when we confess our weakness to the Almighty, who is able to deal with the pollution caused by our sin. He can turn even our wrongs into rights, our failures into victory.

Some say there are non-Christians better than you. Yes, that is true, because God created every human being in his image. Christians are together and individually still better than what we were before we believed and we do not compare ourselves with others neither do we judge others because we live under grace (Mathew 7:1-5). One day, when we see God face to face, we will judge with Him even the angels. For now we are work in progress.

As evangelists, we must stand firm to our beliefs, but we must also be careful not to infringe the right of individuals to make their own choice for their own world view and ethical standards, whatever our good intentions may be. And any conversion is for the purpose of the Creator, not for ours. We, as believers, are not in the business of argument, like we are as scientists in our profession, for a very good reason. The difference of opinion in faith must always be tolerated, remembering that the verdict on any argument will be given when we see God face to face in the new heaven. I can see the smiles on the faces of some of you when I talk about heaven, but to not acknowledge this attitude is to misunderstand our place in the universe. As Christians, we acknowledge that one needs enough space and time to make one's choice, without being forced into it. We do not convert people. Only God does. Above all, our attitude should be that of a true believer. Everything we do, we start with prayer. We love scientists, and we pray for them. No one is won for Christ by argument. It is Love that wins, His love!

Christian Apologetics and the Limits of Science

In arguments, atheists tend to misrepresent the power of science to explain things. A point I always make is that science is not all powerful. The purpose of science is to devise theories, which must always be regarded as mathematical models with a good approximation of the reality, but these models are not the reality itself. Newton's law of gravity is a formula that envisions a world in which the force of attraction is proportional to the masses and inversely proportional to the distance. This was a model, the basis for engineering for a century, until new observations on the speed of light were found that could not fit in it. Then Einstein's formulas came to explain everything known from experiment then. But it is not sufficiently complete for the needs of today, and physicists are now devising new theories again.

Models, although incomplete, are useful to predict behaviour of matter under certain conditions. They are the basis of engineering. Our civilisation is rooted in technology developed on the basis of these scientific models. They are so powerful that scientists over the ages always fell into the trap of declaring them as "all powerful."

As an example, according to the laws ingrained in Maxwell's set of equations, science can explain how an electric motor, consuming energy, can be turned into a generator, returning energy. In fact, the device is a converter from one type of energy to another. But science cannot explain what energy is. We can measure it, but we cannot explain what it is or why it is here, in the universe, in the first place. Where did it come from?

We don't even know what time is. We measure it by using a well-known natural process: the Earth's rotation around its axis for example. But Earth's rotation, strictly speaking, is irregular. Leap seconds have to be added to account for the irregularity. For this reason, our time is now governed by atomic clocks. They measure time with higher precision, using the jumps of the electrons within the atom. We are not good enough to detect irregularities in those jumps, but that doesn't mean they don't exist. Yet we are content with that. According to Einstein's theory, time runs faster on the mountain than in the valley, but it does not bother us either because the difference is negligible for the ordinary everyday tasks.

The space-time theory does not give us a definition of time other than it is what you measure or what the clock reads. But reading the clock is a convention. For example, the atomic clock in Greenwich is not in sync with the GPS clocks in the satellites. It reads a different time. Yet it is a basic, fundamental quantity in most scientific models and engineering calculations. The ships in the old days could calculate their location in the sea by using accurate time. One of the most important jobs on the ship was that of the timekeeper. Nowadays, not only the location of the ships in the sea but also the locations of our cars on the road are calculated by high-precision, synchronised timekeeping in the GPS satellites, which send signals to my gadget. This system achieves an incredible accuracy, down to a meter or less. Yet we do not know what time is. Rather, we think it is an intuitive concept given to us naturally (or perhaps supernaturally). Dare we say? Choose whatever you like, but don't tell me the nonsense that science explains what it is. Stephen Hawking in *A Brief History of Time* writes this: "...maybe what we call imaginary time is really more basic, and what we call real is just an idea that we invent to help us describe what we think the universe is like"

The other thing is that not all scientific models are deterministic. Quantum mechanics, for example, assumes that there are elements of unpredictability or randomness. This is accepted as a fundamental principle in physics today. It suggests that the way matter behaves is open to dependency from outside. Given this reality can we rationally deny the notion that there could be something or someone outside the material world sustaining it at all times?

Another limitation in science lies in the fact that scientific knowledge is currently not contained in one single theory or mathematical model. It is fragmented in a collection of such theories which, strictly speaking, contradict themselves, if someone tries to use them all together to solve a practical problem. Despite all the achievements of modern physics so far, the Standard Model is unfinished. Nevertheless, some scientists unreasonably expect, once it is made complete, it would describe the universe in full. A theory of everything, as it were.

But is a theory of everything possible?

In 1931, the mathematician Kurt Gödel proved one of the most significant theorems in mathematical logic, which affects all other knowledge as well. It states that if a logical system (a system of axioms, which define some knowledge) is consistent (i.e., does not contain contradictions), then it is incomplete. In other words, it cannot produce a yes or no answer to all questions given to it. Some of the answers will be "I do not know." Gödel also proved the reverse theorem: if the system is complete (in other words, it contains all knowledge), it is inconsistent. In other words, it contains contradicting affirmations. Or to formulate differently, a logical system cannot prove itself without being inconsistent. It suggests the meaning of a system can only be found outside the system.

Once tested successfully, the Standard Model will still be limited to the current known facts from observation. By no means can scientific knowledge be considered complete in describing the universe in full. It is impossible to describe the world in full, not just because it is a huge task. In my view, it is impossible in principle because of Gödel's theorem. This should not discourage scientists from searching for more accurate, more powerful descriptions of the material world. This is only to make a point that science has its limits. Isaac Newton once wrote that he was just like a small boy having fun on the seashore, occasionally finding a "smoother pebble or prettier shell" whilst "the great ocean of truth" laid undiscovered before him. All great physicists have that sense of humility before the reality of the material world, realising that they are trying to trap matter like a mouse, but the reality of matter always remains elusive.

To this, we could also add the limitation that comes from the most fundamental principle in scientific methodology on which it actually exists: to operate by experiment, which is the only test for a theory's credibility. That is, science operates only with things that are material and, in that sense, visible (detectable) and measurable. This is a good principle, good methodology. It is the methodology that made modern science come to life. It is also a principle that makes science independent, ethically neutral or 'value-free'. It studies nature just as it is, not as one wants it to be because one has vested interest in using the knowledge that it produces. That is a principle which liberates scientific methods from influence in regard to ideology, politics, and world powers. It liberated science to such an extent, that it led to discoveries that made possible the Industrial Revolution in the last century. I am a witness of how much damage the totalitarian regimes in the Eastern Bloc and Stalin personally caused to science by interfering in it and postulating what kind of results were allowed and what were not, labelled non-scientific.

Now here is my point: The ethical neutrality of science is its strength but also its weakness because it is stripped of moral dimension and could be used for good as well as for bad, to build as well as to destroy, to bring life as well as to kill. But where does the notion of good and bad come from? Science does not and should not engage in producing a moral code. It could study psychology and behaviour of human beings within a given moral system, but it cannot produce the moral system itself. This is why, as Lesslie Newbigin puts it, "scientists are ultimately called to the ethics outside the dome of science."

Atheism likes to claim neutrality, but there is no neutrality in it. It is a choice that one makes for the nonexistence of God. The attempts of metaphysics to engage in morality often end up in creating an atheistic religion, a belief that we somehow indirectly come into a mystic experience, feeling nature is the deity itself. Many scientists worship the creation and not the Creator. Such a deity is just an idol, which is often worshiped through the human personalities of those who govern and on which the logistics of the scientific work depend. But Christians believe in God of the Bible, the Creator of all material things.

I lived for over forty years under Communism, an anti-theistic culture which imprisoned and killed people who committed no other transgression than believing in God. However, a godless society is ultimately bound to degenerate into a cultic and mafia-like way of living, intolerance, violence, restrictions of personal freedom, and dictatorship. I have seen throughout my life the tragedy of people like me who lived without faith. If I were to be left alone to the laws of nature, under anti-theistic Communism, I would have died a long time ago because only the fittest survive under those laws. But I found salvation I did not deserve. It was a gift of life by grace alone.

The Creation Debate and our Origin

There have been lots of debates between atheists and Christians (and among Christians themselves) about the story of Creation in the first book of the Bible, Genesis. For me, the book is a poetic account of who created the universe and why, not about how. Looking at the literary style and the context we can deduce that it was never the intention of the Author to explain exactly how it happened in scientific terms. If it was, then no one would have been able to understand it then, and few would now. Modern science was not given to the writers of the Bible and scientific knowledge has been changing all the time. The story of Creation in the book of Genesis is neither a modern scientific tale nor a chronological text. It needed not be. It is an allegory, full of love, praise, and admiration for the Creator.

Another debatable topic is our origin. As a scientist, I cannot deny the existing evidence for evolution and the link between animals and human beings in it. I cannot think that all creatures on earth before the Fall of man in the Garden of Eden were physically immortal and that they became mortal after that. I do not believe that all the nature has somehow fallen after that in a sense that evil crept in at that point. Whether we like it or not, the suffering of living creatures has always been an open possibility in the plan. That does not mean God was not good. According to the design of the Creator, I believe, two creatures at some point in time had grown physiologically to the stage of self-awareness, ready to respond to the call of the Creator in a way unique among all creatures and have fellowship with him. They were made spiritually alive at the moment they received that call. This was something going beyond the physical world of matter.

The question "Was life created by God or evolved naturally over billions of years?" is wrong in principle, because it assumes, without reason, it is either one or the other. In fact, it could be both. As Denis Alexander put it, "God is either author of the whole book of creation or he isn't." But how did he do it, then? Atheist scientists will be very quick to take the evolution theory as it is today and produce an answer in their usual way: "It is not difficult to imagine this and that." But then, serious, honest scientists would need to support with evidence their exact chain of events took place, and that is very hard to do. It is a work in progress. Some wrongly assume a plausible hypothesis is already an ingenuous theory.

Our short answer to that question is, "We do not know."

Why? Because the biblical account is primarily theological. It tells us only who the Creator is. At the same time, there are so many blanks in the studies of the origin of species that most scientists agree: there is no a complete modern scientific account, at the moment too.

More importantly, whatever natural process God used to create a sufficiently physiologically developed creature with self-awareness, we know that their ability to communicate with

Of Ecclesiastes and More

the Creator came as a result of something beyond the world of matter, an act described as "breathing into the nostrils" of man to give him spiritual life.

Suffering and death were still in the wild when God placed Adam and Eve in an isolated place, the Garden of Eden, away from the wild, where only the fittest survive. I do believe that place was a paradise without suffering and that they could have been physically immortal at that time too. It is not irrational to believe it. Surely, God knew they were going to disobey and plunge back into suffering again as a result. "Why did he create them that way then, with a free will?", one may ask. Surely, he did not give them free will in order to wash his hands and evade responsibility. Surely, the Garden of Eden experience was just teaching humanity to trust a loving God.

Denying the biological continuity between animals and humankind by disregarding the evidence left in the material world is a very difficult doctrine for a scientist to accept. God is not a liar. If we deny the suffering in primordial time, what about the suffering now? Is God now good? He is good to us by offering us eternal life, no matter how much we suffered in human history and still suffer, until we return home to spend eternity with him. God is sovereign and good. He gives life and is entitled to take it back. The elimination of suffering, the Bible teaches, is in God's plan for the new creation (Isaiah 65:17, 2 Peter 3:13, Revelation 21:1).

We do not know at the present time exactly how God created us physically, using the natural laws He created before that, but we can still rejoice by knowing we were formed dust of the ground and were made alive by his breath for his own purpose. We have no vested interest in the ignorance of science and muzzling the truth about our origin. And if one day humanity learns with certainty all the biochemical reactions which took place, transforming the "dust" of the earth over millions of years to our present form of existence as human beings, our life will still be a wonder.

Interpreting the Scripture

Christians accept the Bible to be the Word of God, but they are aware the texts are written by mere mortals, inspired by Him. It is not believed to have been dictated by God with the exception of some, written when humanity made their first steps walking with Him. Yes, there are difficult passages in the Bible, sometimes deterring readers from committing to the whole of it. People often suggest deleting or changing them in order to get a picture of God 'as they like it'. But if we allow ourselves to make change as it suits us, we would not know where to stop because we all differ in our 'likings'. Soon the whole of it will be gone. If we do not have the Bible, His Word, we do not have faith because the words of humans are deceptive, and their memory is short. Jesus, as radical as he was in opposing religious establishment, did not change or abolish the scripture, the Old Testament. He actually fulfilled it. The remarkable story of fulfilling the Old Testament came alive and is now called New Testament. The early Church had many debates on the texts to form their doctrines, but they never contemplated changing what the Apostles wrote. The theologians of the Reformation, who had substantially new revelations, did not change anything in the Biblical texts either. Counteracting non Biblical religious practices, they just spoke out the truths that have always been in the Biblical texts, yet disregarded by the Church.

The Church over the ages did need to have doctrines, which summarise the message of the Bible and filter cultural, racial and historical idiosyncrasies. Some of the existing doctrines in various denominations however are not based on Biblical texts. There is nothing wrong with that as far as the church, making them, does not put them above or contrary to the central message of love and unity in Christianity, found in the Bible. Otherwise the institution that puts them forward cannot call itself Christian without compromising its integrity in the public space. The doctrines of the Church are not static, but they are not 'progressive' either. They are not meant to 'adapt' to fallen human nature. The challenge for the Church is to identify the moral issues in society today, find their solution in the Bible and give direction even if it needs to acknowledge mistakes of its interpretation from the past. The Church, as the body of Christ, should not oppose the development of new theological ideas based on revelation. However the central core of the faith, the Biblical texts, cannot be changed without sinking into moral relativism and confusion, coming from the presuppositions of modern secular thought.

And yes, it has to be interpreted. Scientists often tell me if the Bible has to be interpreted, then there is no universal truth; everyone can interpret it as they like.

Well, no. Let me give you an example with communication theory. There are methods, as you know, by which a message to be sent over a noisy channel can be protected from corruption. By analysing the whole content of the message, a special code, called a "cyclic redundancy code," can be calculated and sent last. On the receiving end, the same calculation is performed, and if the calculated code is not the same as the one sent last, the receiver knows the information has been corrupted. Thus, by introducing redundancy in the information, we are able to detect errors. By increasing the length of the code, adding more redundancy, and using other formulas for coding, it is possible not only to detect errors but also to know where exactly they are in the message and correct them.

Similarly, the Bible has some 'redundancy' in it, which helps making correct interpretations. Same statements are repeated over and over again in different variations, different situations, different historical times, and in a variety of cultures, clarifying different aspects and nuances of the same truth, transcending science, culture, history. The meaning of our interpretation must not be taken out of context but checked against the text around and in other places in the Bible, to see if it is consistent with the meaning of the whole of it. In this way, readers with different backgrounds and ways of thinking over the centuries came to the same or very close interpretation. It is amazing to see so many people from different races, nations, cultures, education systems, and life experiences, from various historical times, united in this common understanding of the message of love there.

It is also amazing how after thousands of years since the patristic writers established the Biblical texts still new revelations have been being drawn out from the texts all the time just as they are. To communicate their revelations theologians do not look for changing the texts. On the contrary, they base their findings on the authority of the Bible as a main source of wisdom. Without it we can easily plunge into relativism on moral issues, on trying to model the character of God according to our own human standards. The core of our belief is that the truths, which are needed for our salvation are placed in the Bible by Him without error.

When reading the Bible one can hit a verse which is difficult to understand or accept. We may think different places contradict themselves. When we pray, God provides clarification, often by paraphrasing sentences in a variety of translations. But it is one thing to paraphrase sentences in order to make them more understandable, without changing the meaning. It is another, to change the meaning because we do not like the message it conveys. Yet even when reading more accessible translations like the *Message*, I still have places I find difficult to understand. That does not put me off. The Bible is the scaffolding of my faith. Human relationships are so complex that they cannot always be defined in human language. We need the Spirit of God to open the eyes of our hearts and help us understand (2 Corinthians 3:6). And there will always be questions to which our answer will simply be, "We do not know." We do not know, because we cannot know God in his fullness, but let us keep his Word a cornerstone of our faith at least just because it records mankind's experience of walking with Him for over ten thousand years.

The Bible is not intended to teach contemporary science, or any science at all. The purpose of any primitive scientific knowledge there is only to provide account for the act of creation. If it were, it would have become obsolete very soon after being written down. Scientific knowledge, we have seen, is always transient in its completeness. The Bible is intended to reveal the spiritual realm by telling stories, which happened in time, but the underlying message is invariant of time.

As Christians, we should not worry about advances in scientific knowledge but rejoice in them. It does not mean God is gradually retreating, diminished in the corner, with the advancement of science, because what happens in nature is also God's work. Yet we believe he also does things supernaturally. He is at liberty to suspend the laws he created.

Science and Faith Together

Science was amalgamated with religion in the natural philosophy of the ancient world and the middle ages. With the emergence of modern science, this integration turned into a painful conflict marked by the trial of Galileo in 1615. The resolution of that conflict was a long process that led to complete independence of both realms of human knowledge when modern science disentangled itself from the legalism and literalism of religion for this very good reason: an ethic neutral enterprise, investigating the material world by testing and experiment should be free from ideological pressure of any kind. However the end result of that approach, despite of all the positive achievements, left the scientists in an isolated chamber without moral and ethics attached to their work. When the shrine of shared ethics remains empty it is always filled with conflicting 'rules of fairness' defined by flawed human beings. The ethical system becomes exposed to the dangers of short-lived secular modernity and relativism.

The Reformation period, which started earlier and was running in parallel with the scientific revolution on its own quest for new revelation and change, brought some reconciliation later, the fruit of which was the Industrial Revolution in the theistic countries of the West. However, the new anti-theist scientists continued the attacks on religion, fueled mainly by the political thinkers of Marxism, libertarianism and secular humanism. Nevertheless Einstein later in the 20th century admitted "there is no law of physics without a lawgiver". He said "Science without religion is lame, and religion without science is blind".

I am convinced that institutional religion with its man-made doctrines will always have friction with modern science for various reasons. However Christian faith, as ordained by God of the Bible, transcends institutions and politics of the day and engages with the moral and ethics from the prospect of the Creator who is Christ, the supreme liberator and redeemer according to His ethics. Christian faith complements science and has no conflict with it. The dialogue between science and faith today is more than just a game of diplomacy and tolerance. All of us have to acknowledge the fact that faith is at the core of our existence as human beings and allows us for better understanding of our place in the universe by providing direction and stability in a confused world. Collin Francis, the physician behind the Human Genome Project, puts it this way: "God is in the beautiful and majestic laws of nature. But he is also the ultimate source of love and forgiveness through Jesus Christ."

5

THE END OF TIME

They were foreigners and strangers
on earth. (Hebrews 11:13)

Our lives here on earth are just a journey. Our destination is
in heaven. We only come to earth once, as aliens, with a job
to do, to prepare. Love, defined by the sacrificial death of Jesus
Christ on the cross, permeates all human life and defines the
meaning of our existence here. We believe in miracles, but this
is not in conflict with our knowledge about the material world.
The difference between the natural and supernatural is blurred
because all our knowledge about the laws of nature is incomplete
at any time, provisional, and the natural world is contingent. In
the Bible, miracles are set apart from natural events not so much
because they violate the laws of nature as to being wonders or
signs for something important that must be remembered. Their
purpose is to reveal the gracious character of God. All knowledge
we obtain about nature must be used in good faith.

Our existence is a mystery. Another way we could
understand heaven is to think of it as a dimension out of
space-time in the spiritual realm, from which humankind has
access to the Creator. This access is not an intellectual state of

enlightenment. It comes through faith and love, received by grace. I chose to accept and live in that grace. Would you? Here is a prayer from the little booklet *Why Jesus*, by Nicky Gumbel. When you speak a prayer like that with a sincere heart, it will walk you on a journey with Jesus Christ, our Lord.

Heavenly Father, I am sorry for the things I have done wrong in my life. [Take a few moments to ask his forgiveness for anything particular that is on your conscience.] Please forgive me. I now turn from everything which I know is wrong. Thank you that you sent your Son, Jesus, to die on the cross for me so that I could be forgiven and set free. From now on I will follow and obey him as my Lord. Thank you that you now offer me this gift of forgiveness and your Spirit. I now receive that gift. Please come into my life with your Holy Spirit to be with me forever. Through Jesus Christ, our Lord. Amen.

Whatever national and personal identity we may have been given by the world, it is temporary, and it is nothing if we do not acknowledge the identity God first intended for us as his adopted children.

God created a connected world, but today, it is even easier to get lost. We are over connected to a vast virtual wilderness: Facebook, Twitter, email, and many others. The internet increases our power to influence others, but at the same time, it also increases the speed with which we and our children get influenced. In this age, when information travels fast and all human activity depends on information processing, we risk being sucked into the information wilderness, marginalised, and made redundant as humans. We may encounter new situations where scientific discoveries and inventions pose a grave danger to humanity. Our history proves we got it wrong so many times. Eugenics, for example, was advocated as a scientific Darwinian approach for improving the human race by many countries, including the United States and Britain. It was later used by the Nazis to justify their horrid treatment of Jews and people with disabilities. We find it now impossible to comprehend how, in the name of improving the race, humans could have treated other people in such a horrible way. But we are not too far away from it today. Genocide of all kind is still taking place in the world today. New eugenics thinking is also on the horizon and threatens our society with far more dangerous scientific adventures as genetic engineering.

We depend on advanced medical science for treating illness and extending life. Genetic engineering now steps in to deal with hereditary diseases. However, improving cognitive abilities and creating "trans-humans" through genetic engineering, advocated by some, might be a step too far in the unknown and a very dangerous thing to do. The question is not "Could we?", but "Should we, and for what reason?" Is that not going to disturb cardinally social and moral conventions? Many super clever people in history had mental health problems. Perhaps having too much cognitive power is inconsistent with having stable, and harmonious mind, able to engage in all aspects of life. Moreover studies show that our behavioural patterns depend so much more on our development, learning and engagement with the world after we are born, than on our physical makeup before that. Besides if we become cleverer, will that make us better human beings on itself? Will we be able to avoid the horror of the Nazi camps? Will that avoid strife and wars between different social groups and nations? During World War II, we were so close to self-destruction with nuclear weapons. How can we ensure that our research and innovations now are safe, and we do not risk killing ourselves or destroying the planet we inhabit?

We are just beginning to understand what we have been doing to this planet, the cradle of our life. We're just beginning to grasp the reality of how far away we are from another world we might be willing to colonise. Our science and technology might never be able to get us there before the Earth comes to its natural end and is engulfed by the fading and expanding sun. There is most certainly nothing we can do to control that process. It may also end earlier by some other natural or manmade catastrophic event. The whole universe, according to some theories, will come to an end by contracting back to nothingness where it supposedly started from and the space and the time will seize to exist.

If we accept the materialistic view of the world, denying the reality of the spiritual world, why should we do anything for the future generations when we know they will not do anything for us? But God, the great "I AM", older and younger than time, is alive and in him we live too! Regardless of whether our civilisation will be in existence or not in the material world of space-time when the universe comes to an end, human beings have a sense of eternity (Eccl 3:11). We see our lives continue in the lives of our children, the future generations. We wish them to continue and do well. And so we wish well to the human race as a whole. We have been given this beautiful planet to live and enjoy and preserve. There is meaning in it and we must take responsibility of good stewards for the home we have been given, though temporary. We might at last grasp the wisdom of the scripture that says, "Though we are many we are one body, because we all share one bread" (1 Corinthians 10:17). We are only kept alive by remembering Christ and anticipating His return. Our best survival strategy, after all, as a species, might be learning how to live here sustainably and love one another as one big family. The only safe way of approaching the Tree of Life for us, therefore, will always be by visiting the cross of Christ first, because God IS.

May you live a life full of passion and wonder, purpose, love and joy. May you live a rich life full of these things, because you only have one life on this beautiful planet called Earth, full of beautiful precious people. And always rejoice that the best is still to come.

Bibliography

Alexander, Dennis. *Creation or Evolution* (2008).

Dyson, George. *Turing's Cathedral* (2012).

Gumbel, Nicky. *Searching Issues* (2013).

Gumbel, Nicky. *Questions of Life* (1993)

Hall, William Webster. *Puritans in the Balkans* (1938).

Hawking, Stephen. *A Brief History of Time* (1988).

The Holy Bible. New International Version, International Bible Society, United Kingdom, 1984.

Lewis, C. S. *Mere Christianity* (1944).

McGrath, Alister E. *I believe* (1997)

Newbigin, Lesslie. *Foolishness to the Greeks* (1986).

Bibliography

Printed in the United States
by Baker & Taylor Publisher Services

Printed in the United States
by Baker & Taylor Publisher Services